UNIVERSALISM EXAMINED AND REFUTED, AND THE DOCTRINE OF THE

ENDLESS PUNISHMENT

OF SUCH AS DO NOT COMPLY WITH THE CONDITIONS OF THE GOSPEL IN THIS LIFE, ESTABLISHED

Luther Lee
Minister of the Methodist Episcopal Church

"If our Gospel be hid, it is hid to them that are lost; in whom the god of this world hath blinded the minds of them which believe not, lest the glorious Gospel of Christ, who is the image of God, should shine unto them." — 2 Cor. iv. 3, 4.

SCHMUL PUBLISHING COMPANY
NICHOLASVILLE, KENTUCKY

COPYRIGHT © 2020 BY SCHMUL PUBLISHING CO.
All rights reserved. No part of this publication may be reproduced or used in any form or by any means—graphic, electronic, or mechanical, including photocopying, recording, taping, or information storage or retrieval systems—without prior written permission of the publishers.

Churches and other noncommercial interests may reproduce portions of this book without prior written permission of the publisher, provided such quotations are not offered for sale—or other compensation in any form—whether alone or as part of another publication, and provided that the text does not exceed 500 words or five percent of the entire book, whichever is less, and does not include material quoted from another publisher. When reproducing text from this book, the following credit line must be included: "From *Universalism Examined and Refuted, and the Doctrine of the Endless Punishment of Such as Do Not Comply with the Conditions of the Gospel in This Life, Established* by Luther Lee, © 2020 by Schmul Publishing Co., Nicholasville, Kentucky. Used by permission."

This Schmul Publishing Co. edition is not a scanned facsimile of a used book. It has not been "updated" or edited into modern English, punctuation or grammar, but is accurate to the author's own style and usage. The text has been carefully proofread for accuracy and formatted for easier reading by today's readers. Every effort has been made to prevent disordered text.

Cover image copyright: <a href="https://www.123rf.com/profile_sakkmesterke">sakkmesterke / 123RF Stock Photo</a>. Used by permission.

Published by Schmul Publishing Co.
PO Box 776
Nicholasville, KY 40340
USA

Printed in the United States of America

ISBN 10: 0-88019-630-0
ISBN 13: 978-0-88019-630-7

Visit us on the Internet at www.wesleyanbooks.com, or order direct from the publisher by calling 800-772-6657, or by writing to the above address.

Contents

Foreword/5
Introduction/11

I
The Original State of Man/15

Man was created holy 17
Proved, I. From the nature of the cause that produced him, 17
  II. From the image in which he was created, 17
  III. From the divine approbation which he received, 19
  IV. From the moral rectitude of his character, Eccl. vii. 29, 20

Man was not originally subject to death, 20
Proved, I. From the first announcement of his mortality, 22
  II. By his expulsion from the Garden of Eden, 22
    III. From the pain of dying, 23
    IV. From the resurrection of the body, 23
    V. From the enmity of death, 24

Objections answered, 25

II
The Fall of the First Man, and Consequent Corruption of Human Nature/27

Proved, I. From the Mosaic history, 28
  II. From scriptural references to the Mosaic history, 29

Objections answered, 33

The depravity of all men in consequence of the fall, 36
    Proved, I. From the fall of the first man, 36
    II. From the universal corruption of morals, 38
    III. From the liability of all men to divine malediction, 40
    IV. From the scriptural view of the unrenewed mind, 44
    V. From the scriptural doctrine of regeneration, 49
    VI. From remaining depravity after justification, 52
    VII. From the general economy of the gospel, 53
    VIII. From the experience of all good men, 57

III
Atonement/59

Proved, I. From the impossibility of salvation without an atonement, 61
    II. From the Mosaic ritual, 73
    III. From the death of Christ, 79
    IV. From those scriptures which attribute salvation to the blood of Christ, 86
    V. From the scriptural view of redemption by Christ, 91
    VI. From mediation, intercession and reconciliation by Christ, 95

Objections answered, 98

IV
Salvation from Punishment/108

Proved, I. From the atonement, 109
    II. From the scriptural view of pardon, forgiveness and remission, 110
    III. From the scriptural view of justification, 119
    IV. From matter of fact—some have been saved, 125
    V. From implication, 127
    VI. From salvation from sin itself, 130
    VII. From the offers which the gospel makes in the present tense, 132
    VIII. From the impossibility of salvation, without being saved from punishment, 132

V
On the Punishment of Sin in a Future State/142

Proved, I. From the sentiments of universalists, 144
II. From the fact that some sins cannot be punished in this life, 146
III. From the design of punishment, 150
IV. From the partial displays of justice in this life, 154
V. From the motives necessary to support virtue, 156
VI. From the descriptions given of punishment, 158
VII. From the existence of hell as a place of punishment, 159
VIII. From the relation punishment bears to salvation in point of time, 186
IX. From the duration of punishment, 192
X. From the moral character of sinners after death, 193
XI. From the existence of devils, 195
XII. From the future reward of the righteous, 207
XIII. From a general judgment, 209
XIV. From judgment after death, 211
XV. From the second coming of Christ, 216
XVI. From the dissolution of nature or the end of time, 227
XVII. From the general consciousness of mankind, 229

VI
On Endless Punishment/233

Proved, I. From the terms everlasting, eternal, &c., 234
II. From a contrast with salvation, 249
III. From the conditionality of salvation, 253
IV. From the danger of coming short of salvation, 261
V. From the resistance sinners make to the means of their salvation, 273
VI. From the limitation of the time of salvation, 276
VII. From implication, 280
VIII. From the scriptures which deny salvation to certain persons and characters, 287
IX. From the scriptures which represent the punishment of the wicked to be their end, &c., 293
X. From the penalty of the divine law, 295
XI. From the relation which sinners will sustain to the divine administration after the day of judgment, 300

XII. From the condition of sinners after judgment, 302
XIII. From the injustice implied in limited future punishment, 304
XIV. From prayer not being offered for the dead, 309

VII
Universalist's Arguments Answered/310

Argument, I. From the perfections of God, 310
The goodness, love and mercy of God, 314
The wisdom of God, 316
The power of God, 321
The holiness of God, 321
The will of God, 322
II. The corrective nature and design of punishment, 323
III. The universality of the atonement, 329
IV. Reconciliation, restoration and restitution, 331
V. The promises of God, 339
VI. The prophecies, 345
VII. The nature of faith and the duty of all men to believe, 345
VIII. The sympathies of human nature, 346

VIII
Objections to Universalism Stated/349

Objection, I. Universalism contradicts itself, 350
II. Universalism is indirect and confused in its proof, 357
III. Universalism is demoralizing, 360
IV. Universalism does not comfort the good, but administers comfort to the wicked, 363
V. Universalism is unsafe, 364

Foreword

I HAVE BEEN ASKED by the publishers to introduce to the reader, the author and the topic of this volume. Since Dr. Luther Lee (1800-1889) was the focus of my doctoral dissertation at Kent State University in 1994, the assumption is that I may be able to enlighten you, the reader, to the author of this particular work. The dissertation was published in 2000 by Scarecrow Press as No. 17 of Donald Dayton and Kenneth Rowe's "Studies in Evangelicalism", with the title of *"Logical" Luther Lee and the Methodist War Against Slavery.* Lee authored *Universalism Examined and Refuted* while pastoring a circuit for the Methodist Episcopal Church in 1831. It has been my experience that knowing about the author of any book always lends a helpful perspective to what I am about to read. To know the circumstances and milieu of the author is to raise the reader's understanding of the material. Hopefully, being introduced to Luther Lee will produce that additional insight for the reader of this volume.

Several facets of Lee's life have captured my interest; especially since he was a completely self-educated man who never entered a schoolroom in his entire life, yet he ended up with an honorary doctorate from Middlebury College. He eventually became an esteemed college professor at Adrian College and the author of twelve books on theological topics. His brother taught him his "letters" on a cedar shingle tablet somewhere in the Schoharie Valley in the state of New York. Orphaned as an adolescent boy, he knew only rough makeshift jobs, eventually working at a tannery until entering the fulltime ministry. Through the influence of a local Methodist Episcopal class leader, Lee found Christ as his Savior in his teens in 1817, near Middletown, NY, preached his first sermon two years later and labored as a local preacher for the next six years in that area. After marrying a schoolteacher in 1825 and serving several small circuits, Lee was appointed in 1831 to the Heuvelton Circuit in upstate New York. There he first encountered the heretical teachings of Universalism, one of many newer ideologies that had taken root in young America.

Universalism drew some of its basic ideas from Methodist theology, and developed quickly in what Charles G. Finney termed the "burned-over district" of western New York, an area that roughly bordered the Erie Canal, extending perhaps fifty miles north and south along a corridor that ran from Buffalo to Albany. The key tenet of Universalism denied the doctrine of eternal punishment. While it had been in America for over half a century, it found fertile soil in which to take root on the rapidly developing country where the Second Great Awakening was influencing the entire population. John Murray, and two later writers, Elhanan Winchester and Hosea Ballou, attempted to conjoin the predestination of Calvinism with the benevolence of God. Since the Gospel taught that Christ had died for the sins of everyone, Universalists insisted that all humankind must go to heaven upon death. Winchester, holding a somewhat restorationist view, argued that the soul passed through a purgatory-like place (although he did not use that term), in which the soul suffers for a period of time before proceeding to its blissful abode. Such teaching naturally appealed to wicked people who preferred not to give up their life of sin, the very type of people that Luther Lee intended to win to Christ. Upon preaching in the town of De Peyster, a Universalist preacher challenged him to a debate on the proposition, "Will all men be finally holy and happy?"

Lee happily accepted the challenge and launched himself onto a path that would earn for him the nickname, "Logical" Lee, due to his mastery of the rules of formal debate and logic, and his amazing knowledge of Scripture and Methodist theology. As the next years rolled by, Lee proved himself to be a master craftsman, skillfully applying the rules of logic and rhetoric to his argumentation and debates, and adapting them to his hearers as well as his debating opponents. The tools he utilized to hone his debating and writing skills can be traced to the required reading for persons studying for the ministry who did not have the benefit of college and seminary preparation. Two British scholars of the day, George Campbell and Bishop Richard Whately, had produced textbooks that were core reading for the ministerial course. Campbell's *Philosophy of Rhetoric* taught the readers how to use rules of rhetoric with the aim of persuading the reader or hearer. Whately's work on logic proved to be equally helpful in preparing men like Lee to be effective defenders of truth. As you read through this book, you will observe how the author lays out his proposition and then cites his evidence from scripture, Biblical commentators and early Church fathers, to buttress his arguments.

The Black River Conference of the Methodist Episcopal Church discovered that in their midst traveled an amazingly brilliant preacher who had mastered Wesley and the early Methodists' minds and methods—one who could out-debate any formidable opponent willing to engage him on almost any theological topic. Those formative years on the frontier prepared him to write a book in refutation of the heretical doctrines. In 1836 he published *Universalism Examined and Refuted, and the Doctrine of the Endless Punishment of Such as Do Not Comply with the Conditions of the Gospel in the Life, Established*, a work that secured his reputation as a Wesleyan scholar within the ranks of the ME Church. While the volume was not intended to be a systematic theology, in it Lee so thoroughly discussed and defended the main aspects of evangelical theology that his work proved to be timeless—it is as relevant today as it was by the third decade of the nineteenth century. He later published his *Elements of Theology*, in 1855, a work that established itself as a core book in the ME preacher's course of study for almost half a century. A comparison of the two volumes, however, reveals that this present work covers almost the entire range of necessary topics for any Christian believer who seeks to understand the plan of salvation. I am pleased that the present publishers have determined that a need exists for this work; it is as relevant to our present day as when it was first published. Hardly a basic moral or theological issue arises today that Lee does not engage in some manner as the book unfolds. He is particularly helpful in that he not only cites the writer or the scripture, but he gives the quote to eliminate the need for the reader to locate the reference.

For the unenlightened reader to whom Luther Lee might be an unfamiliar name in church history, it may be helpful to know that in 1843 Lee, one of the five founders of the Wesleyan Methodist Connection, served for twelve years as editor of the *True Wesleyan*, and as the first General Conference President of the denomination, as well as two subsequent terms. He officiated as the first president of the New York Conference and later as president of the Miami Conference in Ohio. He helped to establish the Leoni Institute, a ministerial training school near Jackson, Michigan and subsequently served as one of the early professors and chair of the faculty and of the board of trustees of Adrian College in Adrian, Michigan. He died in 1889 and is buried in Flint, Michigan.

May God bless the publication and readership of this volume.

—PAUL L. KAUFMAN, PH.D.
Chair, Division of Bible and Theology
Hobe Sound Bible College

Introduction

THE WRITER OF THE following pages, probably, would never have conceived the design of becoming an author on one of the most important subjects that ever engaged the human intellect, had not a train of circumstances compelled him to enter the ranks of the disputers of this world, or abandon what he deemed to be fundamental truth in our holy religion, to the wreckless assaults of its enemies. It is true he had from the earliest period of his christian experience, and especially from the commencement of his public ministry, marked the irreligious tendency of the sentiments against which these pages are directed; yet he would most probably, have deplored the evil, and looked for it to be removed by some more able hand, rather than to have opposed his own efforts to an error which carries with it the full force of the natural inclinations of the unrenewed heart of fallen man, had not the votaries of the error, grown bold through neglect, challenged him to public combat, under circumstances which left him but one alternative, either to give up the truth as indefensible, or "earnestly contend for the faith once delivered to the saints."

From oral controversy recourse was had to the public Journals, and the discussion was continued until it began to attract public attention more generally, and appeared likely soon to come to an important crisis, when suddenly the universalist's columns were closed against it, and no one could be found longer to maintain the contest, oral or written. Under these circumstances the design of publishing the present work was conceived, having already bestowed much labour upon the subject, and having no better method of laying it before the publick, for whose benefit the investigation was first commenced. And after devoting the few leisure hours, to be spared from pastoral duties, to the subject, the work is at last completed, and presented to an enlightened publick, whose right it is to judge of its merits.

Though the author makes no pretensions to perfection in style, yet he humbly trusts he has succeeded, in expressing himself in a manner to be understood by the plain common sense reader, for whose benefit his labours in this work have been principally intended. He has dealt as sparingly in original criticism as the nature of the subject, and the oft and clamorous appeals made to the original language by the abetters of universalism would justify him in doing; and in those instances in which an appeal has been made to the original text, the unlettered reader has not been deserted; for such appeals have not only been made in a manner to be understood by those who have studied no language but plain English, but the same points are supported by a variety of other arguments, which may be understood by all who are capable of reading the common translation of the holy scriptures. If universalism be an error, it must be acknowledged by all to be one of alarming magnitude, fraught with consequences as lasting as the immortal souls it ruins. For assailing such an error, the writer needs no apology, unless it be for not having done it more effectually. Some, indeed, may suppose that enough has been written on the subject; that there is no call for a work of this description at the present time. This has been considered by the author; and after a due examination of the principal works on this important subject; he has come to the conclusion to add one more to the number, for which he offers the following reasons:

1. The works which have already been published have not yet fully put a stop to the errors against which they have been directed, nor do they appear likely to accomplish this object, very seasonably, without additional effort. While others have commenced the assault and battered down some of the bulwarks of error, the writer of these pages wishes to add his humble efforts, hoping that others will follow his example, until her strongholds shall be demolished, and the heresy shall be driven from the records of time.

2. Universalism has so shifted its ground and changed its complexion, that many of the works which, at the time they were written, were directed against it with a deadly aim, are now left to spend their force in the air, the enemy having fled and erected his battery on other ground, from whence he renews his incendiary warfare, and talks as much of courage and victory as though he had never been defeated.

3. Most or all of the works which have been published on the subject, have been directed against some particular author or confined to some one point in the controversy, insomuch, that though there are a number of very able treatises against universalism, yet the writer of these pages has not yet fallen in with any one volume which covers the whole ground of controversy, and pursues and refutes universalism in all its dark retreats, and complicated foldings of error. The author has looked upon it as an object of no small importance, to put into the hands of the publick in one convenient volume, a refutation of

universalism in all its various forms, which it assumes as it is driven from one position to another; indeed, that such a work has not before this time appeared, from the pen of some more able hand, he has looked upon as a defect, to supply which, so far as his humble powers will permit, the present work has been undertaken. How far he has succeeded in the undertaking, he will leave for others to determine, while he indulges the hope, that with a mind honestly inquiring after truth, and with this volume in his hand, the reader will be secure from the assaults of universalism in any form in which it has heretofore made its appearance before the public.

In conclusion, whatever may be the fate assigned to these pages by the impartial judgment of the publick, the author can appeal to the searcher of hearts for the rectitude of his motives, to whom he directs his most fervent prayers, that both writer and reader may be guided into all truth.

THE AUTHOR.

I
The Original State of Man

As it is the primary design of the following pages, to refute the doctrine of unconditional universal salvation, and to establish the doctrine of the endless punishment of such as do not comply with the conditions of the gospel in this life, it will be seen at once, that the original state of man has an important bearing on the subject. If God created man in the same moral state, in which he now exists, with the same imparity of nature and propensities to evil, it might appear reasonable, with our present views of the divine attributes, that he should not only save sinners from, but actually reward them for, all the evils, which are the necessary result of the natural movement of that system, which he put in operation when he bade man awake to conscious and responsible existence. On the other hand, if God created man free from all moral evil, and if his sin and misery are the result of a first transgression, and his continuance in this state the result of his wilful rejection of a sovereign remedy which God has provided in Christ Jesus; these facts are a full vindication of the divine goodness, though sinners perish forever. We will then enter upon our undertaking, by considering the original state of man, in which we shall attempt to maintain that he was created holy; and that he was not subject to bodily dissolution while he remained in his first state of innocence.

First, we say that man was created holy. In support of this position we urge the following considerations.

I. Man was the effect of a holy cause. God created man; and as man was passive, and not active, in his own creation, he could have possessed no nature, powers, nor even tendency of powers, which he did not receive from the plastic hand of his Creator. God imparted to man all that he possessed, when he first awoke to conscious being, even the first breath he drew; hence if man contained in his nature, any moral evil, God must have been its author. Man's body, which was formed of the earth, must have been a lifeless and irrational form of matter; and could not have possessed moral quality, before it was animated by a rational soul; all therefore, that man possessed in his first existence that was moral, was imparted to him when God breathed into his nostrils the breath of life, and constituted him a living soul; therefore, if man was morally corrupt, or contained in his nature any propensity to evil, it must have been infused by Jehovah's breath! Now as God is holy, nothing but holiness could have proceeded from him; man, therefore, must have been holy in his first existence, as he came from the hands of his divine author.

II. "God created man in his own image." Gen. i. 27. By the image of God, in this text, we understand the moral likeness of God, consisting in righteousness and true holiness. No other consistent explanation can be given of the subject. It would be absurd to say that the image of God consists in bodily form, for if form be applied to the

Deity, such form must be bounded by geometrical limits; which is opposed to infinity and omnipresence, perfections which are essential to the Supreme Being. Nor can it be consistently said, that the image of God wherein man was created, consisted in his having authority over the other creatures, which God created as his vicegerent on earth, for this was only a circumstance in his being, and not an image in which he was made. Gen. i. 26. "God said let us make man in our own image, and let him have dominion," &c. Here man's creation in the image of God, and his having dominion are marked as two distinct circumstances; the one refers to his creation, the other to the design of his creation, or to the circumstances in which he was placed after he was created. Man was created in the image of God, but he did not possess dominion until after he was created; therefore, the image of God, in which he was created, could not have consisted in his having authority over this lower world, as God's vicegerent, because the image existed before he possessed the authority: he was created in the image, but the authority was given him *after* he was created. It must appear equally absurd to contend, as some have, that the image of God, in which man was created, consisted *exclusively*, in the immortality of his soul. There is no evidence, that God's immortality constitutes his image, any more than his justice, holiness, or any other perfection of his nature. Immortality is one of the divine perfections, and if one of the perfections of God be embraced in the image, which he stamped upon his rational offspring, it is reasonable to suppose that every communicable perfection of the divine nature must be embraced to render the image complete; wherefore we conclude, that as man was created in the divine image, he received from the plastic hand that formed him, the stamp of every communicable perfection of the divine nature: nor is holiness the least prominent among these perfections, as God has revealed himself in the Bible. But this view of the subject does not depend upon abstract speculations upon the perfections of God, for it is based on the declarations of his word. Eph. iv. 24. "And that ye put on the new man which, after God, is created in righteousness and true holiness." By the new man, which we are here exhorted to put on, we understand the true christian character. This the text informs us, is created after God, i. e. after the likeness or image of God, and this is "in righteousness and true holiness." The image of God, then, consists in righteousness and true holiness; and as man was created in this image, he must have been holy; not merely free from unholiness, but positively holy; for he shone in the divine image, which consist in righteousness and *true* holiness.

III. We infer man's primitive holiness from the seal of the divine approbation which was set upon him by his Maker. Gen i. 31. "And God saw every thing that he had made, and behold it was *very good*." As this was spoken of all the works of God, its meaning must be, that every thing was very good of its kind; the world was a good world, and the man that was created to people it, was a good man. Now as man was a rational being, a moral agent, and destined to lead the moral career of this vast world, when God pronounced him good, it must have been with reference to him, such as he was, a moral being; he must, therefore, have been good in a moral sense. This clearly proves that man was not only free from all moral evil, but that he was positively good, or possessed real moral virtue. If, as some now assert, all moral good and moral evil consist in voluntary action, man being neither holy nor unholy until he puts forth his volitions, the text under consideration which asserts that he was very good, cannot be true; for, in such case, it would be as correct to assert that he was very bad, as it would to pronounce him good. It must be perfectly plain, that, to assert that man was very good, because he was free from all moral evil, would be no more true, than it would be to declare that he was very bad, because he possessed no moral holiness.

IV. One quotation from the pen of inspiration, shall close the subject of man's primitive holiness. Eccl. vii. 29. "Lo this only have I found, that God hath made man upright, but they have sought out many inventions." That this text relates to man's moral rectitude, and not to the erect posture of his body appears from two considerations.

1. This is the sense in which the word upright is uniformly employed in the scriptures. Ps. vii. 10. "My defence is in God, who saveth the upright in heart." Prov. xi. 9. "The righteousness of the upright shall deliver him." See also, Ps. xi. 7. xviii. 23, 25.—xix. 13.—xxxvii. 37. Prov. xi. 20.—xii. 6. The above, to which many more references might be added, are sufficient to show that the term upright, is uniformly used to signify moral rectitude.

2. In the text under consideration the inspired writer represents his discovery of the fact, that God made man upright; to be the fruit of laboured investigation: which could not be the case if he alluded to the upright posture of his body. It would reflect no great honor on the intellect of the inspired penman to understand him as saying, that he had numbered a thousand persons, one by one, examining each, to learn that God had created man to stand erect in opposition to the quadruped race. It is clear then, that God made man upright in a moral sense, and if so, he must have been free from moral evil, on one hand, and possessed positive moral virtue, on the other. With these very brief remarks on man's moral character, as he came from the hand of his Creator, we will proceed to notice his exemption from death, while he remained free from moral evil.

Secondly, we say that man was not subject to natural death or dissolution of body, before he sinned, and consequently, would not have died, if he had not sinned. This we maintain on the principle that moral evil is the cause of natural evil; though in this place, we shall not argue of natural evil in general, but of the death of the body in particular. It is probably, generally known that modern Universalists deny that the death of the body is an effect of sin, and maintain that Adam was created mortal, and that he, and all our race, would have died if sin had never entered the world.

Mr. Hosea Ballou has expressed his sentiments on this subject too plainly to be misunderstood. He says, "natural evil is unquestionably the necessary result of the physical organization, and constitution of animal nature in the elements of which our bodies are composed and in their combination, in our constitution, we evidently discover ample provisions for the production of all manner of disorders to which they are incident, and even of mortality itself. It has long been the opinion of christian divines, that natural evil owes its origin to what is denominated moral evil, or sin, but we feel fully convinced that the very reverse of the opinion is true. The ground we shall take, is, that natural evil owes its origin to the original constitution of animal nature, and that moral evil, or sin, owes its origin to natural evil." *Treatise on Atonement, fourth edition, pages* 31, 32. This position taken by Universalists, so far as relates to the death of the body, appears to be essential to their whole theory. If it be allowed that the death of the body is an effect of sin, two consequences must follow fatal to the modern system of Universalism.

1. If the death of the body be in consequence of sin, it must follow that the consequences of sin are not confined to this world as Universalists assert; for, in such case, it cannot be denied that the separation of the soul from the body must affect it in a future state.

2. As the resurrection of the body depends upon the

sovereign will and power of God, and not upon some germinating principle in man's body, it follows, that if sin has caused the death of the body, it has produced an effect which is in its own nature endless; and which would prove an endless evil, were it not counteracted by the power and grace of God, manifested through Jesus Christ. We will then attempt to prove that man would not have died, if he had not sinned.

I. The first annunciation of man's mortality was in the form of a sentence, inflicted on him for his first disobedience. Gen. iii. 17-19. "And unto Adam he said, because thou hast hearkened unto the voice of thy wife, and hast eaten of the tree of which I commanded thee, saying, thou shalt not eat of it—in the sweat of thy face, shalt thou eat bread, till thou return unto the ground, for out of it wast thou taken, for dust thou art and unto dust shalt thou return." Let it be noted that God first threatened man with death in case he should disobey, and then, after he had disobeyed, he announced his mortality as the fulfilment of his threatening: "*because* thou hast eaten," &c. "dust thou art and unto oust shalt thou return." God charges on man his mortality as the consequence of his own disobedience; hence, if man had not sinned he would not have died.

II. The manner in which God executed the above sentence of death, proves that the death of the body was intended, and, as all must see, that it was in consequence of sin. The sentence of death was executed by expelling the offender from the garden of Eden, and thereby cutting off his access to the tree of life, which stood in the midst of the blooming circle. Gen. iii. 22, 23. "And the Lord God said, behold the man has become as one of us to know good and evil; and now, lest he put forth his hand and take also of the tree of life, and eat, and live forever, therefore the Lord God sent him forth from the garden of Eden." It is clear, then, that if man had not sinned, by partaking of the forbidden fruit, he would not have been expelled from the garden, and cut off from the tree of life; and if he had not been cut off from the tree of life, he would have lived forever, or would not have died; therefore, if man had not sinned he would not have died.

III. The suffering, which is an inseparable accompaniment of death, proves it to be an effect of sin. With our present views of the divine goodness, we cannot suppose that God would permit a race of sinless beings to suffer. If it be consistent with the goodness of God to permit sinless beings to suffer, his goodness can give no security against the endless suffering of sinners.

We say then, sin is the cause of all suffering, directly or indirectly, but death is inseparably connected with suffering; therefore sin must be the cause of death, and if man had not sinned he would not have died.

IV. The resurrection of the body is a part of salvation, which is the gift of God through Jesus Christ; and hence, the death of the body which renders such a salvation necessary, must be a part of the evil of sin, and the curse of the law, from which Christ has redeemed us. 2 Tim. i. 10, "Who hath abolished death and brought life and immortality to light through the Gospel." 1 Cor. xv. 12, 13, 20, 21. "Now if Christ be preached that he rose from the dead how say some among you that there is no resurrection of the dead. But if there be no resurrection of the dead, then is Christ not risen. But now is Christ risen from the dead and become the first fruits of them that slept; for since by man came death, by man came also the resurrection of the dead." These quotations clearly show that the resurrection of the dead is the result of Christ's death and resurrection, overthrowing thereby the empire of death, and bearing away the spoils of the grave. Indeed, if death is not a part of the penalty of the law, and consequently an effect of sin, we think no good reason can he given why the death of Christ was necessary in order to our redemption. If the law did not inflict death, as its penalty for sin, it would not have been necessary for Christ to die to redeem us from the curse of the law, for if the law did not inflict death on the sinner, and yet required the death of Christ in order to his redemption, it inflicted on Christ what it would not have inflicted on the sinner, as a reward of his transgression, had there been no redeemer provided. It is clear then, that as the resurrection of the body has been secured by the death and resurrection of Christ, that the death of the body, which renders such a resurrection necessary, must have been caused by the fall, or must be a part of the evil of sin. To deny this conclusion, would be to say that the mission, death, and resurrection of Christ would have been necessary to secure the resurrection of the dead, had not man sinned; and consequently, that Christ died and rose again, not so much to redeem man from the consequences of his own misconduct, as from the defects of that constitution which was given him by his Creator.

V. Death is said to be an enemy. 1 Cor. xv. 26. "The last enemy that shall be destroyed is death." Now if death was originally intended as the portion of every man, and that too of necessity, from the constitution of our nature, it is not possible to conceive how it can be an enemy, either of God or man. It would be absurd to say that God created man subject to death, with an intention that he should die, and *that* death, which is just as God designed it should be, is, notwithstanding his enemy. As well might it be said that God is his own enemy! Nor can it appear on the above principles, that death is the enemy of man. Had death been originally designed as the means of terminating our earthly existence, and introducing us into a more perfect and permanent state of being, a state of certain and eternal happiness, as Universalists affirm, there would not be that abhorrence of death in the human breast that now exists; death would be welcomed by all, as our deliverer sent to take us to our abiding home, and dying would be as easy as to answer any other demand of nature.

When nature is weary we calmly close our eyes on the light of day, and sink into refreshing slumber; and if man had been designed for death, when nature had performed her work, we should *as calmly* close our eyes on the light of time and retire on the wings of an expiring breath to our proper abode.

We will now bring this chapter to a close by considering some of the objections which have been urged against the doctrine of man's primitive immortality.

1. It has been sometimes objected that if man had been created *immortal*, he could never have become mortal, as matter of fact now proves he is; since immortality implies the impossibility of becoming mortal. To this it is replied, that it is not contended that man was created absolutely immortal. It is admitted that his body contained the same tendency to dissolution that it now possesses, in itself considered; but it is contended, at the same time, that the fruit of the tree of life would have counteracted this tendency, and preserved him in ever during vigor, had he not been cut off from it in consequence of his sin. From this it will be seen, that man's original exemption from death, is not argued from his absolute immortality, nor is it contended that death is the natural tendency of sin, but rather that it is an incidental or circumstantial effect of sin. Through sin man was expelled from the garden of Eden, and thereby cut off from the tree of life, and as this was designed to preserve him in being, his death followed as a consequence of the change sin had effected in his circumstances, rather than by any direct effect it had produced upon his constitution.

2. It has also been objected, that if man did not die, our race could not exist in so great a number of individual beings, since the earth would be too small to contain the

swelling tribes of men, were it not that death removes one generation to make room for another. This, it is said, would diminish the amount of final good to be enjoyed by our race, in proportion as it lessened the number of individuals to enjoy good. To this it is replied, that we are not to suppose that this earth was designed as the place of man's ultimate abode, had death never entered the world; but only as the nursery of his being, in which to prepare to act in a more extended sphere beyond the limits of this terraqueous ball. Matt. xxv. 34. "Come ye blessed of my father, inherit the kingdom *prepared* for you from the foundation of the world." From this, it is clear that heaven or a future state of bliss and glory, was prepared for man as early as when the foundation of the world was laid; therefore, it is certain that man was designed to fill a place in the invisible world, from which it appears reasonable that he would have been duly translated from earth to heaven, had he never sinned, without passing through the disagreeable, loathsome, and painful gate of death through which he now passes into the future world. That this is possible, and more than probable, appears from the fact that some of the most holy have gone in this way from earth, overlooking the gate of death, and at the beck of God lit directly on the battlements of heaven. Enoch, who walked with God, was translated, that he should not see death, and was not found because God had translated him; and Elijah rode to heaven in a chariot of fire, that soared far above the valley of death, and bore the ascending prophet directly into the bosom of heaven!

II
The Fall of the First Man, and the Consequent Depravity of His Descendants

UNIVERSALISTS GENERALLY DENY the doctrine of moral depravity or inherent corruption of our nature, as the consequence of a first transgression, and maintain that every man enters upon the stage of this life, in moral circumstances as favorable as those which attended the first man, with the exception of the influence of bad examples.
 To this view we are opposed; and having in the preceding chapter, considered the primitive state of man, we shall, in the present, offer a few observations on the subject of the fall, and subsequent depravity of all men. It is not however, our design in this work, to travel over the whole ground of controversy on this subject, which has been occupied by voluminous and more able writers; but simply to state a few of the arguments, which, to us, appear to be the most clear and conclusive. In relation to this subject, two points are to be particularly noticed, viz, the fall of the first man, and the consequent depravity of all men.

The fall of the first man, is what first claims our attention. In support of the doctrine of the fall, we urge the Mosaic account of the introduction of evil. This account states that God created man very good, and placed him in a garden in Eden, in the midst of which stood the tree of knowledge, of good and evil, the fruit of which God forbade him to take on pain of death; and that the woman was beguiled by the serpent, partook of the interdicted fruit, and gave also to the man, who was, consequently, involved with her in the transgression. This account, if literally interpreted, must be decisive; hence, those who reject the doctrine of the fall, as generally understood by the church, allegorise the Mosaic account of it. To shew that a literal construction *only* can be made to agree with the sacred record, shall now be the object of a few remarks.

I. The Mosaic account of the fall, is embraced in a series of historical events, all of which, this excepted, are acknowledged to be literal, involving literal and real transactions. The planting of the garden in Eden, stands connected with the creation of the world and the formation of man, in a manner which shows that the one is as literal as the other; hence, if we have a literal account of the creation of a literal heaven and earth, we have also an account of a literal garden, in which the transactions of the fall took place. Gen. ii. 7, 8. "And the Lord God formed man of the dust of the ground, and breathed into his nostrils the breath of life, and man became a living soul. And the Lord God planted a garden eastward in Eden, and there he put the man whom he had formed." Here the planting of the garden is connected with the formation of man out of the dust of the ground, with a positive assertion, that in this garden the Lord "put the man whom he had formed." Now, if the garden was not a literal and real one, the man, whose existence is so intimately connected with it, and who was put in it, could

2-THE FALL OF THE FIRST MAN, AND THE CONSEQUENT DEPRAVITY OF HIS DESCENDANTS | 29

not have been a literal man. If the account of the garden be an allegory, the account of the man who was formed in connection with it, and put into it must be an allegory also. Hence we are constrained to admit that the garden was a literal garden, or else, that we are to this day destitute of any literal account of the origin of the human family. Again, the sacred historian proceeds directly from the scenes of the garden, to record literal transactions which are made to depend thereon, so far as the order of time in which these different events took place, is concerned. The writer after concluding the story of man's expulsion from the garden, proceeds directly to relate literal transactions, which he connects therewith by the copulative conjunction, making it a part of the same narration. The creation of man and the birth of Cain and Abel are acknowledged by all believers in revelation, to be literal events: now, these two events are connected with each other by the intervening transactions of the garden, which must also be literal transactions, or the history would be broken and incorrect. The inspired penman separates the creation of man from the birth of Cain and Abel, by what is said to have transpired in the garden, the eating of the forbidden fruit, &c. Now, if the transactions said to have taken place in the garden, were not literal and real, the link is broken, and the account of the order of events is false; for it represents the creation of man as severed from the birth of the first sons of man by the intervention of a train of other events; whereas no such events took place, if the account of the garden and its reputed scenes are a mere allegory. These considerations are sufficient to show that the account of the transgression and fall of the first man is literal and real.

II. The garden of Eden, with the events which are said to have transpired therein; are referred to in other portions of the holy scriptures, as involving literal facts. Gen. iv. 16. "And Cain went out from the presence of the Lord and dwelt in the land of Nod on the east of Eden." That this is a literal reference to Eden, cannot be doubted by any one, who considers the connection in which it stands. Abel was a keeper of sheep, but Cain was a tiller of the ground: Cain brought of the fruit of the ground an offering unto the Lord, and Abel brought of the firstlings of his flock: God had respect unto Abel's offering but not unto Cain's, in consequence of which Cain was wroth and slew his brother; for which he was banished, and went to the land of Nod on the east of Eden.

Here reference is made to the geographical boundaries of Eden, to describe the settlement of Cain. Now can any one suppose that the Holy Ghost dictated a reference to a place which had no real existence, to describe the local situation of another place, real in existence, from their geographical affinity; and yet, to such a consequence are we driven, if we deny the literality of the Mosaic account of the fall. If Eden was not a literal place, where was the land of Nod situated, which lay on the east of it?

Gen xiii. 10. "And Lot lifted up his eyes and beheld all the plain of Jordon [sic], that it was well watered every where, even as the garden of the Lord, like the land of Egypt." In this text the plain of Jordon is described by being compared to the garden of the Lord, by which Eden is doubtless meant. Eden was watered by four rivers to which reference is made, to describe the well watered plain of Jordon. Now if Eden was not a literal garden, then the plain of Jordon is described by being compared to a place that never existed. That Eden is here referred to as a literal place, and not as a mere description given of it, as an ideal garden, is evident from its being connected with Egypt, which must be acknowledged to be literally a place. "As the garden of the Lord like the land of Egypt." The meaning appears to be this: As the garden of Eden was watered by four rivers, and as the land of Egypt was watered by the flowing of the Nile, so the plain of Jordon was well watered.

Isa. li, 3. "For the Lord shall comfort Zion: He will comfort all her waste places, he will make her wilderness like Eden, and her deserts like the garden of the Lord." Here the garden of the Lord or Eden is referred to, for the purpose of describing the prosperity of the church, when the moral wastes shall be made glad by the tidings of salvation, and when her borders shall be enlarged by the conversion of the gentiles to God. As the garden of Eden presented an assemblage of nature's excellencies, ever clad in a verdant and flowery mantle, strewing her delightsome walks and pleasant shades with flowers and fruits; so shall Zion bloom with moral flowers, and shed her fragrance on the world, when her light shall come and the glory of the Lord shall rise upon her. But who does not see, that in order to sustain the Prophet's figure, Eden must have a real and literal existence? If Eden had only an allegorical existence, and God make Zion like Eden, then, the latter day glory of christianity [sic], which has been predicted by prophets, looked for by saints, and prayed for by all the faithful, vanishes into an allegory, and ends in a mere phantom that will at last elude the grasp, and disappoint the hopes of the long expecting church. There are other texts which speak of the garden of Eden, that might be noticed. Ezekiel xxviii. 13. "Eden the garden of God." Chap. xxxvi. 35. "And they shall say, this land, that was desolate, is become like the garden of Eden." Joel ii. 3. "The land is as the garden of Eden." These references to the garden of Eden, by inspired authors, clearly show that the garden described by Moses, as the first abode of man, had a literal and real existence.

But the scriptures not only contain references to the garden of Eden, but direct reference is made to the scenes said to have transpired therein, as we will now show.

Job xxxi. 33. "If I covered my transgressions as Adam."

Job, no doubt, here refers to Adam's attempt to hide himself among the trees of the garden as described, Gen. iii. 8. "And they heard the voice of the Lord God walking in the garden in the cool of the day, and Adam and his wife hid themselves from the presence of the Lord God, amongst the trees of the garden." Now who does not see that the account of Adam's sin, and attempt to hide himself, must be a narration of literal facts, in order to justify such allusions to them.

On the above text Dr. Clarke has the following note. "Here is a most evident allusion to the *fall*: Adam *transgressed* the commandment of his maker, and he endeavored to *conceal* it; *first* by *hiding himself* among the trees of the garden; *secondly* by laying the *blame* on his *wife*." 2 Cor. xi. 3. "But I fear, lest by any means, as the serpent beguiled Eve through his subtilty, so your minds should be corrupted from the simplicity of Christ." Here the seduction of Eve is directly referred to by an inspired Apostle, in the use of the same terms employed in the original account. Eve said, "the serpent beguiled me;" and Paul says, "the serpent beguiled Eve," referring to it as a literal fact. Again, it is said that "the serpent was more subtle than any beast of the field; while Paul declares that it was through his subtlety that he beguiled the woman. From this, it must be clear that the Apostle understood the account of the first transgression as a literal history; and it is not possible for us to conceive how any one can think otherwise, who has any confidence in his inspiration.

1 Tim. ii. 14, "And Adam was not deceived, but the woman being deceived, was in the transgression" The Apostle is here speaking of the subjection of the woman to the man. "I suffer not a woman to teach, nor to usurp authority over the man." For the subjection of the woman, the Apostle assigns two reasons. The first is, the man was *first formed*. The second reason is contained in the text

under consideration. "Adam was not deceived, but *the woman, being deceived, was in the transgression.*" This plain reference to the deception of the woman, and that too, in proof of an important principle, involved in the matrimonial relation, must clearly show, beyond all doubt, that the account of the fall of man is literal and real. If the account of the fall be a mere allegory, and the deception of the woman, consequently, be not a literal fact, it could furnish no argument in support of the authority of the man, over the woman. Indeed, to say that wives should be in subjection to their husbands, *because* "the woman, being deceived, was in the transgression," while, in fact, no such deception and transgression ever took place, the whole being a mere allegory, is too futile to charge upon such a master of logic as the Apostle Paul. Such an imputation, to an inspired Apostle, would not only be trifling, but profane. When the Apostle asserted that wives should be in subjection to their husbands, *because* "the woman, being deceived, was in the transgression," had some grave Universalist matron objected to his conclusions, saying that the story of Eve's deception and transgression, was a mere allegory, without any foundation in literal fact, he certainly would have been confounded, unless he contended for a literal interpretation of this portion of the Mosaic history.

Before we close our remarks upon this subject, we will devote a few observations to what has been said in opposition to the above literal exposition of the garden of Eden, and of the fall of its once happy inmates. On this subject Mr. Hosea Ballou has made the following remarks. After giving a summary statement of the scriptural account, he adds: "This, in short, the scriptural representation of the first sin, and I consider it to be figurative. Should it be said that this garden was a literal garden, that the tree of life was a literal tree, and that the tree of knowledge of good and evil was also literal; I should be glad to be informed what evidence can be adduced in support of such an idea. Where is the garden now? Where is the tree of life now? Where is the tree of knowledge, of good and evil, now? Are these trees now growing on the earth as literal trees? We are not informed in the scripture that this garden was carried off to heaven, or that either of the trees was removed. It is written that God drove the man whom he had made out of the garden and placed cherubims and a flaming sword at the east of the garden to prevent the man from approaching the tree of life. If the garden were literal, why could not Adam have gone into it on the north, south, or west side?" *Treatise on Atonement, page* 35.

Mr. B. appears to argue, in this case, altogether by asking questions; but it should be recollected that if no answer could be given to the above interrogations, they would not disprove the existence of a literal garden, since a mere want of information on any subject cannot prove its falsity, or non-existence. It has often been said that "a novice may ask questions which a wise man cannot answer," though we do not consider this to be the case in the subject before us; we consider Mr. B's questions perfectly capable of solution. If we understand him, he intends *three* objections to the literal existence of the garden of Eden in the extract we have above given, which we will briefly notice.

1. Mr. B. appears to object to a literal exposition of the subject, on the ground that there is no evidence to support it. He says, "I should be glad to be informed what evidence can be adduced in support of such an idea." In answer to this we say, if no other evidence could be adduced, the text itself is sufficient, until some evidence be offered to prove it to be figurative; since every document is to be literally interpreted, unless good reasons can be rendered for a different construction. Taking this view, Mr. B's call for evidence in favour of a literal construc-

tion, comes with a very ill grace, until some more cogent reasons shall be offered on the opposite side of the question than any thing we have been able to discover in his performance on the subject. But we think the evidence in favor of a literal interpretation of the subject is ample, and if Mr. B. or any who embrace his views wish "to be informed what evidence can be adduced in support of such an idea," so far as our efforts are concerned, they may have their desires gratified by consulting the pages over which the reader has just passed.

2. Mr. B. appears to found an objection to a literal interpretation of the subject, on the circumstances that neither the garden nor the trees are now known to exist on earth. He asks: "Where is the garden now? Where is the tree of life now? Where is the tree of knowledge now? Are these trees now growing on the earth as literal trees?" That the garden now exists no one will pretend, but this is very far from proving that it never did exist. It is perfectly consistent to suppose, that when man was expelled from the garden, and the ground cursed for his sake, that it should decay and cease to bloom. If Mr. B's mode of reasoning be sound, it will disprove many other portions of the sacred history, for it would probably cost our opponents as much trouble to inform us where the land of Nod is, to which Cain retired, and where he built the city of Enoch, as it would for us to inform them where Eden was situated. When Mr. B. or any of his friends will inform us where Cain built his city, we will point to the place where Eden once bloomed; for, as Cain's settlement was east of Eden, Eden, in turn, must have been west of the city of Enoch, and when our opponents will point to the latter of these places, we will inform them by what rule they may find the place of the former.

3. Mr. B. supposes that if it had been a literal garden, from which Adam was expelled, he might have re-entered at another point. His language is: "It is written that

God drove the man out of the garden, and placed cherubims and a flaming sword at the east of the garden, to prevent the man from approaching the tree of life. If the garden were literal why could not Adam have gone into it on the north, south, or west side?" To this a very plain answer is given in the language of inspiration. Gen. iii. 23, 24. "The Lord God placed at the east of the garden of Eden cherubims and a flaming sword *which turned every way* to keep the way of the tree of life." If then the flaming sword turned *every way* to guard the tree of life it must have cut off Adam's approach from every point. But it may be asked, why the cherubims and flaming sword were placed at the east of the garden if they were intended to guard it on all sides? We answer, because it was doubtless on the east that Adam retired, when God drove him out of the garden; but while the flaming sword was placed at the east, appearing in front of the garden, to guilty and retiring man, it turned *every way* to prevent his re-entering from another direction. On the subject of the cherubims, Dr. Clark has made the following remark. "These angelic beings were, for a time, employed in guarding the entrance to paradise, and in keeping the way or road to the tree of life. This I say, for a *time*, for it is very probable that God soon removed the tree of life, and abolished the garden; so that its situation could never after be positively ascertained." We trust we have now shown that the first man fell from a state of holiness and happiness, into a state of sin and misery, by an act of disobedience against God; we will therefore pass to what most readers will, doubtless, consider the more difficult part of our undertaking in this chapter.

Secondly, we propose proving that all men are now born into the world with a fallen and corrupt nature, in consequence of the fall of the first man.

I. We argue the general corruption of human nature from the fall and corruption of the first man, from whom all men have received their existence by way of natural descent.

We have shown, in the preceding chapter, that the first man was created in righteousness and true holiness, that he bore the impress of the hand that made him, and shone in the likeness of his divine author. Now as righteousness and true holiness constituted the moral character or nature of man, as be came from the hand of his Creator, it must follow that this divine image was designed for his descendants, and would have been communicated to them, had he not sinned and lost it himself, while all men were yet in his loins. If then the image of God, wherein the first man was created, was designed to have been transmitted to his offspring, it must appear reasonable that nothing short of a full possession of this image, can answer the claims of the law of our creation; for it would be absurd, to say that God created man in a higher state of moral perfection than is necessary, to answer the claims, and secure the glory of the moral government which, he exercises over the human family; or that he bestowed on man a degree of moral holiness, which he did not secure from desecration by the direct interposition of moral obligation, or which might be squandered and lost on the part of man, without incurring moral guilt. It is clear, from this, that any state of human nature which comes short of that moral perfection, or that divine image which God bestowed, when he created man, must be regarded as a lapsed state, coming short of that righteousness which the perfect law of our Creator requires; and, consequently, a sinful state, "for all unrighteousness is sin." If, then, a want of the image of God, which consists in righteousness and true holiness, constitutes a fallen and sinful state, it only remains to show farther, that man does not, by nature now possess this divine image. Now, when Adam sinned, he must have lost the image of his maker; for it would be absurd to suppose that the image of God, consisting in righteousness and true holiness, could be possessed by man, and he be a sinner at the same time, guilty before God, and a subject of divine punishment. As well might it be said, that God could consistently condemn, and pour a divine curse upon his own image! As well might it be said that sin and holiness once formed a harmonious alliance! That Adam was righteous and truly holy, and unrighteous, polluted and guilty, at the same time. It is certain, then, that Adam could not have retained the image of his maker after he sinned, and being destitute of it himself, he could not communicate it to his offspring; for no being can communicate to another that which he does not himself possess.

We have now shown that the image of God, wherein the first man was created, was designed to have been transmitted to his descendants, and that any want of it, on their part, constitutes a degenerate state of human nature. We have, also, shown that this image was lost by the first man, to whom it was committed, not only for himself, but also in trust for his off-spring, and that he therefore could not transmit it to his descents who, consequently, cannot possess it by nature, or as the natural descendants of Adam. Human nature, therefore, is degenerate and corrupt, coming short of that state of moral perfection which it possessed, when it came from the holy hands of God, glowing in the brightness of his own moral image.

II. In support of the doctrine of the inherent corruption of human nature, we urge the universality of actual or outbreaking sin.

It will not be denied, that "all have sinned and come short of the glory of God," that "all are under sin," that "all have gone out of the way," and that "by the deeds of the law, no flesh shall be justified in the sight of God" Rom. iii. 9, 12, 20, 23. These pointed declarations of divine truth, must convince all who have any confidence in revelation, that all men commit sin, whether they have a corrupt nature or not; and if any should take the trouble to read these pages, who reject the scriptures, for their benefit we make an appeal to the consciousness of all men; and ask, where is the man who is not conscious of having, at some time deviated from the perfect rule of right? We think there is no danger of successful contradiction, when we assert that all men sin, and commence sinning too, as soon as they are capable of feeling the claims of moral obligation, or discerning between good and evil. This general overflowing of corruption, running through all the channels of human society, must have somewhere a cause or fountain from whence it emanates. That this fountain is the corruption of our nature, or the natural bias of the human soul to that which is evil, in preference to that which is good, we maintain on the ground, that it cannot be rationally attributed to any other cause. Why is it that all men sin as soon as they are capable? Those, who deny the doctrine of original sin, assert that it is the result of bad example, or a bad education, or both. Now, as these are the only reasons, or, at least, the most plausible reasons given by our opponents, if the ground is shown to be untenable, it will follow that we are to look for the fountain, from whence this general wickedness proceeds, in the corruption of human nature. Now, that neither bad example, nor a bad education is the cause of the general wickedness that prevails among men, must appear from one consideration. They themselves are dependent on a state of general wickedness for their own existence, as an effect is dependent upon the cause that produces it. Generally bad example and education cannot exist, without a pre-existing state of generally corrupt morals; for until men are generally wicked or immoral, example and education cannot be generally bad; hence, to say that general wickedness has resulted from bad example and education, is to put the effect for the cause. The argument must stand thus: Men are generally wicked because example and education are generally bad, and example and education are generally bad because men are generally wicked. This leaves one or the other without a cause, for which we must resort to the corruption of human nature. If bad example, or bad education has caused the general wickedness of men, what caused general bad example and education at first? If it be denied that men are more inclined to evil than good, we have here an effect—the general corruption of example and education, for which there is no assignable cause; and if it be admitted that this general corruption of example and education be the result of a natural bias in man to evil, the argument is ceded, and the doctrine of the corruption of human nature is established.

Other reasons might be rendered, why bad example and education cannot have produced the general wickedness that has prevailed in the earth, but enough has been said, on this point, to show, that until our opponents can invent some more rational cause for the general wickedness of mankind than they have yet been able to assign, it will remain a standing memorial of the corruption of our nature through the fall, to the entire overthrow of the Pelagian heresy.

III. Those scriptures, which represent *all men* as being liable to some sort of divine malediction, in consequence of Adam's sin, clearly prove the corruption of human nature through the fall.

Rom. v. 15. "For if through the offence of one many be dead, much more the grace of God, and the gift by grace, which is by one man Jesus Christ, hath abounded unto many." The many, which are said to be dead in this text, embraces the whole human family; for they form a perfect parallel, to the many, unto whom the grade of God is said to abound by Jesus Christ. All are then dead *through the offence of one*. By this one man, through whose offence all are dead, we are undoubtedly to understand the first man, Adam. Now, if by death, in the text, we are to understand the death of the body, which we have shown in the preceding chapter to be an effect of sin, it will follow that we die in consequence of Adam's offence; from which one of two consequences must follow. First, the law inflicts a penalty on those who are perfectly conformed to its divine claims, or else, secondly, the one offence of Adam corrupted human nature so as to produce in his offspring a non-conformity to the law. Should it be said that men produce in themselves a nonconformity to the law, by their own personal sin, and that therefore the law does not inflict its penalty on those who are conformed to its claims, in the sentence of death upon all men, it is replied, first, that this would be to suppose that all men die, temporally, for their own offence, and not "*through the offence of one*," as the text affirms. Secondly, infants die before they are capable of producing in themselves a non-conformity to the law. Now, to suppose that the law inflicts a penalty on such as are conformed to its requisitions, would be subversive of all righteous government! The thought cannot be indulged for a moment. As the law, then, cannot inflict a penalty on such as are conformed to its claims, and as it does inflict a penalty on all, in consequence of Adam's offence, it must follow, that it produced in all his posterity a non-conformity to the law, which implies a lapsed and corrupt state of human nature. Should it be denied, that the death of the body is intended, in the text, and maintained that it is a moral death that is come upon all, "through the offence of one," the argument is ceded, this being the sentiment for which we contend; therefore, whether temporal or moral death, or both be understood, in the text, the argument remains conclusive. In the 16th verse, the Apostle says: "And not as it was by one that sinned, so is the gift; for the judgment was by one to condemnation." This clearly shows, that by the offence of one man, Adam, judgment has come upon all, condemning them to death of some sort—"the judgment was by one to condemnation"—and as we have seen, that the law could not condemn or inflict a penalty upon those who are conformed to it, the offence of Adam must have produced in his offspring a non-conformity to the law, or by it judgment could not have come upon them, condemning them to death either temporal or moral.

In the 18th verse, the Apostle expresses the same idea, if possible, in clearer language. "By the offence of one, judgment came upon all men unto condemnation." It is settled, then, on the authority of inspiration, that condemning judgment was passed upon *all men*, in consequence of the offence of *one*, i. e. Adam. All men thus condemned, were conformed to the divine law, or they were not; but if they had been conformed to the law, we have shown that they could not have been condemned, therefore they were not conformed to the law. There is then in man, a non-conformity to the law of God, which appears from the fact, that all men have fallen under its condemnation. Now, as condemnation unto death, came upon men, before they were guilty of personal sin, and does now come upon infants, who are incapable of committing sin, it follows that this want of conformity to the law of God, is an inherent defect in human nature, and as it cannot be charged upon the Creator, the conclusion is irresistible, that it was caused by the sin of the first man, the Father and federal head of the human family, by whose offence "judgment came upon all men to condemnation." The 19th verse gives a still more direct view of the subject. "By one man's disobedience many were made sinners." It will not be contended by those who deny the corruption of human nature through the fall, that many were made sinners, by a direct imputation of Adam's guilt to his offspring. How then were many made sinners by the offence of one? The only consistent answer to this question, is found in the principles already laid down: a corrupt state of human nature was produced by the sin of the first man, and inherited from him, by all men. Is it asked how men can be considered sinners, merely because they inherit a corrupt nature by Adam, which they have not caused, and which they cannot prevent; it is answered, that this inherited corruption of nature constitutes a want of conformity to the perfect law of God, which requires holiness in the inner part, the same "righteousness and true holiness" which man possessed when he came from the hand of his Creator; and this want of conformity to the law is unrighteousness; a coming short of right, and "all unrighteousness is sin." 1 John v. 17. There is another sense in which it may be true that "by the offence of one, many were made sinners." "The offence of one" corrupted human nature, and this corruption of human nature leads to actual transgression. There is no other sense in which it can be consistently said, that, "by the offence of one, many were made sinners." If, as some contend, human nature has not suffered by the fall, and if all sin consists in voluntary actions, "the offence of one man cannot have been the cause of the sinfulness of many. It would be futile to say that the first offence led to the sinfulness of mankind generally, by the influence of the example it furnished; for such was the nature of Adam's offence, and such the condition in which it placed him and his descendants, as to preclude the possibility of a repetition of the same act. Not only so, but what influence can Adam's offence have on the morals of men, in producing sin at this late period of the world? Most certainly none at all, unless it be by a bias to sin which it has produced in human nature. If men are now naturally inclined to sin, in consequence of a bias, which human nature has received through the fall of Adam, it is the very thing for which we contend; but if human nature is not thus inclined to evil, then *many* cannot have been *made sinners* by the *disobedience* of one, and the Apostle stands corrected by the inventors of new doctrines.

IV. Those scriptures, which describe the unrenewed mind of man, clearly imply his native depravity. Jer. xvii. 9. "The heart is deceitful above all things and desperately wicked."

The strength of the argument, drawn from this and similar texts, which we shall introduce under this head, depends upon what is understood by the term *heart*. If by the heart is meant nothing more than the voluntary actions of men, the argument would lose much of its force; but if we understand by it the whole moral man, it follows that human nature itself is corrupt. Now, that by the heart is meant the mind, soul, or whole moral man, appears from the fact that those attributes and characteristics which belong to the soul, are ascribed to the heart, as will be seen by the following references. 1 Kings, iii. 12. "A wise and understanding heart." Rom. i. 21. "Foolish heart." Ex. xxxv. 5. "Willing heart." Psa. ci. 4. "A froward heart." Matt, xi.29. "Meek and lowly in heart." Prov. xxi. 4. "A proud heart." Psa. li. 17. "A contrite heart." Ex. vii. 14. "Hardened heart." Rom. ii. 5. "Impenitent heart." Psa. li. 10. "Unclean heart." Isa. xxxv. 4. "A fearful heart." Deut. xxviii. 47. "Joyfulness and gladness of heart." Lev. xxvi. 16. "Sorrow of heart," &c. &c. The above quotations clearly show that the scriptures do not mean the volitions of the mind, exclusively, when they speak of the heart, but that the whole mind or soul is intended; for wisdom, understanding, humility, pride, contrition, impenitence, purity, joy, sorrow, peace, &c. imply powers, passions and qualities, which are not attributable to volition alone, or to voluntary actions, but which belong essentially to the mind or soul. By the heart, then is meant, not the affections or volitions only, but the soul or whole moral and intellectual man; or the seat of the understanding, will, or volitions, affections and passions. Now as the "*heart*," which is the seat of the understanding, will, affections and passions, is said to be "deceitful above all things and desperately wicked," it follows that the whole man is depraved, and that entire human nature has become corrupt.

Gen. vi. 5. "And God saw that the wickedness of man was great in the earth, and that every imagination of the thoughts of his heart was only evil continually."

This text clearly makes a distinction between the heart and the volitions, or thoughts and purposes of the mind; the former is the source or fountain; the latter are the streams proceeding therefrom. The expression, "thoughts of his heart," marks the thoughts, as not being the heart, but as belonging to the heart, or proceeding therefrom. Now as every imagination of the thoughts of the heart is evil, it follows that the heart itself must be corrupt. Can that heart, from whence proceeds evil without any mixture of good, and without any intermission of the evil, be free from evil itself? When the heart can send forth that which it does not possess in itself, and when an effect can exist without a producing cause, then, and not before, this can be true. Should it be still contended that the evil has its existence alone in the volitions of the heart, and that the thoughts are evil, not in consequence of the source from whence they proceed, but from the objects to which they tend; it is replied, that this does not in the least alleviate the difficulty; it still leaves us without a reason why the volitions should all be evil, and every thought tend to an evil object. Can every volition of the human soul be evil, directing every thought towards an evil object, without ever once missing the mark; and still, the soul itself contain no bias to evil? As well may we suppose that something may exist or take place without an adequate cause; which, to say the least, is very unphilosophical.

Rom. vii. 18, 19, 20. "To will is present with me, but how to perform that which is good I find not, for the good that I would, I do not, but the evil which I would not, that I do. Now if I do that I would not, it is no more I that do it, but sin that dwelleth in me." Whether the Apostle is here speaking of himself as a christian, or as an awakened sinner; or whether he is simply personating one awakened to a sense of his danger, as a sinner, yet under the influence and guilt of sin, groaning for the pardoning mercy of God and "renewing of the Holy Ghost," by which he is to be delivered from the law of sin and death, are questions which do not materially affect the present argument; the latter however is our opinion. The text, we think, clearly teaches that human nature is corrupt, and that too beyond the will or volitions of the mind. Three things are to be particularly noticed.

1. The Apostle informs us that he could will that which was good. This, no doubt, was through the help of the Holy Spirit, under whose arrest and awakening energies his mind was labouring. Now, as to will was present, while he did not the good that he willed, it follows beyond the possibility of doubt that the sinner's depravity and helplessness does not consist merely in the perverseness of his will.

2. The Apostle declares that he finds not how to perform that which is good, and that he does that which he would not. This argues that there is in human nature a strong bias to evil, against which the will has to contend. If, as some contend, the sinner has a natural ability to do all that the perfect law of righteousness requires, without supernatural aid, the perverseness of his will only preventing, it is not possible to conceive how a man can sin by not doing the good which he wills, and by doing the evil which he would not.

3. The Apostle explains how he does that which he would not, by saying it is sin that dwelleth in him. "If I

do that I would not, it is no more I that do it, but sin that dwelleth in me." This clearly points out the corruption of human nature. The Apostle does evil: "The evil which I would not that I do." This clearly points out actual sin. But why does he do it? He declares that it is the work of sin that dwelleth in him. What then is this indwelling sin? It cannot be his volitions or voluntary actions, for he assigns it as a cause why he acts as he does, and it would be absurd to make the Apostle say that his actons [sic] were the cause of his actions; hence, there is in man an indwelling corruption which does not consist in action, and this we say, in the language of the church, "is the corruption of the nature of every man, that naturally is engendered of the offspring of Adam, whereby man is very far gone from original righteousness, and of his own nature inclined to evil, and that continually." (*Methodist Discipline, Article,* VII.)

Psa. li. 5. "Behold I was shapen in iniquity and in sin did my mother conceive me." On this text Dr. Clark has the following pointed remark. "Notwithstanding all that *Grotius* and others have said to the contrary, I believe David to speak here of what is commonly called *original sin*; the propensity to evil which every man brings into the world with him; and which is the fruitful source whence all transgression proceeds." That this is the true sense of the text is clear from the following more critical remarks made by Rev. Richard Watson. "What possible sense can be given to this passage on the hypothesis of man's natural innocence? It is in vain to render the first clause, 'I was *brought forth* in iniquity,' for nothing is gained by it. David charges nothing upon his mother, of whom he is not speaking, but of himself: he was conceived, or if it please better, was born a sinner. And if the rendering of the latter clause were allowed, which yet has no authority, 'in sin did my mother nurse me,' still no progress is made in getting quit of its testimony to the moral corruption of children; for it is the child only which is *nursed*, and if that be allowed, natural depravity is allowed; depravity before reasonable choice, which is the point in question."

We respond to the above: "What possible sense can be given to this passage," if no reference be had to inherited depravity? On such a supposition, it must stand a mere blank in the midst of a most interesting and pathetic subject. David is making confession of his sin, and imploring pardon for the same, and while thus confessing his actual sins, which he had committed, he adds an acknowledgement of his native corruption. "For I acknowledge my transgression, and my sin is ever before me; Against thee and thee only have I sinned and done this evil in thy sight: Behold I was shapen in iniquity and in sin did my mother conceive me." Understand the Psalmist in the above sense and the connexion is clear, the confession full, and the climax regular and grand. We understand him as saying, I have committed sin; I have not only sinned, but my sin has been of the most daring character, it has been committed against thee O God, Majesty of heaven! yea, I confess more; I have not only done wickedly, but my very nature is sinful; these outbreaking sins have been only the streams issuing from a fountain of corruption within, existing in my very nature which was shapen in iniquity and conceived in sin. When my mother conceived me, she conceived a sinful nature, and when I was formed into an organized being, my moral shape or likeness, was after the form of iniquity; i. e. in the image of a fallen spirit, and not after the image of God in which the first man was created.

Rom. viii. 7. "The carnal mind is enmity against God, for it is not subject to the law of God, neither indeed can be." The whole connexion in which this text stands, goes to show that by the "carnal mind" we are to understand the soul of man in its natural state, unrenewed by the quickening grace of God. The Apostle here notes the difference between a natural state and a renewed state. "To be carnally minded is death, but to be spiritually minded is life and peace; for the carnal mind is enmity against God. So then they that are in the flesh, cannot please God. But ye are not in the flesh if so be that the spirit of God dwell in you." To be carnally minded then, is to be destitute of the spirit of God by which he renews and sanctifies the soul; hence, the carnal mind is one unrenewed by the spirit of God: not "born of the spirit." Now, that this carnal mind, or state of enmity against God is the natural state of the soul, is evident from its being opposed to a state of grace and salvation. The scriptures speak of a two fold state: our natural state, and a spiritual or renewed state. "That which is born of the flesh is flesh, and that which is born of the spirit is spirit." John iii. 6. The first state must be our state by nature, the second state is a supernatural, gracious, and renewed state. The first state is a fleshly state in which we cannot please God; a carnal state, which is enmity against God: the second state is a state of reconciliation to God, a state of conformity to the divine will and likeness. Therefore, the carnal mind, which is enmity against God, being the natural state of the soul, it follows that man is by nature an enemy to God, or possesses a natural and inherent want of subjection or conformity to the divine law, which requires holiness in the inner parts. The texts above quoted, are to be regarded as mere specimens, of the many which, in similar language, describe the human soul in its natural state as a fallen spirit, full of wickedness, estranged from God, possessing unholy affections and passions.

V. Those scriptures which speak of the necessity, and describe the nature of regeneration, clearly imply the corruption of the human soul through the fall. John iii. 3. "Except a man be born again he cannot see the kingdom of God." that [sic] this text has reference to a moral change for the better, of some sort, we trust will not be denied by any; and that it is the change which constitutes the difference between a christian and a sinner, in the popular sense of these terms, appears from a consideration of the agent by which the change is effected; the spirit of God is the agent by which sinners are renewed and sanctified; hence, the Apostle says, "he hath saved us by the renewing of the Holy Ghost. The words of Christ "born again" exactly correspond to the words of the Apostle "renewing of the Holy Ghost," both implying the same change. That the necessity of such a change, as is implied by being born again, arises from the corruption of human nature, and not merely from the wickedness of human conduct, appears from the reason assigned by him, who "knew what was in man," "that which is born of the spirit is spirit, and that which is born of the flesh is flesh. Marvel not that I said unto you ye must be born again." Here the natural birth, which is of the flesh, and by which we are introduced into the world, is opposed to the spiritual birth by which we are introduced into the kingdom of God or church of Christ; and the *necessity* of the latter is made to depend upon the *circumstances* of the former: we must be born again" *because* that which *is born of the flesh is flesh*," to which an Apostle adds, "they that are *in the flesh* cannot please God." From this it most unequivocally appears that we inherit something by natural birth, or by natural generation which excludes us from the kingdom of God, being naturally unfit for its possession and enjoyments, and this unfitness is by birth, and not by subsequent wicked conduct. Therefore, moral depravity, in its first stage, consists in something which we inherit, and not in what we do.

It is worthy of remark, that the change under consideration is termed a *renewal*, a *new creation*, &c.; terms which can have no meaning unless the change is in fact a reparation of lapsed human nature. Titus

iii. 5. "He hath saved us by the washing of regeneration, and renewing of the Holy Ghost." Col. iii. 9, 10. "Ye have put of the old man with his deeds, and have put on the new man, which is renewed in knowledge, after the image of him that created him." 2 Cor. v. 17. "If any man be in Christ he is a new creature." Eph. ii. 10. "We are his workmanship *created* in Christ Jesus." Eph. iv. 24. "And that ye put on the new man which after God is *created* in righteousness and true holiness." These texts which are adduced merely as a specimen of the many which might be quoted on the same point, imply a renovation of nature as well as of life or conduct, and we repeat it, that they have no meaning, unless they imply a reparation of lapsed human nature; and if they imply this, the doctrine of inherent depravity is established.

To evade the force of this argument, and the consequences fatal to their system, which it must draw after it if admitted, universalists have sometimes referred the change commonly termed being born again, regeneration, &c. to the resurrection of the body; maintaining that all will experience it on that auspicious morn when the trumpet shall sound and the dead shall be raised. This attempt at evasion is so futile as not to deserve a refutation, were it not that it is sometimes uttered with an appearance of sincerity, by men who, of all others, ought to be serious. It is a sufficient reply, to remark that every text above quoted, and many more which might be quoted, speak of a change which takes place in this life. When Christ taught Nicodemus that he must be born again, he showed him that it must take place in this life, by terming it being born of *water* and of the *spirit*; the spirit working the change in the heart, and the water, externally applied in baptism, signifying the "washing of regeneration" within. And Paul who said, "they that are in the flesh "cannot please God," also said to those who were yet living, "ye are not in the flesh but in the spirit." Again the Apostle says, He *hath saved* us by the washing of regeneration—not, *will* save us, &c. We *are* his workmanship—not, *shall be*; ye *have* put off the old man and *have* put on the new man—not, *will* have, &c. &c.

VI. The corruption of human nature is proved by those scriptures which teach that there is in man remaining pollution, after justification or pardon.

2 Cor. vii. 1. "Having therefore these promises, dearly beloved, let us cleanse ourselves from all filthiness of the flesh and spirit, perfecting holiness in the fear of God." On this text it may be remarked, first, that it is addressed to christians, as such. Secondly, the expression in the text, *"let us cleanse ourselves from all filthiness of the flesh and spirit, perfecting holiness in the fear of God,"* clearly supposes that they were not, or that it was possible that as christians they might not have been, cleansed from all filthiness of the flesh and spirit, and that they were not as perfect in holiness as was their privilege to be; there may be, therefore, remaining in man a degree of moral corruption after he is justified by faith, or has his sins forgiven. It also follows that there is, with man, such a thing as an imperfect state of holiness.

1 Thes. v. 23. "And the very God of peace sanctify you wholly; and I pray God your whole spirit and soul, and body be preserved blameless unto the coming of our Lord Jesus Christ."

This text supposes that those to whom it relates, were sanctified in *part*, and not in *full*; or, at least, it supposes that sanctification in *part* and not in *full*, is a possible condition; for it would be absurd to pray to be sanctified *wholly* if there were no such thing as being sanctified in *part* without being wholly sanctified. Furthermore, as the Thessalonians, to whom the Apostle wrote, were, beyond all dispute, believers in Christ Jesus, it follows that men are not *necessarily* sanctified wholly in spirit, soul and body, when they are converted to God; or when they are justified through the forgiveness of sin; hence, there may be a degree of unholiness remaining in the spirit, soul, and body after justification.

On this point Mr. Watson has given the testimony of his opinion in the following language. "That a distinction exists between a regenerate state, and a state of entire and perfect holiness, will be generally allowed. Regeneration, as we have seen, is concomitant with justification; but the Apostles, in addressing the body of believers, in the churches to whom they wrote their epistles, set before them, both in their prayers they offer in their behalf, and in the exhortations they administer, a still higher degree of deliverance from sin, as well as a higher growth of christian virtues."

Now, this remaining corruption in the hearts of believers, after the pardon of sin, is totally irreconcileable [sic] with the native purity or indifference of human nature. When God pardons a sinner, he forgives all his sins that have been committed in past life; hence if human nature is not corrupt, and if all sin consists in voluntary actions, when a sinner is pardoned there could be no remaining corruption, or pollution, and the soul would be just as holy, just as free from moral defilement, as it would be if sin had never stained the universe.

This puts the doctrine of Christian perfection on the ground of our native innocence and purity, and not on the ground of that blood which *"cleanseth from all sin."* Though the Methodist Episcopal Church have been proverbial for holding and preaching the doctrine of perfection, yet it was never held among us on this ground, and we should in our very souls deprecate the day when, in this form, it should find its way into the church.

VII. The whole gospel economy proceeds on the ground of man's natural depravity, or corruption of nature. It will not be denied, that the whole gospel system is founded on the mission of Christ, and proceeds to offer salvation to the human family on the ground of what he has done and suffered for us. He came to "seek and save that which was lost"—he "gave himself a ransom for all," and tasted "death for every man." That "as by the offence of one" (Adam) "judgment came upon all men to condemnation, even so by the righteousness of one" (Jesus Christ) "the free gift came upon all men unto justification of life." "Neither is there salvation in any other; for there is none other name under heaven, given among men, whereby we must be saved;" for he is the "saviour of all men, especially of those that believe." There are two leading truths on the very face of the gospel, on the ground of which the whole gospel system proceeds. These truths are the following: First, all are lost and stand in need of salvation.—Secondly, Christ is the saviour of all, able and willing to save all that need, who will come unto him that they may have life. These truths, which lead the van, and draw after them every other part of the gospel theory clearly suppose a fallen and corrupt state of human nature; for they can be truths only in view of the truth of our inherent depravity. If man is not corrupt in nature, and if all sin consists in voluntary actions, it is perfectly possible to avoid all sin, so as to need no atonement for sin; no restorer, no mediator, no interposition of Jesus Christ to reconcile us to God. It would be profane to say that men are unreconciled to God so as to need a mediator, and lost so as to need salvation, in the same state in which God created them; having never broken his law nor in any way sinned against him: hence, if men are not by nature corrupt, it is possible to live free from all sin, so as not to need the atoning blood to wash away our sins, or the Holy Ghost to renew our hearts. This would be subversive of the whole gospel system. To such beings the story of Jesus' sufferings and death would be preached in vain; the invitations of the gospel would be heard only as addressed to others, and the proffered agency of the Holy Ghost would be declined, and the mission of Christ and the whole gospel system, would prove an unnecessary and an uncalled for interference with human allotment. The following very appropriate remarks, on this point, are from the pen of Mr. Fletcher. "In every religion there is a principal truth or error, which, like the first link of a chain, necessarily draws after it all the parts with which it is essentially connected. This leading principle in Christianity, distinguished from deism, is the doctrine of our corrupt and lost estate: for if man is not at variance with his Creator, what need of a mediator between God and him? If he is not a depraved, undone creature, what necessity of so wonderful a restorer and savior as the Son of God; If he is not enslaved to sin, why is he redeemed by Jesus Christ? If he is not polluted, why must he be washed in the blood of that immaculate lamb! If his soul is not disordered, what occasion is there for such a divine physician? If he is not helpless and miserable, why is he perpetually invited to secure the assistance and consolations of the Holy Spirit? And in a word, if he is not born in sin why is a new birth so absolutely necessary, that Christ declares, with the most solemn asseverations, without it no man can see the kingdom of God?"

Should it be replied to this, that men are not free in their volitions and actions, that their conduct is the result of an unseen yet resistless fate, rendering their sin certain and unavoidable; and that, therefore, the Gospel can proceed on the ground of the sinfulness of all men, without supposing a preexisting corruption of nature; it is at once replied that this would overthrow the whole gospel theory by annulling the sinner's guilt from which the gospel proposes to save him, and by making God the author of the sin which he, in the gospel, proposes to overthrow and destroy. To suppose that God has made provision, in the gospel, for all men on the ground that he has secured the sinfulness of all men by a previous decree, or on the ground that he causes the sinfulness of all men by a direct and governing agency, would be worse than trifling. Not only so, but the gospel proceeds with instructions, warnings, promises and threatenings, all on the ground that man is a moral agent.

Should it be said, that the gospel proceeds on the ground of the certainty of foreknowledge, God foreknowing that all would sin, instead of on the ground that all are lost by nature, it is replied, that it is not a fact that all do commit personal sin. Infants are not capable of committing sin; for they cannot be held responsible by a righteous moral law, for personal obedience, as is evident from the fact, that they have neither understanding, memory, nor consciousness. If infants are saved, they must be saved by Jesus Christ; for he is the only "name given under heaven among men whereby we must be saved;" and if infants are saved by Jesus Christ, they are saved as sinners, for the whole gospel system proceeds on the ground that those for whose benefit it was instituted, are sinners. "For the son of man is come to save that which *was lost.*" Now as infants can be saved by him only on the ground that they are fallen and sinful beings, it follows that, if they are not by nature corrupt and sinful, they must be lost; hence, to deny the doctrine of inherited depravity, is to deny the whole infant race all interest in the blood of the lamb, exclude them from the gospel plan of salvation and consign them to a fate, over which the darkness of uncertainty hangs as black as the brow of eternal night. Our souls shudder at the thought! What! shall our infants, who have had an earlier exit from earth, find no home in heaven? No saviour in the person of Jesus Christ? And shall they have no part in the song of the redeemed? To deny the sinfulness of human nature, then, is to deny that Christ died for infants; and hence, it is to deny them salvation through his blood and exclude them forever from the ranks of the redeemed; and to suppose that infants are not saved by Jesus Christ, is so slanderous on the character of our heavenly Father, and would so detract from the work and kingdom of the Messiah, that it cannot be deserving a serious refutation. Our opponents must either admit the sinfulness of human nature, or deny that infants have any interest in the Saviour of the human family, and we venture that but few, if any, will be found of sufficient hardihood openly to avow the latter.

VIII. In conclusion, on the subject of depravity, we appeal to the experience of all the good, who have resolved on living conformably to the strict piety and pure morals inculcated by our holy religion, and ask, if they have not found foes within, as well as without? If their disordered and scattered affections, so difficult to control and concentrate in the one supreme object, God; if their unholy passions so difficult to restrain and correct, which, at touch kindle into forbidden anger, and settle into deliberate and hateful revenge, or melt into compliance with the most low and debasing indulgencies [sic], do not teach that the soul to which such affections and passions belong, is a fallen and corrupt spirit? This appeal may have but little influence with the abandoned, who have never attempted to subdue their unholy propensities, who have yielded to the current of evil without resistance; but he, who has ever made an attempt at the pure religion of the gospel, will feel its force.

While the life of the christian is a warfare, a warfare not with the world and satan only, but with the affections and passions which are the attributes of his own soul, a warfare with the elements of his own nature, he will carry with him an ever present evidence of the corruption of human nature; an evidence that will last until the victory is complete and he finds himself wholly redeemed from the ruins of the fall.

III
Atonement

HAVING IN THE PRECEDING chapter considered the fallen state of the human family, we propose now to treat of their redemption by Jesus Christ. The doctrine of atonement has been referred to in arguments and remarks which have preceded; but we purpose to devote the present chapter to a more full consideration of this very important subject. The doctrine of a vicarious atonement, has a very important bearing on the controversy to which these pages are devoted; for if it can be shown, that the sufferings of Jesus Christ were a vicarious sacrifice for sinners, by virtue of which, and by which only, they can be restored to the divine favour and image, or be made holy and happy, two consequences will follow, fatal to the whole theory of modern universalism.

1. If sinners can be saved *only* through the merits of Christ's death, it must follow, that if such atonement had not been made, offenders must have been lost forever; and hence, that the proper penalty of the law or punishment of sin, is an endless curse.

2. It must follow on the above principles, that if it can be proved that sinners can, and do, forfeit the benefits of the atonement by a non-compliance with the conditions on which the gospel offers salvation, and consequently endure the punishment from which the death of Christ was intended to save them, they will still be lost as fully and endlessly as they would have been had Christ never died for their redemption.

To avoid these consequences, *modern* universalists deny the doctrine of a vicarious atonement, made by Jesus Christ, and maintain that his mission into this world, sufferings and death, were not intended to reconcile God to men, nor to render their salvation consistent with the claims of justice and the maintenance of the authority of the divine administration, but simply to reconcile sinners to God; winning their hearts by a display of divine love, and by bringing to view, through the gospel, the goodness and glories of the divine character. The above, we believe to be a correct statement of the opinion generally held by universalists on the subject of the atonement, as the following extracts will show. Mr. Hosea Ballou objects to the doctrine of a vicarious atonement, on the ground that it is improper for the innocent to suffer for the guilty. While treating upon this subject, he says: "We wish to inquire into the propriety of an innocent person's suffering for one who is guilty. It is scripture, reason and good law, never to condemn the innocent in order to exculpate the delinquent." *Treatise on Atonement, page* 74. Mr. B. says again, *page* 121. "God's love is antecedent to our love to him, which refutes the notion of God's receiving the atonement." The author, in stating his own views of atonement, *page* 120 says: "Atonement and reconciliation are the same, reconciliation is the renewal of love, and love is the law of the spirit of life in Christ Jesus. It is by the force and power of the law of love in Christ, that the soul is delivered from the government of the law of sin. The process of this deliverance is the work of atonement. The power which causes us to hate sin and love holiness, is the power of Christ, whereby atonement is made." Nearly the same sentiment is advanced by Mr. Pitt Morse, a late author, who has published a small volume of sermons, in reply to "Lectures on Universalism, by Joel Parker." On page 45 and 46 Mr. Morse remarks: "Let it be distinctly understood, that universalists do not contend that Christ saves men from the curse of the law, in any other way than by delivering them from their sins. He" (Mr. Parker) "probably understood the atonement according to the sense in which it is usually explained, viz. the satisfying divine justice by Jesus Christ giving himself a ransom for us, undergoing the penalty due our sins, and thereby releasing *us* from that punishment which God might justly inflict upon us. But we (universalists) do not so understand the atonement. It is generally taught that God receives the atonement. It is something received by man. What can it be? Atonement is reconciliation to God." The above extracts, are calculated in some respects, to give a false view of the commonly received doctrine of atonement; yet they fully answer the purpose for which they are here intended, viz: to shew that universalists do not believe in the merits of Christ, as the ground of the sinner's hope; that they reject *in full* the doctrine of atonement, as generally believed. In opposition to the views contained in these extracts, we maintain that Christ suffered and died in the place of sinners; in a manner to deliver them from the punishment due their sins, and that the merits of his death, as our atoning sacrifice, is the ground, and the only ground of our restoration to holiness and happiness. We will now proceed to the proof of our views on this subjects.

I. The necessity of a vicarious atonement, may be urged in proof of the doctrine itself. That God does save sinners in some way, by restoring them to holiness and happiness, will not be denied, especially by universalists. It being admitted on all hands that God does save sinners, it follows that he saves them by, or without, atonement; hence, if it can be shown to be inconsistent with the principles of the divine administration to save transgressors without satisfaction on their part, which is out of their power to make for themselves, the fair inference will be that Christ, by his mediation, has made the necessary atonement for them; since no one will contend that there is any other mediator between God and men, save the man Christ Jesus, "who gave himself a ransom for all." The main points to be considered in this argument, are, the nature and penalty of the divine law, the impossibility that any law should provide for the remission of its own penalty, and the absurdity of supposing that God can pardon transgression by mere prerogative without an atonement, consistently with the moral government which he has established over his creatures.

That we are under some law to our Creator, will not be denied by any. "If we deny the existence of a divine law obligatory upon man," says Mr. Watson, "we must deny that the world is under divine government; for government without rule or law is a solecism." The law, by which we should be governed, is the will of our Creator. When God brings any rational being into existence, such being must be under obligation to the hand that made him, and as every power is the work of the Creator, nothing short of the employment of the whole, in accordance with his will, can requite the claim of the divine author.

Taking this view, we see that no rational being can exist without law to God, which law commences with the commencement of our rational existence, and continues through the whole extent of our being—while life, and thought, and being, last. That God has made known his will to us in the scriptures, and that men have violated that will, universalists will not be willing *openly* to deny.

We will then enquire into the nature and extent of the penalty of this violated law.

The penalty of God's law is death. Death was the penal sanction of the first precept given to man. Gen. iii.47. "In the day thou eatest thereof thou shalt surely die." Ezek. xviii. 20. "The soul that sinneth it shall die." Rom. vi. 23. "The wages of sin is death." Rom. viii. 6. "To be carnally minded is death." James i. 15. "Sin when finished bringeth forth death." Now, death, whether natural or moral, must be in its own nature endless. What is death? It is the negation of life, the absence of that life to which it stands opposed. If death is made to consist in moral depravity, it is the negation of that holiness, that conformity to the divine will and likeness, which constitutes moral or spiritual life. If death is made to consist in the dissolution of the body, it is the negation of those vital energies which constitute animal life. When a person dies morally or naturally, it is the principle or power of the opposite life that is overcome; life becomes extinct and death reigns. Now when a person is dead, on this principle, self-resuscitation is utterly impossible, life has become extinct and nothing but death reigns and pervades the whole system; hence death left to the tendency of its own nature must hold on to its subjects with an eternal grasp, unless it be said that death can produce life, or that inertia can produce animation; for as there is nothing but death now pervading the once animated sphere of the fallen, the energies of life can move there no more forever, unless they can spring from death, or out of nothing rise.

It is certain then, so far as moral or spiritual death is concerned on which this argument is predicated, that persons once dead must remain dead forever, unless God, who said "thou shalt die," speak to the dead and say, thou shalt live, and thereby revoke the sentence of his righteous law. We see then that there is no way of being delivered from the penalty of the law but by a pardon;

for when the penalty of the law takes effect in the death of the sinner, as that death is in its own nature endless, holding the criminal under its dominion, any subsequent deliverance by the communication of life by God, from whom it must proceed, must be regarded in the light of a pardon, since, in such a case, the offender does not endure all that the sentence imports; death being endless of itself. If then there is no salvation but by a pardon, we are led to enquire on what ground such pardon is to be looked for.

There are but three grounds of pardon which, in view of this argument, can be taken with any appearance of plausibility; viz. by some provision in the law, by the prerogative of God, or by an atonement. When the two former of these grounds shall be shewn untenable, the latter will appear true.

Does the law, then, make provision for the remission of its own penalty? This question is answered by St. Paul, Gal. iii. 21, 22. "If there had been a law given which could have given life, verily, righteousness should have been by the law, but the scripture hath concluded all under sin, that the promise, by faith of Jesus Christ, might be given to them that believe." In this text, the Apostle asserts, in effect, that no law has been given which can give life, hence, the law, which inflicts death, can contain no provisions for the removal of death and the restoration of the dead to life; for in such case the law would give life, which is the point the apostle denies. A law without any penal sanction would be of no force, and might be violated with impunity; and a law, making provision for delivering offenders from its penalty, would be the same, in effect, as a law without any penal sanction; since, in such case no penalty would take effect; therefore, the idea of a law making provision for delivering offenders from its own penal sanctions, is a solecism.

Is pardon, then, to be expected by the prerogative of

God? We proceed, to the answer of this question, on the ground that God is immutable, just, wise, and good, which will not be denied by any, who believe in the God of the Bible. These perfections of the divine nature are so many objections to the theory which asserts the pardon of transgressors, by the *mere prerogative* of God without an atonement.

1. If God be immutable, what he does or sanctions at one time, he must do or sanction at all times, under circumstances involving the same moral principles. God having sanctioned the death of the sinner, by attaching death to his law as a penalty, to counteract it by interposing a pardon would be to act differently at different times, under circumstances which involve the same moral principles, which would clearly imply mutability or change; unless something be urged as the ground of the pardon which renders the case of the offender a different one from what the law contemplates, as is the case, on the supposition that Christ has made an atonement. Taking this view, it must appear that for God to pardon merely prerogative, not only implies his mutability, but also involves the divine administration in principles which contradict and oppose each other. It makes God say in his law, the soul that sinneth it shall die, and at the same time say, by an act of pardon, the sinner shall not die; both of which cannot be true.

2. Divine justice, on the above principles, must be violated, either in the penalty of death, or else, in the pardon which averts the penalty. The law claims the death of the transgressor; hence, if the law be just, justice claims the death of the offender; and justice as well as law says, the soul that sinneth, it shall die. On the other hand, if justice does not claim the death of the offender, the law claims more than justice and must be unjust, and, consequently, God must be unjust; for he could not be just in giving an unjust law. Now as justice claims the death of the sinner,

his deliverance by a pardon, founded on mere prerogative, would be a violation of justice; for justice cannot claim the death of a sinner and sanction his life at the same time, all in view of the same moral principles. The conclusion is that if God pardons sinners by mere prerogative, he must have been unjust in sanctioning his law with the penalty of death, or else in the pardon which sets aside a just penalty.

3. If God is all-wise, he must have seen it proper and for the good of the moral system that transgressors should die, or he would never have sanctioned his law with the penalty of death; for God could not be wise in giving to his law a penalty, the execution of which would be improper and opposed to the best interests of his government. Now, if perfect wisdom saw that it would be proper and for the best interests of the moral system that offenders should die, the same perfect wisdom cannot see that it is proper and for the best interests of the moral system that the same offenders should live: It is either proper and for the best interests of the di- vine government that sinners should die, or it is not; if it is proper and for the best, God would be unwise to pardon them; but if it be not proper and for the best, that sinners should die, God must have been unwise when he gave his law the sanction of death. The conclusion is, that if God pardons offenders by mere prerogative, he must have acted unwisely when he sanctioned his law with the penalty of death, or he acts unwisely when he prevents the execution of such penalty by extending a pardon to the offender.

4. The same mode of reasoning may be employed in relation to the goodness of God, for it must appear obvious to all, that the same goodness which would pardon a sinner to save him from death, which is the penalty of the law, would have withheld such a sanction from the law; or to reverse the order, *that* goodness which would

sanction the law with the penalty of death, would not prevent its execution, but suffer the offender to die. But we forbear to pursue this subject, supposing enough has been said.

Should it be conjectured that the above reasoning stands opposed to our own views of pardon through the atoning merits of Jesus Christ, we answer, that a pardon upon consideration of an atonement, consisting in a substitute for the sinner's death, involves moral principles very different from a pardon by mere prerogative. When the doctrine of pardon is urged on the ground of atonement, it supposes a consideration or reason which the law does not contemplate in the denunciation of its penalty against all offenders; and such new consideration justifies a different procedure in the divine administration. God may say that sinners shall die, in view of the relation which they sustain to the divine government, merely as his creatures in rebellion against his authority, and yet pardon the sinner redeemed by Christ, in whose behalf Christ has offered himself a redemption price, without implying any mutability in God, or change in the moral principles of his government; since, in this case, the change is not in God, nor in the principles of his government, but in the sinner, or in the relation which he sustains to the divine administration. Again, God may see it just and wise to condemn to death, sinners unredeemed, or sinners rejecting offered grace through a redeemer, and at the same time see it consistent with justice and wisdom to save redeemed sinners through faith in Jesus Christ.

Before we dismiss this point, it may be well to bestow a few remarks on the argument sometimes offered in support of the notion of a pardon by the prerogative of God, drawn from the example of civil governments. It is said that civil governments pardon offenders with the approbation of the good and wise, and that if it be right for civil governments to pardon, it must be admitted that the divine government can pardon. To this we reply, that it must be admitted that the best human governments are imperfect; and it cannot be safe to rely upon deductions drawn from the doings of an imperfect government, in proof of what a perfect government will do. In order to show the absurdity of the argument, let it be noted:

1. That no human government vests in the hands of the executive the right of pardon, with the expectation that it will be universally exercised, so that no offender be punished; for, in such case, it would be more consistent to repeal the law, or not to enact penal laws, and thereby save the executive the trouble of granting pardons. But with respect to the divine government, it must be contended that God will exercise the prerogative of pardon universally, or the argument will not answer the purpose for which it is intended. The argument then stands thus: civil governments, in *some cases*, pardon offenders, therefore, the divine government will pardon *all* offenders. A universal conclusion is here drawn from a restricted proposition. By reversing the argument, it will prove just as much, yea more, on the opposite side of the question, thus: civil governments generally punish offenders by inflicting the penalty of the law; therefore, God will punish all offenders. This latter form of the argument possesses the greater force, just in proportion as the number of instances, in which civil governments inflict the penalty of the law, is greater than the number of instances in which they remit the penalty.

2. The right of pardon, in civil governments, is necessary in view of the liability of all human tribunals to err. The real facts in a case cannot always be brought to light before a human tribunal, while two judges or juries may come to different conclusions in view of the same facts. Under such circumstances, the executive

should have the right of pardon that he may exercise it in doubtful cases; whereas, no such reason for its exercise can exist in the divine administration, for God sees all things just as they are.

3. If civil governments pardon offenders, whose guilt is notorious, it is not on the ground that justice or goodness to the offender requires that a pardon be granted to him; for a pardon, granted on such ground, would be an admission that justice and goodness are violated in every case in which pardon is not granted. On what ground, then, is pardon extended to offenders whose guilt is manifest? We answer, on the ground that the enforcement of law, in that particular case, is not necessary to secure the purposes of government, or on the ground that in that particular case, the penalty of the law may be remitted without endangering the stability of government or the good order of community. But it may be asked, if a pardon, on such ground, would not be as much a violation of moral justice, as we have supposed it to be for God to pardon by mere prerogative? We answer, by no means. A civil pardon is not an absolution of moral guilt, nor a *final* deliverance from any just punishment, but merely a suspension of punishment, referring the criminal to the law of God, by whom he shall be judged for the same offence, and from whom he will receive all the punishment he deserves; but should God pardon offenders, it would be to exempt criminals from all judgment and punishment, for there is no higher tribunal to call them to an account. We think we have now established the following propositions:

1. Such is the nature of the divine law and its penalty, that no creature, having once incurred its penalty, can ever be delivered from it, except by a pardon from the law giver.

2. The law makes no provision for the remission of its own penalty.

3. God cannot, consistently with his own perfections, and the principles of his moral government, extend pardon to offenders by mere prerogative.

The irresistible conclusion which strikes us in view of these propositions is, that sinners must remain forever under the curse of the law, or be saved through mediation or atonement; which atonement, must be in some sense, regarded as a satisfaction to divine justice in their behalf. By whom then has this atonement been made? We answer, by Jesus Christ, by man, or by some other being. One of these propositions must be *true*; hence, if we can show two propositions out of the three to be *false*, the remaining one will most certainly be true.

Can man, then, make an atonement for his own sins? This is impossible, in view of the following facts:

1. Man has nothing to present, as an atonement, or to render to divine justice as a redemption price, on which the law had not a previous claim. Were man capable of obeying the law, perfectly, from this time forward and forever, and should he do it, it would not atone for his past sins; for all this the law claims without any reference to his past disobedience, and would have claimed, if he had never disobeyed. We have already seen that the law claims man's entire obedience, through the whole period of his existence; but if the sinner should, at any time, commence a course of obedience, and pursue it forward, in view of his past disobedience, he could obey God, only during a part of his existence, and hence, must forever come short of answering the claims of the divine law.

2. We have shown in a preceding chapter, that man is a fallen and corrupt being by nature; he is, therefore, incapable of any such obedience without first being redeemed and renewed by grace.

But it may be asked, is not repentance all the restitution that is required of sinners? We answer, repentance is *no* restitution, and cannot, in the least, be regarded in the light of an atonement. If repentance be regarded, as it is by those who deny the doctrine of atonement, as a mere reformation from open vice, it would appear a singular atonement indeed. It amounts to this, in principle: I have offended against a good law; now how shall I escape punishment? I will satisfy the claims of the law by an atonement. But what shall I render as a satisfaction? It I can be excused I will leave off committing the offence. Such notions of atonement are too lax to deserve further notice. But should repentance be viewed as a work of the heart, under the exercise of a godly sorrow for sin, producing confession of sin and reformation in life, it will still come short of being an atonement, for the following reasons:

1. Repentance is a work or an exercise which cannot exist without the previous existence of sin, and can be exercised by none but sinners. Now, that which is dependant upon sin for its very existence, the necessity and existence of which is laid in sin, cannot be an atonement for sin. Again, as repentance is an exercise of the heart and soul, under a sense of guilt and exposure, producing a heartfelt sorrow for sin, it cannot constitute an atonement for sin; for the law had a previous claim on the entire heart, requiring the exercise of all its powers, not in repentance, but in the more noble work of loving the Creator. "Thou shalt love the Lord thy God with all thy heart, and with all thy soul, and with all thy mind, and with all thy might." We have already noticed that in order to an atonement, something must be engaged on which the law had not a previous claim, which is not the case in the work of repentance.

2. Repentance is not only insufficient in itself, but, in view of the fallen state of man, it cannot be exercised without the gracious influence of the Holy Spirit, which supposes a state of grace previous to repentance; hence, the atonement must be made before repentance can take place, and that which can exist only subsequently to an

atonement, cannot be the atonement itself. We see then that man cannot make an atonement for sin, nor give a ransom for his own soul.

We ask, then, has some other being save Jesus Christ, made an atonement for sinful man. This question, we think, will be answered in the negative by all parties. The thing is impossible in itself, for the following reasons:

1. It would be absurd to suppose, that an atonement could be made in any other nature save that in which the offence was committed, and for which the atonement is offered.

2. If the difference in nature formed no objection to the mediation of a being from some distant orb, or some heavenly sphere, still, no being could be found capable of making an atonement. We have already seen that every created being is under obligation to devote all his powers to God, for his own personal existence, and as no created being can possess any powers which he has not received from God, he can possess no power, on which God has not an entire claim; hence, no created being can do more than duty requires, and therefore can merit nothing to place to the account of others who may be deficient. Taking this view of the subject, we may search all worlds, heaven, earth, and hell, and we cannot find a ransom for our race, save in the person of Jesus Christ; the Word who was made flesh, who was "God manifested in the flesh." Now, as we have, shown that there can be no deliverance from the penalty of the law but by an atonement, and as we have also shown that an atonement can be made by no being save Jesus Christ, it follows that he, who died on the cross, was our atoning sacrifice, and that we are constrained to rely on the merits of his death, as the ground of our hope, or retire to the shades of despair as dark as the gloom of an endless death.

We see, from this, how falsely that system, which denies the doctrine of atonement, has been called a system of *universal salvation!* Never was there a greater misnomer! It involves principles which, if true, would damn the world, and yet it is called *salvation!*

II. The types and symbols of the Mosaic Ritual, which typify Jesus Christ, are of such a character as to point him out as a sacrifice for sin, and an expiation for the sinner's guilt. Let us consider some of the offerings for sin directed by the Levitical Law.

Lev. iv. 27, 28, 29, 30, 31. "And if any one of the common people sin, he shall bring his offering, a kid of the goats, a female without blemish for his sin which he hath sinned; and he shall lay his hand upon the head of the sin offering, and slay the sin offering in the place of the burnt offering. And the priest shall take of the blood thereof with his finger, and put it upon the horns of the altar of burnt offering, and shall pour out all the blood thereof at the bottom of the altar; and he shall take away all the fat thereof as the fat is taken away from off the sacrifice of peace offerings, and the priest shall burn it upon the altar for a sweet savour unto the Lord; and the priest shall make an atonement for him, and it shall be forgiven him."

If God did not require a sacrifice for sin, as an expiation of the sinner's guilt there can be no meaning in the whole of the above performance. The sinner laid his hand upon the victim that was to be slain, denoting a symbolical transfer of sin from the sinner to the sin offering; the latter dying in the place of the former. Nor can it be pretended that the offering was a mere fine for the sinner's trespass, for in such case it would have been an offset, in itself considered, which was not the case as appears from two circumstances.

1. The victim received all its validity, as a sacrifice for sin, from the place and circumstance of the offering, and not from any intrinsic value it possessed in itself, as being equal to damages sustained by the sinner's trespass. Had the victim been offered in any

other place, save in the sanctuary, it would not have been accepted as an atonement for sin. The sanctuary was regarded as the place of the divine presence, for in it God had recorded his name; and this being the place where the sacrifice was made, marked it as *an offering to God on the part of the sinner.* The offering was made by the priest, who must be acknowledged to be the type of Jesus Christ, in his great sacrificial work. Had the sacrifice been presented by any other person save the priest, it would have been no atonement; whereas neither the place nor the person making the offering could have affected its value, if it was to be regarded as a mere fine for trespass. Again, nothing else, of the same or even greater value, than the victims prescribed by the law could have been accepted in their place, as a sin offering, which shows that the law did not have reference to their value as a fine for an equal amount of damage done, but that they were by divine appointment, rendered acceptable in their death, as a substitute for the sinner's death, who had forfeited his life by his sin.

2. The offender was not released on the ground of having paid an equivalent for his sin, which must have been the case if his offering was regarded as a mere fine for his trespass; but he received a pardon of the offence on the presentation of his sin offering. It is said "the priest shall make an atonement for him and it shall be *forgiven* him. This clearly proves that an atonement for sin was directed by the law, to be made to God to procure his pardon, and not to man, exclusively to procure his reconciliation to God. It also proves that the atonement, directed by the law, was an expiation of the sinner's guilt, effecting his deliverance from the punishment he deserved, not however by an absolute payment of the debt, but by procuring a pardon. God pardoned the sinner on the ground of the sin offering or atonement, directed to be made by the

priest of the sanctuary, which was rendered acceptable by two circumstances.
1. It was of God's own appointment.
2. It had reference to, and typically pointed out, the sacrificial death of Jesus Christ, "who gave himself a ransom for all, by whom we have now received the atonement." These remarks may serve as a comment on all the offerings for sin, ordained under the Levitical priesthood, which are too numerous to be particularly mentioned; the annual atonement, however, is of sufficient importance to entitle it to some special notice. Lev. xvi. 5, 7, 8, 9, 10, 21, 22. "And he shall take of the congregation of the children of Israel two kids of the goats, for a sin offering and he shall take the two goats and present them before the Lord at the door of the congregation. And Aaron shall cast lots upon the two goats; one lot for the Lord and the other lot for the scape goat; and Aaron shall bring the goat upon which the Lord's lot fell, and offer him for a sin offering. But the goat, on which the lot fell to be the scape goat, shall be presented alive before the Lord, to make an atonement with him, and to let him go for a scape goat into the wilderness. And Aaron shall lay both his hands upon the head of the live goat, and confess over him all the iniquities of the children of Israel, and all their transgressions in all their sins, putting them upon the head of the goat, and shall send him away by the hand of a fit man into the wilderness; and the goat shall bear upon him all their iniquities unto a land not inhabited." On this offering Dr. Clark has made the following remarks: "It is allowed on all hands that this ceremony, taken in all its parts, pointed out the Lord Jesus dying for our sins, and rising again for our justification; being put to death in the flesh, but quickened by the spirit. Two goats are brought, one to be slain as a sacrifice for sin, the other to have the trans-

gressions of the people confessed over his head, and then to be sent away into the wilderness. This animal, by this act was represented as bearing away, and carrying off, the sins of the people. The two goats made only one sacrifice; yet only one of them was slain. One animal could not point out both the divine and human nature of Christ, nor show both his death and resurrection, for the goat that was killed could not be made alive. The divine, and human natures of Christ were essential to the grand expiation: yet the human nature alone suffered; for the divine nature could not suffer; but its presence in the human nature, while agonizing unto death, stamped those agonies, and the consequent death, with infinite merit. The goat therefore, that was slain, prefigured his human nature, and its death: the goat that escaped, pointed out his resurrection. The one shows the atonement for sin as the ground of justification; the other Christ's victory, and the total removal of sin in the sanctification of the soul." On the above ceremony of making the annual atonement for the sins of the people, we remark, in addition to the quotation from Dr. Clark already given,

1. That the offering must be regarded as an atonement for sin and expiation of the sinner's guilt, from the plain and simple language in which it is set forth: "And Aaron shall lay both his hands upon the head of the live goat, and confess over him all the iniquities of the children of Israel, and the goat shall bear on him all their iniquities into a land not inhabited." Here is an actual removal of sin, not by suffering its punishment, but by an atonement or expiation. Is it said that this bearing away of the sins of the people by the scape goat was not real, but symbolical, or typical? It is replied, that this does not in the least invalidate the argument; for if the Mosaic ritual, in pointing to better things to come, symbolically represented the removal of sin by an atonement, then, it must

follow that the better covenant provides a real atonement which does in fact remove sin and save from the punishment it deserves.

2. This atonement was made for past sins, and not in anticipation of sins which might be committed in future, nor to prevent the future commission of sin, which universalists contend is the only way in which Christ saves from sin. The high priest confessed the iniquities of the people, laying his hands upon the head of the goat, and the goat bore them away. We ask, what sins the high priest confessed? If they were sins which had not been and were never after committed, he confessed that of which they were never guilty, and his confession must have been false; and if they were sins which were afterwards committed, then, the confession and atonement produced no effect, since, the sins confessed and atoned for existed the same as though no confession and atonement had been made, and the offenders were punished for them, if there is no salvation from merited punishment. This proves that the notion that atonement saves only from the commission of sin in the future, is false. On the same principle, we ask, what sins the scape goat bore away? If they were sins which were never committed, he bore away just no sins at all; for he could not have borne away that which had not been, was not, and never should be; and if they were sins which were afterwards committed, then he did not bear them away, since they were afterwards committed and the people suffered for them, if an atonement does not save from the punishment due to sin. It is clear then that the atonements, made under the law, were, at least, typically an expiation of sins that were passed.

3. The atonements, made under the law, were symbols and types of the atonement or offering of Jesus Christ, who gave himself a ransom for all. This position is clearly sustained by the reasoning of the Apostle, Heb. ix. 1, 9, 11, 12, 13, 14, 22, 23, 24, 25, 26. "Then verily the first

covenant had also ordinances of divine service, and a worldly sanctuary, which was a figure for the time then present, in which were offered both gifts and sacrifices, that could not make him that did the service perfect as pertaining to the conscience. But Christ being come a high priest of good things to come, by a greater and more perfect tabernacle, not made with hands; neither by the blood of goats and calves, but by his own blood, he entered once into the holy place, having obtained eternal redemption for us. For if the blood of bulls and of goats, and the ashes of a heifer sprinkling the unclean, sanctifieth to the purifying of the flesh, how much more shall the blood of Christ, who through the eternal Spirit offered himself without spot, to God, purge your consciences from dead works to serve the living God. And almost all things are by the law purged with blood; and without shedding of blood is no remission. It was therefore necessary that the patterns of things in the heavens, should be purified with these; for Christ is not entered into the holy place made with hands, which are the figures of the true; but into heaven itself, now to appear in the presence of God for us: nor yet that he should offer himself often, as the high priest entereth into the holy place every year with blood of others; for then must he often have suffered since the foundation of the world: but now once in the end of the world hath he appeared to put away sin by the sacrifice of himself."

This language of the apostle is too plain to be misunderstood or to need explanation. It must be seen that he draws a comparison between the offerings under the law and the one offering of Jesus Christ, and represents the former as shadowing forth the latter, and the latter as the substance, object, and end of the former; exceeding them in character and value in the same proportion in which a substance outweighs a shadow, or a thing itself transcends its mere pattern or symbol. He refers directly to the annual atonement made by the high priest: "Nor yet that he (Christ) should offer himself often, as the high priest entereth into the holy place every year with blood of others." This offering he represents only as a temporary relief, saying, Chap. x. 3. "But in those sacrifices there is a remembrance made of sins every year," but the offering of Christ he represents as being more perfect, saying, "he entered in *once* into the holy place, having obtained eternal redemption for us," having "now *once* in the end of the world appeared to put away sin by the offering of himself." Much more might be said under this head, but we trust sufficient has been advanced to show that the sacrifices of the Mosaic ritual point out Jesus Christ, as a real atonement and expiatory sacrifice for sin. Deny the vicarious and expiatory character of the sufferings and death of Jesus Christ, and the ceremonial worship of the Jews loses its charm, their sanctuary is divested of its significant grandeur, their smoking altars lose their sanctity, the confession upon the head of the scape goat becomes foolish mummery, and their sacrifices of slaughtered hecatombs are rendered useless, barbarous and cruel.

III. The scriptures teach, directly, that the sufferings and death of Jesus Christ, were in the place of the punishment which was due to sinners; he suffering in their stead, bearing the punishment which they otherwise must have borne and from which they, consequently, may now be delivered on gospel terms. By this, however, we do not mean that Christ suffered the same in kind and degree that sinners would have suffered, but simply that what he suffered was a substitute for what they must have suffered without the atonement. Isa. liii. 5, 6, 8, 11, 12. "He was wounded for our transgressions, he was bruised for our iniquities, the chastisement of our peace was upon him, and with his stripes we are healed. The Lord hath laid upon him the iniquity of us all; for the transgression of my people was he stricken. He shall bear their iniquities, ana he bore the sin of many and made intercession for the transgressors."

That this whole chapter relates to Jesus Christ there is no doubt, and if it does not teach that he suffered for sinners, bearing a punishment for their sins, it is because the sentiment cannot be couched in the English language. Why was he wounded for our transgressions and bruised for our iniquities, if it was not to save us from being thus wounded and bruised? It is worthy of remark, that in this interesting chapter, Christ is represented as suffering for us by divine appointment, and under the divine sanction: "the Lord hath laid on him the iniquity of us all" —"when thou shalt make his soul an offering for sin." Now, if it was not the divine purpose to save us from the punishment our sins deserve by laying our iniquities on Jesus Christ, and making his soul an offering for sin; if after all this, we must inevitably suffer *all* that our sins deserve, then what Christ suffered for us must have been over and above what justice requires, and, consequently, unjust and cruel.

But we recollect of having seen an attempt made by universalists to evade the force of the above quotations from the Prophet. It has been said that this prophecy was fulfilled in the miracles which Christ wrought for the relief of the afflicted; in proof of which they quote Matt. viii. 16, 17. "He healed all that were sick, that it might be fulfilled which was spoken by Esaias the prophet saying, himself took our infirmities and bare our sicknesses." That this is a quotation from the same chapter, we admit, but it is not a quotation from any portion which we have quoted, or on which we rely as proof of the point in question, but is borrowed from the 4th verse which reads thus: "Surely he hath borne our griefs and carried our sorrows." These are the words which the Evangelist applies to Christ's healing the sick, which can furnish no ground for making the same application of the whole chapter, some of which most clearly refers to his death and not to the works of benevolence which he performed during his ministry. There is a vast difference between his bearing our grief and carrying our sorrows, or as the Evangelist renders it "taking our infirmities and bearing our sicknesses, and being wounded for our transgressions" and "bruised for our iniquities; or being "numbered with the transgressors" and bearing "the sin of many." But this question is settled by the fact that two other Evangelists quote from the same subject and apply it to his crucifixion, Mark. xv. 27, 28, "And with him they crucify two thieves; the one on his right hand and the other on his left, and the scripture was fulfilled which saith, and he was numbered with the transgressors." This is a quotation from the 12th verse which reads thus: "He hath poured out his soul unto death, and he was numbered with the transgressors, and he bare the sin of many." Luke xxxii. 37. "And he was reckoned among the transgressors." It is clear then that the prophet describes the death, as well as the life, of our blessed Lord, and forcibly points it out as a sacrifice for sin.

In the above position we are, if possible, more amply sustained by the apostles in the New Testament, who express the same sentiment in nearly the same language, evidently borrowing their descriptions from the above paintings of the prophetic pencil.

1 Cor. xv. 3. "For I delivered unto you first of all, that which I also received, how that Christ died for our sins according to the scriptures." Several points in this text, deserve notice.

1. The substance of the apostle's declaration is *"Christ died for our sins."*

2. This, doctrine of the vicarious death of Christ, he

declares, he received: "I delivered unto you that which I also received." It was not a thought of his own, nor the invention of man, but he received it from God who called him to preach Christ crucified.

3. This doctrine of Christ's death for our sins, he says, he "delivered unto them first of all," showing that he considered the doctrine of Christ's vicarious death one of the first principles of the Gospel, of the first importance, on which the sinner's hope rests, and upon which the whole Gospel fabrick is reared.

4. This doctrine of Christ's death for our sins, he declares, is *"according to the scriptures."*

Let it be understood that, by the scriptures here, the Old Testament only can be intended, and what we have said on this subject, reasoning from the law and the prophets, is confirmed. As the apostle declares that Christ's death for our sins was according to the scriptures of the Old Testament, it follows that the sin offerings made under the law were representations of his death, and pointed him out as suffering for sinners; and that the prophet, in foretelling his passion, referred to the same object of his death saying, "When thou shalt make his soul an offering for sin he shall see his seed," &c.

1 Peter ii. 24, 25. "Who his ownself bare our sins, in his own body, on the tree, by whose stripes ye are healed; for ye were as sheep going astray." This is almost a literal quotation from the prophet, whose words we have already considered, and goes farther to show that we are sustained by the New Testament writers, in our application of the prophet's language to the death of Christ as a sacrifice for sin. The apostle here is so plain and precise that it seems hardly possible to misunderstand or misapply his language.

1. He states that Christ bore our sins.
2. To show beyond all dispute that he bore them liter-

ally, and not in some symbolical or allegorical manner, he notes the manner in which he bore them, in three particulars. *First*, he bore them "his own self." *Secondly*, he bore them "in his own body." *Thirdly*, he bore them "on the tree," i. e. on the cross.

3. Lest some sceptick should still question the meritorious character of Christ's sufferings the apostle adds "by his stripes ye are healed."

Rom. iv. 25. "Who was delivered for our offences and raised again for our justification." Here, the Apostle clearly asserts Christ's death for sinners, and their deliverance or salvation from the guilt of sin by his resurrection; i. e. he died to atone for our sins, and rose again to intercede for us, by pleading the merits of his death; we, therefore, may be justified, i. e. saved from the guilt and, consequently, the punishment of sin, through his resurrection.

2 Cor. v. 21. "For he hath made him to be sin for us who knew no sin, that we might be made the righteousness of God in him." On this text, it may be remarked,

1. By Christ's being made sin for us, we are to understand that he was made a sin offering for us, or an offering for our sin.

2. The design of this was that we might be made the righteousness of God in him, by which we understand, being made the partakers of God's justifying and renewing grace, whereby we are rendered righteous. This is termed the righteousness of God, because the pardon of sin on the ground of the sin offering of Christ, whereby we are justified from sins that are past, is the prerogative and act of God, and because the internal work of renewing the heart and sanctifying the soul, whereby we are rendered righteous in heart and life, is the work of God's Holy Spirit.

1 Peter iii. 18. "For Christ also hath once suffered for sins, the just for the unjust, that he might bring us to

God, being put to death in the flesh but quickened by the spirit."

1. This text declares that Christ suffered for sins.

2. It was not his own sins for which he suffered, for he was without sin, but he suffered "the just for the unjust," his sufferings were therefore vicarious.

3. The object of his sufferings was that he might bring us to God; his sufferings, therefore, must have been necessary in order to our salvation.

4. To show that the salvation of sinners depends upon the merits of Christ's death, and not upon the influence of his example and truth, revealed in his gospel aside from his death, the apostle refers the whole to his passion: "He suffered for sin, that he might bring us to God, *being put to death in the flesh.*"

Heb. ix. 28. "So Christ was once offered to bear the sins of many." Chapter ii. 9. "But we see Jesus" &c. "that he by the grace of God should *taste death* for *every man.*" This class of texts might be multiplied to almost any extent, but it is unnecessary to add, enough has been produced to show, beyond dispute that Christ did suffer for sinners, and that he suffered and died by divine appointment on the part of the Father, and as a free-will offering on his own part. The death of Christ then must have been an atonement for sinners, essential to their salvation, or it would never have been voluntarily endured by himself or sanctioned by the Father. If Christ did not die to save men from the guilt and punishment of sin, what was the object of his death, and wherein are we benefitted [sic] by his passion any farther than we might have been by his mission, had he appeared on earth, lived, preached, established a system of religious truth, appointed others to preach it after him, and retired to his native clime without heaving a sigh, uttering a groan, or shedding a drop of blood? If his death was not an atonement for sin, essential to our salvation, we can conceive of no benefit arising from his death, which we might not have enjoyed without it. When it has been asked for what purpose Christ suffered and died, if it was not to make an atonement for sin, our opponents have answered that he suffered to furnish an expression of the Father's love to a lost world. To this we reply that if the death of Christ was not an atonement for sin, essential in order to our salvation, it was no expression of God's love to us but an expression of cruelty towards his beloved Son, in whom be declares himself well pleased. Suppose, as the universalist's view of the atonement does, that God was perfectly reconciled to us, and that nothing in his perfections or principles of administration, rendered it inconsistent for him to extend saving mercy to offending man, and, hence, that no offers of grace are now made to sinners which might not have been made without the death of Christ, and it not only strips his death of all that importance which is given to it in the scriptures, but renders it useless and cruel. But it is said that the death of Christ was not designed to procure the favour of God, but to benefit the sinner, acting directly upon his mind as an evidence of the divine love. To this we reply, that if it were viewed in this light it would not be calculated to produce such an effect. What is there in the sufferings of Christ calculated to convince us of the divine goodness, and to win our rebellious hearts to God, if we are assured at the same time that they were intended to produce no other happy effect, farther than to convince us that God is good and that he loves us? Look at the picture as this view presents it. God informs rebellious man that he is good, that be loves them, and that he is able and willing to save them; but incredulous man will not believe that God is love. The Father of mercies adds, hear, ye unbelieving children, and I will convince you that my very nature is love, and that my bowels yearn over the miseries of a fallen world; I have one only well beloved son, and to convince you that I am all goodness, I will send him into the world, and he shall suffer and die before your eyes. He is innocent, he is neither guilty of crime nor worthy of pangs; nor is his death necessary in order to render it consistent for me to save you, but is only necessary to convince you of my tender love. Look now on his pangs, hear him cry out under the most excruciating tortures, and see him sweat great drops of blood, and then ask your unrelenting hearts if I am not pure unmingled love, who can inflict such sufferings on the *innocent* merely to convince the *guilty* and *hell deserving* of my goodness towards them. What soul would not turn away with horror, frightened to despair, lilt such an exhibition of divine love, or rather divine wrath?

IV. The scriptures attribute the salvation of sinners to the sufferings, death and resurrection of Christ; or in other words to the atonement which he has made. John i. 29. "Behold the Lamb of God that taketh away the sin of the world."

1. This text attributes the removal of the sin of the world to Jesus Christ, which can in no wise be true unless he was, in some way, an expiation for sin, removing its guilt, and delivering the offender from its punishment. If, as universalists contend, Christ does not save from guilt and punishment, only by saving from the future commission of sin, in no sense can it be said that the sin of the world is taken away by him. It might be said, on this principle, that he *prevents* the future sin of the world, which would be committed were it not for his interposition; but it cannot be said that he *takes away* the sin of the world, for that which has not been committed bas no existence and cannot be removed, and that which has been committed is not taken away, on the above theory, since it asserts that Christ does not save from its guilt and punishment. Now, as this text can be true only on the ground of the sacrificial death of Christ it is to be regarded as proof

that such death was an expiatory offering, by which the guilt of sin is removed and its punishment averted.

2. The manifest allusion, which the text contains, to the sacrifices of the law shows that John referred to the sacrificial death of Christ, as the means by which he takes away the sin of the world. "Behold the LAMB of GOD." He is termed the Lamb of God, no doubt, in reference to the Paschal Lamb, or to the sacrifice of two lambs for a daily offering. Ex. xxix. 38, 39. "Now this is that which thou shalt offer upon the altar, two lambs of the first year, day by day continually. The one lamb thou shalt offer in the morning and the other lamb thou shalt offer at even." Now, as lambs were offered for *daily* sin offerings, which offerings were typical of the *one* offering of Jesus Christ, he is called the Lamb of God that taketh away the sin of the world, of whom the prophet says, (Isa. liii. 7.) "He is brought as a lamb to the slaughter."

Dr. Clark's note on the text under consideration deserves particular attention.

"'Behold the Lamb of God,' &c. This was said in allusion to what was spoken Isa. liii. 7. Jesus was the true Lamb or sacrifice required and appointed by God, of which, those offered *daily* in the tabernacle and temple, Ex. xxix. 38, 39, and especially the *Paschal* lamb, were only the types and representatives. The *continual* morning and evening sacrifices of a lamb under the Jewish law, was intended to point out the continual efficacy of the blood of atonement: for ever at the throne of God, Jesus Christ is ever represented as a Lamb newly slain. Rev. v. 6. But John, pointing to Christ, calls him *emphatically, the Lamb of God*—all the lambs which had hitherto been offered had been furnished by *men*; this was provided by God, as the only sufficient and available sacrifice for the sin of the world. In three essential respects, this lamb differed from those by which it was represented. 1st. It was the *Lamb of God*: the most *excellent*, and most *available* 2d. It made an *atonement* for *sin*: it carried sin away in *reality*; the others only *representatively*. 3d. It carried away the *sin* of the world; whereas the other was offered only in behalf of the *Jewish people*."

Rom. v. 9. "Much more then, being now justified by his blood, we shall be saved from wrath through him." In this text, the blood of Jesus Christ is asserted as the ground of our justification; and that justification implies the removal of our guilt, and remission of our punishment, is clear from its being followed by salvation or deliverance from wrath, being "*justified by his blood* we shall be *saved from wrath* through him." This most clearly marks the death and blood of Christ as an atonement and expiation of the sinner's guilt; for on no other principle can we be justified by the blood of Christ, any more than by the blood of Paul or of Peter.

John vi. 51, 53, 54, 55. "And the bread that I will give is my flesh, which I will give for the life of the world. Except ye eat the flesh of the son of man, and drink his blood, ye have no life in you. Whoso eateth my flesh, and drinketh my blood, hath eternal life; for my flesh is meat indeed and my blood is drink indeed." We presume it will not be necessary to attempt a refutation of the Romish doctrine of transubstantiation, as inferred from the above text, for the satisfaction of universalists, who pay less attention to the holy sacrament than any other class of professing Christians, with the exception of the honest Quakers. And without any reference to this absurd notion, as to the manner of partaking of the body and blood of Jesus Christ, how clearly does the quotation attribute salvation to the broken body and spilt blood, or in other words, to the sufferings and death of Jesus Christ? When Christ speaks of giving his flesh and blood for the life of the world, it is evident that he has reference to the offering which he made upon the cross. And as he declared "except ye eat the flesh of the son of man, and drink his blood"—i. e. except ye partake of the merits of his death, through faith in his name— "ye have no life in you;" his broken body and spilt blood are here represented as the source of eternal life: "Whosoever eateth my flesh and drinketh my blood hath eternal life." And in no other way can the death of Christ be the source of life to the world, only by being an atonement for sin, by which sinners are "redeemed from the curse of the law," which is death, "for the wages of sin is death, but the gift of God is eternal life through Jesus Christ our Lord."

1 John i. 7. "But if we walk in the light, as he is in the light, we have fellowship with one another, and the blood of Jesus Christ his Son cleanseth us from all sin." It can hardly be necessary to make a remark to show that this plain declaration attributes to the blood of Christ the power of removing sin. The entire washing of the soul from the pollution of sin, is here ascribed to the blood of the cross. And from what sin does the blood of Christ cleanse? Most certainly from that which has been committed; for it would be trifling to talk of being cleansed in anticipation of pollution. It is from "all sin," which includes sin of every kind and degree. The blood of the cross, therefore, is an expiation for sin, and has the power of removing its guilt, washing away its pollution, and averting its punishment.

Heb. ii. 14. "For as much then as the children are partakers of flesh and blood, he also himself took part of the same; that through death he might destroy him that had the power of death, that is, the devil." This text has often been produced by universalists, to show that sin and the punishment of the wicked will have an end, by proving that the devil will be destroyed. But before it can prove any thing to their purpose on this point, they must prove that destruction, in the sense of the text, means annihilation, and this they cannot do; since, it is often said that the wicked shall be destroyed, who, they contend, will be made holy and happy forever. But while the text does not teach the destruction of the devil, in the sense of annihilation, it furnishes the most conclusive evidence that the success of the Redeemer's kingdom, in the overthrow of the devil, and in rescuing from the bondage of sin and death, all that believe in him, and cleave to his cross, is the result of his sufferings and death: "that through death he might destroy him that had the power of death." Whatever different views may be entertained concerning the devil's having the power of death, and in relation to his destruction, they cannot effect the argument; since, all must admit that the text teaches, that the death of Christ was necessary in order to the accomplishment of the object of which it speaks, and that this object is one inseparably connected with the salvation of sinners. The death of Christ, then, was intended to destroy him who had the power of death, and thereby to deliver those who through fear of death were subject to bondage; the death of Christ, therefore must have been a substitute for the death of those who were delivered from death by it.

Eph. i. 7. "In whom we have redemption through his blood, the forgiveness of sins, according to the riches of his grace." Col. i. 14. "In whom we have redemption through his blood, even the forgiveness of sins." Here are two texts which, in the use of the same language, attribute our redemption and forgiveness of sins to the blood of Christ. Without the shedding of blood, therefore, there would have been no redemption nor forgiveness of sins, and without these there could have been, no salvation. Our entire salvation, therefore, is attributed to the blood of the cross. 1 Pet. i. 18, 19. "Ye were not redeemed with corruptible things, as silver and gold, but with the precious blood of Christ, as of a lamb without blemish and without spot."

Rev. i. 56. "Unto him that loved us, and washed us from our sins in his own blood, be glory and dominion forever and ever." Chap. v. 9. "And they sung a new song, saying, thou art worthy to take the book and to open the seals thereof; for thou wast slain, and hast redeemed us to God by thy blood out of every kindred, and tongue, and people, and nation." Chap. vii. 14. "These are they which came out of great tribulation, and have washed their robes and made them white in the blood of the Lamb." Such plain declarations of the efficacy of the blood of the cross, in washing away our sins, clearly point out the death and blood of Christ as an atoning and expiatory sacrifice for sinners, and show that our entire salvation depends upon what he has done and suffered for us.

V. The doctrine of a vicarious atonement is fully confirmed by those scriptures which speak of Jesus Christ as a redeemer, and man as being redeemed by him.

Matt. xx. 28 and Mark. x. 45. "The son of man came not to be ministered unto, but to minister, and to give his life a ransom for many."

1 Tim. ii. 6. "Who gave himself a ransom for all." The English word *ransom* contained in the above quotations is thus defined by Dr. Webster.

"RANSOM, *n.* 1. The money or price paid for the redemption of a prisoner or slave, or for goods captured by an enemy. 2. Release from captivity, bondage or the possession of an enemy. 3. In *law* a sum paid for the pardon of some great offence and the discharge of the offender; or a fine paid in lieu of corporeal punishment. 4. In *scripture*, the price paid for a forfeited life, or for delivering or release from capital punishment. 5. The price paid for procuring the pardon of sins and the redemption of the sinner from punishment."

"RANSOM, *v. t.* 1. To redeem from captivity or punishment by paying an equivalent. 2. To redeem from the possession of an enemy by paying a price deemed equivalent. 3. In *scripture*, to redeem from the bondage of sin, and from the punishment to which sinners are subjected by the divine law. 4. To rescue, to deliver.["]

If then Christ "gave himself a ransom for many," "for all," in the above sense, there is no room for farther controversy. The texts above quoted teach that Christ has ransomed sinners from the bondage of sin and the punishment to which they are subjected by the divine law, by paying his life a price for theirs.

It may also be asked, if the word *ransom* is a proper translation of the original Greek.

The word which the Evangelist employs, rendered *ransom* by our translators, is *lutron* which is thus defined in the Greek and English Lexicons: Lutron, *ransom, redemption, atonement, price of deliverance*. The word which the apostle uses in the above text is *antilutron* and is thus defined: "Antilutron, (from *anti*, inturn, and *lutron*, a ransom,) the price of redemption, ransom."

It is clear then that Christ has ransomed us by giving his life a ransom for ours.

This view is farther supported by those scriptures, which express the same sentiment by the terms redeem, redemption, &c.

Rom. iii. 24. Being justified freely by his grace, through the *redemption* that is in Christ Jesus." 1 Cor. i. 30, "But of him are ye in Christ Jesus, who, of God, is made unto us *redemption*." Gal. iv. 45. "God sent forth his Son, made of a woman, made under the law, to *redeem* them that were under the law." Tit. ii. 14. "Who gave himself for us, that he might *redeem* us from all iniquity." Heb. ix. 15. "And for this cause he is the Mediator of the New Testament, that by means of death, for the *redemption* of the transgressors that were under the first testament, that they which are called might receive the promise of eternal inheritance."

It is clear, from these texts, that Christ has redeemed us, that he is the redeemer and we the redeemed. We ask then, what is it to redeem, or what is redemption? So far as the English word is concerned there can be hardly room for dispute.

The word *redeem* Dr. Webster defines as follows:

"REDEEM, *v. t.* 1. To purchase back; to ransom; to liberate or rescue from captivity or bondage, or from any obligation, or liability to suffer or to be forfeited, by paying an equivalent. 2. To repurchase what has been sold; to regain possession of a thing alienated, by repaying the value of it," &c. With this corresponds his definition of the word *redemption*, which he defines thus: "REDEMPTION, *n.* repurchase of captured goods or persons; the act of procuring the deliverance of persons or things from the possession and power of captors by the payment of an equivalent. ...In *theology*, the ransom or deliverance of sinners from the bondage of sin and the penalties of God's violated law by the atonement of Christ." Indeed, these terms are so well understood that it can hardly be necessary to produce authority to establish their meaning; and yet, if Christ has redeemed us in this sense, the controversy is ended in plain English, and the doctrine of vicarious atonement is established. Now, that it is in this sense that Christ has redeemed us, appears from the following considerations:

1. These English terms well express the sense of the original Greek.

In Rom. iii. 24. in the expression, "through the redemption that is in Christ Jesus," the apostle uses the word *apolutroseos* which our translators have rendered *redemption*, and which literally signifies deliverance from captivity.

In Tit. ii. 14. in which it is said Christ "gave himself for us that he might redeem us," the verb which is rendered *redeem* is, in the original, *lutroselia* which is derived from *luo* to pay, and signifies to ransom or to redeem, and the very derivation of the word shows that it signifies to redeem by paying a redemption price.

In Gal. iv. 4, 5. where the apostle says, Christ "was made under the law, to redeem them that were under the law," the original word which is rendered *redeem*, is *exagorase*. This word is compounded of *ex, from* and *agorazo, to buy* and signifies *to buy from*, or *out of*, implying that Christ has redeemed, *i. e.* brought us from or out of the claims or power of the law, so as to deliver us from the penalty which it inflicts on transgressors as the apostle states. Chap. iii. 13. "Christ has redeemed us from the curse of the law."

2. The connection in which these terms are used is sufficient to convince the plain English reader, without any reference to the original, that redemption by price or purchase is intended. It is said that "Christ *gave himself for us* that he might redeem us." 1 Pet. i. 18, 19. "Ye were not redeemed with corruptible things, as silver and gold, but with the precious blood of Christ." These forms of expression clearly imply that a price was paid for our redemption, and that the sufferings and death of Jesus Christ constituted such a price.

This view is farther supported by other expressions which represent us as being purchased, bought, &c. Acts xx. 28. "Feed the church of God, which he hath *purchased* with his own blood." 1 Cor. vi. 20. "Ye are *bought* with a *price* therefore glorify God in your body and in your spirit which are his." 2 Pet. ii. 1. "There shall be false teachers among you, who privily shall bring in damnable heresies, even denying the Lord that *bought* them." In the first of these texts, the church is said to be *bought*, and the *blood of Christ* is stated to have been the *price paid*. In the second of the above texts, the Corinthians are said to be *bought* with a *price*, and what was that price more or less than the sufferings, and death of Christ, "who gave himself a ransom for all?" In the third of the above quotations, some persons are said to deny the Lord that *bought* them, they must, therefore, have been bought.

VI. The vicarious and propitiatory character of Christ's sufferings and death, is farther established by those scriptures which represent him as a *mediator, intercessor* and *reconciler* 1 Tim. ii. 5, 6. "There is one God and one mediator between God and men, the man Christ Jesus, who gave himself a ransom for all." The word, *mesites*, mediator, literally signifies a *middle person*, whose office it is to reconcile the parties between whom he acts, who are supposed to be at variance. The apostle says Gal. iii. 20. "A mediator is not a mediator of one, but God is one." That is, a mediator does not act exclusively for one party, but equally for both parties, between whom he mediates. This was true of Moses, of whom the apostle was speaking; he spake to the people on the part of God, and intercedes with God on the part of the people. The same is true of Jesus Christ who is a mediator between God and all men, he being both God and man, God manifest in the flesh, acts for both parties in effecting a reconciliation. Christ as mediator reconciles God to men by his death for their sins, and men to God by the word of his gospel and the renewing of the Holy Ghost. That he is our mediator, to render God propitious to us, as well as to reconcile us to God, is evident from the manner of his exercising his mediatorial office, marked by the apostle in the above text. "There is one God and one Mediator between God and men, the man Christ Jesus, *who gave himself a ransom for all*." Christ then, as mediator, gave himself a ransom (*antilutron*, the price of redemption) for all. To whom was this ransom paid? it was not paid to man, to purchase his favour and reconciliation to God, by the payment of a price! The apostle informs us to whom Christ gave himself a ransom, Heb. ix. 14. "Who" (Christ) "through the eternal spirit offered himself without spot to God." Christ then, as mediator offered himself *to* God *for* man. The offering was made to God to render him propitious and to procure, consistently with the principles of divine government, that grace by which sinners are renewed, pardoned, and reconciled to God. Heb. vii. 25. "Wherefore he is able to save them to the uttermost that come unto God by him, seeing he ever liveth to make intercession for them." Does Christ intercede with men, in the sense of this text, to reconcile them to God? Or does he intercede *with* God *for* man, to render him propitious, that they may receive reconciling grace? Let God, by the mouth of his apostle, answer this question. Heb. ix. 24. "Christ is not entered into the holy place made with hands, which are the figures of the true, but into heaven itself, now to appear in the presence of God for us." It is clear, then, that Christ intercedes with God for us. Eph. v. 2. "Christ hath loved us, and hath given himself for us an offering and sacrifice to God for a sweet smelling savour." This not only fully refutes the notion held by universalists, that men only, and not God, are reconciled by Christ, but it establishes, beyond doubt, the fact that an atonement *for the sins of men* has been made *to God*, the object of which is to render him propitious to his offending offspring, by enabling him to "be just and the justifier of him that believeth in Jesus." If, as universalists contend, God never was unreconciled to man but was always propitious, without reference to a vicarious atonement, man only being an unreconciled party, the offering and intercession of Christ should have been made *to* and *with* man; for it would not be necessary for Christ to offer himself to God, and intercede with him in behalf of man if God was not unreconciled, man only being the subject of reconciliation through the mediation of Christ. But in opposition to this absurd notion, the scriptures uniformly represent Christ as offering himself *to* God *for* man and as interceding with him in behalf of his rebellious offspring.

This view is farther supported by Rom. iii. 25. "Whom God hath set forth to be a propitiation, through faith in his blood, to declare his righteousness for the remission of sins that are past, through the forbearance of God." On this text we remark,

1. That to propitiate is to conciliate or to appease one offended and render him favorable. In this sense Christ is our propitiation, turning away from us the wrath of God.

2. That God is the offended party, with whom Christ propitiates for us to turn away his displeasure from us, is evident from the fact that the object of his propitiation is the remission of our sins; he "is set forth to be a propitiation to declare his righteousness for the remission of sins that are past, through the forbearance of God." Now, as the remission or pardon of sin is the act of God, and as this is the object of Christ's propitiation, it is clear that God is the offended party and that he is rendered propitious, even to the remission of our sins, by the interposition of his son. Jesus Christ.

3. That this interposition of Jesus Christ, in our behalf, is on the ground of his having died for us, appears from the fact that it is *through faith in his blood* that the blessing sought for us, is received. "Whom God hath set forth to be a propitiation *through faith in his blood* for the remission of sins." This shows that the whole rests upon his having shed his blood for us, or upon the merits of his death.

To this we may add the testimony of St. John.

1 John ii. 1, 2. "If any man sin, we have an advocate with the Father, Jesus Christ the righteous, and he is the propitiation for our sins, and not for ours only but also for the sins of the whole world."

1. This text speaks of our sinning against God by which we most certainly incur the divine displeasure. Rom. i. 18. For the wrath of God is revealed from heaven against all ungodliness and unrighteousness of men."

2. The text declares that Christ is the propitiation, *hilasmos*, atoning sacrifice, for our sins.

3. That Christ as our propitiation or sacrifice for sin renders God propitious, or reconciles him to us, is clearly shown by his being *our advocate with the Father*; "If any man sin we have an advocate with the Father, Jesus Christ the righteous." If it is not the office of Christ, as mediator between God and man, to reconcile God to us as well as to reconcile us to God, if God requires no sacrifice for sin to render him propitious to sinners, and if he is never unreconciled to us we need no advocate with the Father; the pleadings, in such case, should all be on the other side to persuade men to be reconciled to God. If the case of a master and servant should be presented to the reader, the master always kind and propitious, never unreconciled to his servant; the servant rebellious, manifesting the blackest ingratitude and the most inveterate enmity towards his master; but notwithstanding all this the master still smiles and asks for no redress of wrongs only that his rebellious servant should return to his duty and to his arms that are extended to embrace him: now, should the son of the kind master undertake the work of mediation, to effect a reconciliation between them, what would the reader think to see him undertake to effect a reconciliation by making an offering to the master on the part of the servant, and by turning advocate for the rebellious servant and pleading in his behalf with the kind master, who was never unreconciled, instead of spending all his energies to bring the rebellious servant to his duty? As much as such a procedure would shock the common sense of every beholder, yet this is the very point of light in which Jesus Christ is presented, in view of the above text, by those who deny the necessity of Christ's atonement and intercession for us in order to render God propitious.

Before we close our remarks on this subject, it may be

well to offer a few observations, in answer to some of the principal objections which are urged against the preceding views of a vicarious atonement.

1. It has been objected to the doctrine of a vicarious atonement that it would be unjust for the innocent to suffer in the place of the guilty.

To this objection we reply,

1. To suffer, endure privation or inconvenience for the good of others, is uniformly represented as virtuous and benevolent. "I could wish," said Paul, "that myself were accursed from Christ, for my brethren, my kinsmen according to the flesh." Rom. ix. 3. "I am the good shepherd: the good shepherd giveth his life for the sheep." John. x. 11. To endure a smaller evil to save others from a greater one, or to secure to them a greater good, is certainly an act of benevolence; it is benevolence in the light of the Bible, it is benevolence in the sight of the world; such conduct has been made the subject of eulogy by orators and the matter of song by bards. It is worthy of remark, that it is not pretended that Christ suffered as much in quantity as sinners would have suffered, through coming ages, had they been left unredeemed; his sufferings, therefore, save men from a greater amount of evil than he endured for them, while, on the other hand, it brings to them a greater amount of good than be had to forego in accomplishing the work of their redemption. Thus, it is clear, that to suffer for others under the circumstances in which Christ suffered, is an act of virtue and benevolence, unless it can be shown that such sufferings are an infringement upon the prior claims of a superior. When it can be shown that by such sufferings some just claim, some paramount obligation is violated, then, and not till then, will such sufferings appear unjust. Now, we maintain that this is not true of the offering which Jesus Christ made of himself once for all; no prior claim or law, by which the act could be determined an unjust

one, was violated. Let it be particularly noted, that Jesus Christ suffered voluntarily on his own part, and in accordance with the will of the Father at the same time. Nothing is more clear than that the Father and the Son both willed the offering which Christ made "of himself once for all." This being understood, we say, if, as those who hold the doctrine of vicarious atonement believe, Christ was God as well as man, equal with the Father, he must have been the source of all law, so that no law could be of higher authority than that of his own will; hence, as he willed to suffer, he suffered under the highest authority, and, therefore, the act cannot be determined to be unjust by a paramount law. But if, as Socinians contend, Christ was a mere created being, bound by the law of his Creator, then, there could be nothing unjust in the offering, since, he suffered in accordance with the will of the Father, the act being sanctioned by the highest authority in the universe, while he voluntarily suffered on his own part, for the good of others, delivering them from a greater evil than he endured, and bringing to them a greater amount of good than he sacrificed; which we have shown to be an act of virtue and benevolence, provided no law or prior claim is thereby violated. View the subject in this light and the charge of injustice on the doctrine of vicarious atonement disappears.

2. While our theory of vicarious atonement is thus vindicated from the charge of injustice, the charge returns upon those who have originated it with a force beyond the power of their theory to resist.

That Jesus Christ did suffer and die voluntarily, and at the same time in accordance with the will of the Father, cannot be denied. This has been sufficiently shown in the preceding arguments, to which we will here add, John x. 17, 18. "Therefore doth my father love me, because I lay down my life for the sheep that I might take it again. No man taketh it from me, but I lay it down of myself: I have power to lay it down, and I have power to take it again: this commandment have I received of my Father." It is clear then that Christ did lay down his own life in which he had the sanction of the Father. Now suppose the act was unjust, on the supposition that his death was vicarious, i. e. in the place of the sinner's death, we ask in what respect it would be less unjust on the supposition that it was not vicarious? Is it *unjust* for Christ to die to redeem the world, by giving his life a ransom for the forfeited lives of sinners, while it is *just* for him to die under circumstances in every respect similar, with the exception that his death is not a ransom for the lives of sinners? If Christ suffered vicariously for sinners, his death contemplated a greater amount of good than it could have done had he died merely as a martyr for the truth; hence, if our opponents prefer the charge of injustice against the doctrine of Christ's vicarious death, they aggravate the circumstance of injustice in proportion as they lessen the amount of good to be secured by it, by denying its atoning merits.

Should it be said that the injustice consists not in the death of Christ, but in the salvation of sinners on the ground of the suffering of the innocent, which salvation could not have taken place, consistently with justice, without such atonement, we reply, that God does save sinners either with or without a vicarious atonement. If he saves them without such atonement, consistently with justice, (and no one will contend that he saves them unjustly,) justice cannot object to the salvation of the sinner after such atonement has been made; therefore, there can be no injustice in the salvation of sinners on the ground of the merits of Christ's death.

II. It has sometimes been objected to the doctrine of the vicarious sufferings and death of Christ, that if Christ made a full atonement for the sinner, as his substitute, then the sinner cannot be held responsible to the law, his substitute having satisfied its claims. This ground has been taken by antinomian limitarians to prove the absurdity of a general atonement, and by universalists to prove that universal salvation must follow from a universal atonement; both of which positions are equally absurd.

The fallacy of this argument appears to consist in blending the atonement itself with the conditional benefits which flow from it; or, in overlooking the conditions on which men, as moral agents, are made the partakers of the benefits of the atonement. The atonement was unconditionally made; i. e. no condition was required of man in order that the atonement might be made, for when we consider man as a fallen being, it is clear that the atonement must first be made, and man become a partaker of its benefits to some extent, before he can be capable of complying with any condition; it must, therefore, appear that the atonement is not only unconditional, but that some of its benefits must be unconditional also. But while we admit that the atonement, and, even some of its benefits, are unconditional, we deny that all its benefits are unconditional; it therefore becomes necessary to distinguish between its conditional and unconditional benefits. We shall not attempt, here, to point out all the benefits of the atonement, separating the conditional from the unconditional, but will simply remark, with reference to adults, leaving infants entirely out of the question, that the atonement is unconditionally applied, so far as to restore man to a state of moral agency and to render him capable of complying with the conditions of the gospel, on which the full and ultimate benefits of the atonement are proffered. We have remarked upon the unconditional benefits of the atonement merely for the purpose of illustration; the main point on which this reply rests, is the fact that its full and final benefits are conditionally offered in the gospel. If this point can be sustained the objection vanishes. The question is, then, whether it be a part of the divine plan of human redemption, that the atonement should be so applied as to deliver sinners from all obligation, or whether it was intended to render the forgiveness and salvation of sinners consistent with the best interest of the moral system, on certain conditions to be complied with on the part of the sinner himself? If our opponents will prove that it was the intention of Jesus Christ, in dying for man, to deliver him from all obligation, satisfying the claims of the law fully and unconditionally, and that God has accepted the atonement in this full sense, without the reserve of a single condition to be complied with on the part of man, we shall then be obliged to yield to the force of the objection under consideration, and take ground with the high toned antinomian limitarians and deny that the atonement was made for all men; or else, admitting the universality of the atonement, strike hands with the universalists and say that all will and must be saved. On the other hand, if we can prove that it was not the design of the Father in the gift of his Son to die for us, and that it was not the design of Jesus Christ in giving himself for us, to deliver us from all moral obligation, nor yet that the benefits of the atonement should be unconditionally applied to us, in their full extent; that the atonement was never intended to deliver us from our obligation to obey God, but only from the penalty of the law after it has been transgressed, and from this only on certain conditions to be complied with on the part of the sinner himself: then, it must follow that the objection is unfounded, that the sinner is held responsible to the divine law though Christ has died as his substitute, and that he is liable to the divine penalty until he complies with the conditions of the gospel on which salvation is offered. To suppose to the contrary, after the above positions shall have been established, must be the name as to assert that the atonement must, of necessity, produce an effect which was never intended by God in the gift of his Son, or by Jesus Christ in the offering of himself, which is vanity in the extreme. Must an atonement, if made, do more than its author intended it should? If an atonement has been made, which God intended should save men from the penalty of a violated law, only on certain conditions, is it logical or theological to infer, that because such an atonement has been made, it must therefore save men from all obligation to obey the law, and from all liability to punishment, without reference to any conditions? If God has given his Son to make an atonement, whereby we may be saved on certain conditions, is it just, true, or modest, for us to start up and assert that he must, therefore, save us irrespective of all conditions? We see then, as we have already stated, that the question at issue must turn on the original intention of the atonement. If it was intended to deliver man from all moral obligation, and to save him, irrespective of his moral agency, then, the ground taken by our opponents on this point is tenable; but if, as we maintain, the atonement was not intended by God to deliver men from their obligation to obey the law, nor yet to save them from the penalty of the law, only on certain conditions prescribed in the gospel, then, the objection falls, and our theory of conditional salvation steers clear of antinomian limitarianism on one hand, and licentious universalism on the other hand.

Having now, as we believe, fairly stated the question at issue, we will attempt to decide it by an appeal "to the law and to the testimony."

John iii. 16. "For God so loved the world that he gave his only begotten Son, that whosoever believeth in him should not perish, but have everlasting life." If the Saviour understood his own mission, this text must be conclusive in proof of a conditional application of the atonement. Indeed, we think it clearly asserts the doctrine of the atonement, while it guards it from abuse on either hand.

1. The text asserts that God was moved by love to the *world*, in the gift of his Son. Now as by the *world*, in this text, nothing can be meant less than the whole human family, the atonement is shown to be universal, in opposition to limitarianism.

2. As the object of this divine gift was the salvation of *such only as believe*; or in other words, as the design of God in giving his Son was to save men *only through faith*, salvation is proved to be conditional; from which it appears that universal salvation does not *necessarily* follow from a universal atonement, as universalists assert. The expression, "that whosoever believeth in him should not perish, but have everlasting life," clearly supposes that to perish is the opposite of everlasting life, so that they cannot both take effect in the same subject. It also supposes that the sinner may believe or that he may not; or that some sinners may believe and have everlasting life, and that others may not believe and perish. It is clear, then, that God did not intend that the atonement should deliver men from all moral obligation, or save them from the penalty of the law, so far as adult sinners are concerned, only on condition of faith in Jesus Christ, by whom the atonement was made; therefore, to urge such consequences as necessarily following from the doctrine of atonement is no less than an attempt to wrest the atonement from the simple object for which God intended it, and apply it to other purposes never contemplated by its divine author, and foreign to the divine plan of human redemption; and we think that an objection founded in such arrogance and profanity, as this is proved to be, may be dismised [sic] without further consideration.

III. It has been objected to the doctrine of atonement, that it excludes the benevolence of God from the plan of salvation; for, say objectors, if God required a full atonement, and if such atonement was made by Jesus Christ, then, justice must be satisfied and there can be no room for the exercise of benevolence on the part of the Father. To this we reply,

1. That God did not require an atonement through any want of love to his fallen creatures, but because it was inconsistent with his perfections, and the principles of his moral government, to save offenders without an atonement.

2. It being inconsistent with the perfections of God to save sinners without an atonement, as we have shown in our remarks on the necessity of an atonement, God's benevolence or love to his fallen creatures led him to devise the plan of salvation through the gift of his Son, our atoning sacrifice; "for God so loved the world that he gave his only begotten Son that whosoever believeth in him should not perish, but have everlasting life." We see then that the doctrine of atonement is so far from excluding the divine benevolence from the plan of human salvation, that the atonement itself is the brightest display of divine love that ever dazzled the vision of angels or men.

We will now bring our remarks on the subject of atonement to a close. The vast importance of the subject, the deep personal interest growing out of the advantages already experienced, through faith in the atonement, by every experimental christian, in connection with our hopes for the future world, based alone on the merits of Christ's death, have led us on until we have extended our remarks beyond what we anticipated; and we hope the reader will find his patience supported from the same source, while he gives this chapter a thorough and candid perusal.

As christians we can never give up the atonement. What! renounce the atonement, which has already washed away the guilt of sin and given us peace with God through faith in our Lord Jesus Christ—renounce the efficacy of the blood of the cross, the cleansing power of which we have already felt in our souls by blessed experience—renounce the atonement, trusting in which holy Martyrs shouted in the flames—renounce the atonement, which has dispelled the horrors of death and shed the light of eternity on the night of the grave—renounce the atonement, while redeemed spirits which have already gained the blest shore, ascribe their salvation to the blood of the Lamb as they surround the throne with son of deliverance, saying, "Unto him that loved us and hath washed us from our sins in his own blood, be glory and dominion forever and ever: thou art worthy for thou wast slain, and hast redeemed us to God by thy blood"— No, heaven forbid it! Holy Ghost inspire us, and the atonement shall be our rallying point forever.

IV
Salvation from Punishment

AFTER HAVING ESTABLISHED, as we believe, the doctrine of atonement, and shown that Christ's sufferings and death were a sacrifice for the sins of men, by which alone they can be saved; we propose in this chapter to enquire more particularly into the nature of salvation itself, by showing that gospel salvation implies a deliverance from the punishment we deserve.

On reverting to the remarks with which we prefaced the preceding chapter, it can hardly be necessary to observe that universalists generally deny that the gospel proposes salvation from the punishment of sin after it is committed. Indeed, such a position appears to be essential to their theory, for as it is so easily proved that some men will be punished according to the demerit of their crimes, they have no way to evade the force of the argument drawn from thence, in favour of endless punishment, only to admit the premises and maintain that punishment, to the extent of the divine penalty, is consistent with the final holiness and happiness of all men. This has a very important bearing on the subject; for if, as universalists assert, every sinner is punished to the extent of his desert, it must follow that sin does not deserve endless punishment, or else that all must be endlessly punished, "for all have sinned and come short of the glory of God." Now, as no one will contend that all men must be lost without the possibility of being saved, it must follow that the Gospel provides for the remission of *just* punishment, or else, that sin does not deserve *endless* punishment. If we can show that gospel salvation implies deliverance from the punishment due to sin, it will follow that such as are punished to the extent of the divine penalty, cannot enjoy gospel salvation and consequently must be forever lost. On the other hand, if our opponents can prove that the gospel offers no release from the punishment due to sin, which is actually committed, but on the contrary, that every sinner must suffer all he deserves, we shall be constrained to admit that the divine law does not inflict endless punishment, or give up our own hope and retire, with the rest of our sinning race, to the shades of despair on which one ray of hope can never dawn. Having thus fairly stated the question at issue we will proceed to prove our own views, in the use of such arguments as to us appear best suited to the object.

I. What has been said, in the preceding chapter in support of the doctrine of atonement, goes equally to prove that the gospel provides for the remission of the righteous penalty of God's holy law. The doctrine of atonement and salvation from the punishment of sin, must stand or fall together. Deny the doctrine of forgiveness and the necessity of atonement vanishes at once; and the declaration that "God so loved the world that he gave his only begotten Son that whosoever believeth in him should not perish but have everlasting life," that "he laid on him the iniquity of us all," that "by his stripes we are healed," that "Christ suffered for us the just for the unjust," that "he was delivered for our offences and raised again for our justification," that he "is the propitiation for our sins," that he "has entered into heaven itself now to appear in the presence of God for us," that "he ever liveth to make intercession for us," that he "is the author of eternal salvation to all them that obey him"—we say, deny the doctrine of forgiveness and these declarations can have no meaning; the cross is made of none effect; the sufferings and death of Christ answer no important end in the economy of salvation, and his blood becomes as the blood of another man! All, then, that has been said in the preceding chapter, in proof of the doctrine of atonement comes with equal strength to the support of the doctrine of forgiveness. But as some may yet question the doctrine of atonement, as there stated and defended, we will attempt to prove that the gospel proposes salvation from punishment, by arguments independent of those by which we trust we have fully established the doctrine of atonement.

II. Those scriptures which speak of pardon, forgiveness, remission, &c. clearly prove the point in question. Neh. ix. 17. "Thou art a God ready to *pardon*, gracious and merciful, slow to anger and of great kindness." That pardon, in this text implies deliverance from punishment is clear from the other expressions with which it is connected. It is not only declared that God is ready to pardon, but that he is gracious, merciful, slow to anger and of great kindness. To be gracious, is to be favorable to those who have no claim on our beneficence; and to be merciful is to be lenient to those who are guilty; hence, these terms connected, as they are, with pardon, clearly show that remission of penalty is intended. But what farther confirms this sense of the text is, that God's being ready to pardon stands connected with his being slow to anger. By the anger of God, we understand his displeasure towards sinners. Judg. ii. 12. "And they forsook the

Lord God of their fathers, and followed other gods, and bowed themselves unto them, and provoked the Lord to anger." 2 Kings xxii. 16, 17. "Thus saith the Lord, behold I will bring evil upon this place, because they have forsaken me, and have burned incense unto other gods, that they might provoke me to anger with the works of their hands." This anger or displeasure at sin shows itself in punishment. Ps. xc. 7. "We are consumed by thine anger." Jer. xxv. 37: "The peaceable habitations are cut down, because of the fierce anger of the Lord." Lam. ii. 22. "In the day of the Lord's anger none escaped, none remained." If, then, God's anger is his displeasure at sin, and if this anger shows itself in the punishment of the sinner, how clear is it that when God is said to be slow to anger, in connection with his being ready to pardon, remission of punishment is intended by a pardon.

Ps. xxv. 11. "For thy name's sake, O Lord, pardon mine iniquity for it is great." Here the Psalmist prays God to pardon his iniquity and assigns as a reason for his prayer that his iniquity is great. We ask, in the name of reason, what particular good is here sought if it be not salvation from guilt and punishment? It is not preservation from the commission of sin in future, for the supplicant asks pardon for his *great iniquity*, which must have been already committed. Now we can form no idea of a blessing under the name of a pardon for past sin which does not imply salvation from the punishment which sin deserves. Isa. lv. 7. "Let the wicked forsake his way, and the unrighteous man his thoughts, and let him return unto the Lord and he will have mercy upon him, and to our God, for he will abundantly pardon." The abundant pardon of God bestowed on the wicked and unrighteous, as expressed in this text must mean some important blessing. Pray what does God do for a sinner when he abundantly pardons him, if he does not remit the punishment he deserves? Universalists have sometimes asserted, when pressed on the doctrine of pardon, that it means salvation from the commission of sin in future; but this text fully refutes such a notion. Reformation from the commission of sin is here made a condition of the pardon promised in this text. The wicked must *forsake his way* and the unrighteous must *forsake his thoughts*, and they must *turn unto the Lord* before this pardon is available; hence, the pardon can relate only to past sins. A pardon cannot consist in that which must take place before such pardon can be received. As God requires us to break off from our sins *first*, to suppose the pardon promised in the text means no more than restraining grace, would be to understand him as promising to save us from the commission of sin, on condition that we will first save ourselves from the commission of sin. Jer. xxxiii. 8. "And I will cleanse them from all their iniquities, whereby they have sinned against me, and I will pardon all their iniquities, whereby they have sinned and whereby they have transgressed against me." Nothing can be more plain than that pardon is here applied to the removal of past sins, and not to the prevention of the commission of sin in future.

Micah vii. 18. "Who is a God like unto thee, that pardoneth iniquity, and passeth by the transgression of the remnant of his heritage? He retaineth not his anger forever, because he delighteth in mercy." The term pardon is here attended by three other expressions which fix its meaning. God pardons iniquity, and to show that the remission of punishment is intended, it is added that he *passeth by transgression*; that he *retaineth not his anger forever* because *he delighteth in mercy*. Enough has been said to show that God does pardon sin. Reasons have already been offered for understanding the pardon of an offence to imply the remission of the punishment it deserves, to which we will add the following:

1. We have no authority to use or understand the term,

pardon, in any other sense than that for which we contend. Dr. Webster says its meaning is, "to remit as a penalty," or "to excuse as a fault;" or "the release of an offence, or of the obligation of the offender to suffer a penalty or to bear the displeasure of the offended party," or the "remission of a penalty." What linguist has ever told us that the word pardon means, to take away the love of sin, or to save from sin by preventing its commission in future, without, in the least, implying a deliverance from the punishment of sin which has been committed? Who understands the word pardon in this sense, when it is employed in the affairs which exist between man and man? Suppose the executive of the state to be vested with authority to pardon criminals convicted of crime and condemned to punishment; and should a convict, in one of our state penitentiaries, solicit his excellency's interference and obtain his pardon, what would be the disappointment of the expecting criminal, should he be informed that a pardon implies no remission of merited punishment; that he must still suffer the full penalty of the law? What wise counselor would hazard his reputation, before the Supreme Court in a plea on executive prerogative, by maintaining that the constitutional right of pardon gives the governor no power to remit any penalty which the law inflicts, but simply to save offenders from the guilt of their crimes, in any way he can, without saving them from any punishment they deserve; or that it gives him the right to save them from the love of their crimes; or what is still more important, to save them from committing crime in future? It is presumed that no one would plead thus; and yet every counselor, who embraces modern universalism, must take this ground to be consistent with his own theory.

2. That the term pardon is used in the scriptures to signify the remission of punishment appears from the manner in which the negative particle is associated with it. It

is said of wicked Manasseh, 2 Kings xxiv. 4. that "he filled Jerusalem with innocent blood which the Lord would *not* pardon." The meaning of this text must be exactly the reverse of what it would be, if it were said that God would pardon the same offence; hence, if the text now means that God would not remit the punishment that Manasseh's crimes deserved, which no doubt is its true meaning, then, when it is said that God does pardon, the true meaning must be that he remits a just punishment. On the other hand, if when it is said that God does pardon sin, it means no more than that he saves the offender from the love of his crimes, or from the commission of sin in future, in this case, in which it is said he *would not pardon,* the meaning must be that God would not save Manasseh from the love of his sin, or from a repetition of the same bloody and horrid crimes. This consequence we think no universalist will dare openly to avow; and yet it is a consequence which no one can evade, who denies that pardon implies a remission of punishment.

The above view is farther supported by those scriptures which speak of the forgiveness of sin. This class of texts is so numerous that we can only produce a small portion of them as a specimen of the whole. Mark ii. 5. "Jesus said unto the sick of the palsy, son thy sins be forgiven thee." Luke xxiii. 34. "Then said Jesus, Father forgive them, for they know not what they do." Ps. lxxviii. 38. "But he being full of compassion forgave their iniquity, and destroyed them not; yea, many a time turned he his anger away and did not stir up all his wrath." This last text is deserving of particular attention. The forgiveness of iniquity is here attributed to divine compassion, "he being *full of compassion* forgave them." If forgiveness does not imply remission of punishment, it must be difficult to see why it should result from the fullness of divine compassion any more than from wisdom, justice, or holiness. But to show more fully what is meant by forgiveness, the text specifies in what way it manifested itself, as well as the source from whence it proceeded: "he forgave them their iniquities and *destroyed them not.*" Here destruction is marked as the just punishment of their iniquity, and their preservation is represented as the result of their forgiveness. And to show that this is the common mode of the divine procedure, the text adds, "many a time turned he his anger away and did not stir up all his wrath." As forgiveness proceeds from the divine compassion, so punishment proceeds from the divine anger; hence, by his turning away his anger, is meant his forbearing to punish them for their sins; and by his not stirring up all his wrath, is meant his punishing them less than their sins really deserved; all of which supposes salvation from the punishment of sin after it has been committed.

Dan. ix. 9, 19. "To the Lord our God belong mercies and forgiveness though we have rebelled against him; O Lord hear, O Lord forgive." Ps. xxxii. 5. "Thou forgivest the iniquity of my sin." Ps. xxxii. 1. "Blessed is he whose transgression is forgiven, whose sin is covered." This text is quoted by the apostle, Rom. iv. 7, and applied to the gospel mode of justification by faith. Ps. ciii. 2, 3. "Bless the Lord O my soul and forget not all his benefits, who forgiveth all thine iniquities." Ps. cxxx. 3, 4. "If thou Lord, shouldest mark iniquity, O Lord who shall stand, but there is forgiveness with thee that thou mayest be feared." In this text, *forgiveness* is opposed to God's *marking iniquity,* so that when God marks iniquity, in the sense of this passage, he does not forgive; and when he forgives he does not mark iniquity. Taking this view, the text contains three reasons for understanding forgiveness to mean the remission of punishment.

1. Marking iniquity can mean nothing less than taking account of our sins, and holding us to answer the penalty of the law for the same; hence, as forgiveness is exactly the reverse of marking iniquity, it must mean

passing by our sins in some way without inflicting the punishment they deserve. But suppose that forgiveness means no remission of punishment, but simply a preservation from the commission of sin in future, as marking iniquity is opposed to forgiveness, it must consist in leaving men to commit sin without restraint. This indeed would be an uncommon way of marking iniquity. The notion is too absurd to be indulged for a moment.

2. The text under consideration, intimates that no man could stand, i. e. be saved, or enjoy the divine favour, if God should mark iniquity, i. e. if God should judge and punish us for all our sins. Now, if every man does and must suffer for all the sin he commits, and if the infliction of the full penalty of the law is consistent with salvation, then God does mark iniquity and men stand too, which is opposed to the text: "If thou Lord shouldest mark iniquity, O Lord who shall stand."

3. The text makes forgiveness the ground of that filial fear which the scriptures every where inculcate: "There is forgiveness with thee that thou mayest be feared."

This supposes that the doctrine of forgiveness is essential to the true fear of God, which cannot be explained consistently, only on the ground that forgiveness implies the remission of punishment. None could stand if God should mark iniquity; hence, if forgiveness stands opposed to his marking iniquity, it is by this that we stand. This marks forgiveness as the only ground of our hope, and hope is essential to that fear of God which he requires; for he, who has no hope of the divine favour, cannot exercise a filial fear towards God: his fear would be that of a devil and not that of a christian. Thus we see that the full punishment of sin, if endured, cuts the offender off from all hope in the divine favour, and that forgiveness implies the remission of such punishment, giving hope to offenders, that they may fear God, with that fear which is equally opposed to presumption and despair.

It is unnecessary to multiply quotations to prove that God forgives sin; a few only shall be added in proof that we have not mistaken the nature of forgiveness. Matt. vi. 12. "Forgive us our debts as we forgive our debtors." Luke xi. 4. "Forgive us our sins for we also forgive every one that is indebted to us." Here we are taught to pray to God for the forgiveness of our sins, in the same sense in which we forgive one another. To understand, then, what God does for us when he forgives our sins, we need only ask ourselves what we do for our fellows when we forgive them. If, when we forgive those who are indebted to us, or who have trespassed against us, we discharge the debt or relinquish the punishment which we might inflict on them, then, when God forgives our sins, he remits the punishment we deserve; but if, when God forgives our sins, he does not remit the punishment we deserve, then he does not require us to forgive our enemies in this sense; for he has directed us to pray, forgive *us*, i. e. in the same manner, as we forgive our debtors.

Eph, iv. 32. "And be ye kind, one to another, tender hearted, forgiving one another even as God for Christ's sake hath forgiven you." Col. iii. 13. "Forbearing one another, and forgiving one another, if any man have a quarrel against any, even as Christ forgave you, so also do ye." Nothing can be more plain than that we are here taught by the apostle, that we are to forgive those who have injured us in the same sense that God forgives sinners, or that God forgives sinners in the same sense in which we are to forgive those who have injured us. Taking this view, who does not see that gospel forgiveness implies the remission of the punishment of sin? Deny this and you involve consequences fatal to religion; you give full license to exact to the utmost the punishment of those who have injured us, and retaliation and revenge are thus let loose unbridled upon society. Could mercy be expected at the hand of those who believe that forgiveness implies no remission of punishment? Do universalists act up to their belief on this point, or are their hearts better than their creeds? That class of texts, which speak of the remission of sin teaches the same sentiment.

Luke xxiv. 46, 47. "Thus it is written and thus it behooved Christ to suffer, and to rise from the dead the third day, and that repentance and remission of sins should be preached in his name among all nations." Matt. xxvi. 28. "For this is my blood of the new testament which is shed for many, for the remission of sins." Luke i. 77. "To give knowledge of salvation unto his people, by the remission of their sins." Acts ii. 38. "Repent and be baptised every one of you, in the name of Jesus Christ for the remission of sins, and ye shall receive the gift of the Holy Ghost." x. 43. "Through his name, whosoever believeth on him, should receive the remission of sins" Rom. iii. 25. "Whom God hath set forth to be a propitiation through faith in his blood, to declare his righteousness for the remission of sins that are past."

These quotations are sufficient to show that the scriptures teach that Gospel salvation implies remission of sin. What then is *remission*? Or what does God do for us when he remits our sins? We maintain that he remits the punishment which our sins deserve. To remit an offence is to pardon the offender which we have already shown implies a deliverance from punishment. The Greek word, *aphesin*, which our translators have rendered remission, is derived from *aphiemi*, which signifies to send away; hence, when God remits our sins, he in some sense dismisses or sends them away, and it is not possible to conceive in what sense this can be done, unless it is by a pardon, which annuls the guilt of sin, and consequently, dismisses the sinner from the suffering which is its just punishment. There is not the least ground to maintain that remission of sin implies the preventing of its commission in future, for it is said, in one of the above quoted texts, that Christ is set forth to be a propitiation "for the remission of sins that are *past;*" hence, it is sins that have been already committed that are remitted.

III. The plain scriptural doctrine of justification, by grace through faith, clearly implies salvation from the punishment which sin deserves. Avoiding all scholastic and technical terms in the statement of the doctrine of justification we will endeavor to give it a scriptural and common sense definition, by saying that the scriptures employ the term justification in opposition to condemnation and to liability to punishment, so that when a man is condemned, in a scriptural sense, he is not justified, but is liable to punishment; and when a man is said to be justified, he is not condemned, or is delivered from condemnation, and consequently, not liable to punishment. Rom. V. 18. "Therefore, as by the offence of one, judgment came upon all men to *condemnation* even so by the righteousness of one, the free gift came upon all men unto *justification* of life." In this text condemnation is opposed to justification, and the latter is a deliverance from the former, which fully confirms the above view of justification. If, however, another proof text is necessary on this point, we have it at hand in the 9th verse. "Much more then, being now *justified* by his blood, we shall be *saved from wrath* through him." This text asserts salvation from wrath, which is but another word for punishment, to be the result of justification; hence, justification must be the opposite of condemnation, and salvation, which follows from justification, must be the opposite of the punishment to which condemnation exposes or consigns us. It is settled, then, that justification is the opposite of condemnation by which we are exposed to punishment.

John iii. 18. "He that believeth not is condemned already." Indeed it would be trifling to prove for the satisfaction of universalists, that all sinners are under condemnation and exposed to punishment, for they contend that every man must be punished for all the sin he commits without the possibility of escaping it, which is the very sentiment against which we are contending. While we contend that all sinners are under condemnation, and exposed to punishment, we maintain that the gospel proposes salvation from such punishment on certain conditions. It being agreed on both sides that all sinners are under condemnation and exposed to punishment, it follows that from such condemnation and punishment they must, in some way, be delivered, for nothing is more plain than that they cannot go to heaven under condemnation and a liability to punishment. How then are sinners delivered from the condemnation and punishment to which their sins have exposed them? So far as this controversy is concerned, there can be but two ways of deliverance proposed. Universalists maintain that the offender suffers all that his sin deserves, while we resort to the doctrine of justification, by grace through faith, maintaining that this doctrine, as above stated, is totally irreconcilable with the notion that men are delivered from guilt and condemnation only by suffering all the punishment which sin deserves. It is plain that both of these positions cannot be true. If men can and do suffer the full punishment of sin, in a limited period, at the expiration of which they are exempt from condemnation and punishment, on the ground of having suffered all they deserve, then, they are *justified by the law through suffering*, and, consequently, cannot *be justified by grace through faith*. On the other hand, if sinners are justified by grace through faith, they cannot be condemned and punished, for we have shown that justification is opposed to condemnation. Again punishment *does* absolve the sinner from guilt, or it *does not*. Now if punishment does absolve the sinner from guilt, he is not and cannot be justified by grace through faith; but if punishment does not absolve the sinner from guilt, the idea of the sinner's suffering all he deserves, as prerequisite to salvation, vanishes forever; for, in such case, let him suffer as long as you please, he will still be just as guilty as at the moment he endured the first pang, and, consequently, just as much deserving of punishment; he must therefore be justified and saved from punishment on some other ground than that of enduring all he deserves, or suffer forever. Taking this view, it only remains to show that sinners are justified by grace through faith and through faith only, and the argument will be conclusive. This point has already been proved by the scriptures quoted to shew that justification is the opposite of condemnation, but we will give the point farther confirmation in this place. We would remark that the grace of God, manifested through Jesus Christ, is the ground of our justification or acceptance with him. Rom. iii. 24. "Being justified freely by his grace, through the redemption that is in Christ Jesus." Titus iii. 7. "That being justified by his grace, we should be made heirs according to the hope of eternal life." That faith is the gospel condition of justification, is too plain to need argument, the point having been once argued and established by St. Paul. Gal. ii. 16. "Knowing that a man is not justified by the works of the law, but by the faith of Jesus Christ." iii. 8. "And the scriptures foreseeing that God would justify the heathen through faith, preached before the gospel unto Abraham." Rom. iii. 30. "Seeing it is one God which shall justify the circumcision by faith, and uncircumcision through faith." v. 1. "Being justified by faith, we have peace with God." Gal. iii. 11. "That no man is justified by the law, in the sight of God, it is evident, for the just shall live by faith." These pointed declarations from the pen of inspiration, concerning the gospel mode of justification, must determine it to be by grace through faith; and as we have just shown that it is totally irreconcilable with the idea, that the sinner suffers all the penalty he deserves, it follows that the gospel provides for the deliverance of the guilty from the punishment they deserve, and that those who are saved with gospel salvation, do not suffer all the punishment due to their sins.

It will be worse than in vain, to attempt to evade the force of this argument by supposing that justification does not cover the ground of past transgression, but that we are only saved from the commission of sin in future by grace through faith, and that we are thereby justified, i. e. saved from condemnation by being first saved from the commission of sin, for which all must be condemned by whom it is committed. To this exposition of the doctrine of justification we object on the following ground:

1. It destroys the very notion of justification itself. In such case, the sinner is not justified in view of his past sins, for which he suffers a full penalty, and in view of the future he is not and cannot be justified, and can need no justification, having never been under condemnation. Nothing can be more clear than that justification relates to the sinner's past delinquency, and that it is a deliverance from the guilt and punishment of sin. Acts xiii. 39. "By him all that believe are justified from all things, from which they could not be justified by the law of Moses." Here, men are said to be justified by faith from that from which they could not be justified by the law of Moses. Now, from this it must follow that the Jews, under the law of Moses, could not live without transgression, so as to be justified by the non-commission of sin, or else that the gospel, which justifies from what the law could not, makes provision for saving men from past sins; either of which is fatal to the notion that the gospel justifies only by saving from the commission of sin in future. To suppose that men were not able to live under the law of Moses so as to be justified by the non-commission of sin, and at the same time maintain that there is no justification from sin after it is

committed, only by suffering its punishment, would be no better than to assert outright that God punishes his creatures for that which they cannot avoid, and, consequently, for which they are not responsible or in the least to blame; which would be unjust, and, therefore, cannot be allowed. It is certain, then, that it must be possible for men to live under every divine dispensation so as to be justified; or, more properly speaking, to avoid condemnation, provided they improve to the best of their abilities all the means of moral culture which such dispensation affords. From what then are those who believe in Christ justified, from which they could not be justified by the law of Moses? We answer, while the law of Moses prohibited the commission of sin, it made no provision for delivering offenders from the moral guilt of their crimes after the law had been once violated; but this the gospel does, so that he that believeth is justified from all things, from which he could not be justified by the law of Moses. Rom. v. 16. "The judgment was by one to condemnation, but the free gift is of many offences unto justification of life." This text applies the free gift of God's grace, through Jesus Christ, to the justification of the condemned from the guilt of past offences, in a manner too plain to need farther comment.

2. We object to the idea, that justification through faith relates *only* to the future; justifying, not from the past, but by preventing the commission of sin for time to come, on the ground that such a justification would be essentially by works. If men are not justified by grace through faith from the guilt of the past, but are only led to break off from their sins and obey God in future, and are, therefore, said to be justified because they have not committed sin, i. e. because they have answered the claims of the law, then, they are justified by the works of the law. If they are not, it would be difficult to understand what can

be meant by justification by the deeds of the law. Is it said that the law is kept by faith, and therefore, the justification is by faith? We answer it would be a perversion of language to say that a man is justified by faith *merely* because faith is concerned in his compliance with the requisitions of the law, by which alone he can be justified. Let it be noted, that if a man could keep the law without faith, he would be justified thereby, but if he could have faith without keeping the law, on the above principle, he would not be justified; therefore the works of the law are indispensable, but faith is not indispensable to justification; it is only an auxiliary in the work of keeping the law by which he is justified. Not only so, but if we should admit that it is by faith, because the law is kept by faith, still it would not make out justification by faith in a gospel sense; for there would be no justification without the works of the law: whereas, St. Paul says, Rom. iii. 28 "Therefore we conclude that a man is justified by faith, *without the deeds of the law.*" Let it not be supposed by this, that good works are not necessary after we are justified by faith, in order to retain it. On this point we cannot express our views better than in the 10th Article of the Church. "Although good works, which are the fruits of faith, and follow after justification, cannot put away our sins, and endure the severity of God's judgments: yet are they pleasing and acceptable to God in Christ, and spring out of a true and lively faith insomuch that by them a lively faith may be as evidently known, as a tree is discerned by its fruit."

The points which we have labored to establish in this argument are the following:

1. Justification, as held forth in the gospel, is opposed to condemnation, so that those who are justified, in a gospel sense, are absolved from guilt and delivered from punishment.

2. This justification is by grace through faith, and not

by the works of the law or by enduring its penalty; as must be the case if men are punished for all the sin they commit, and are said to be justified, *only* by keeping the law, or by the non-commission of sin in future.

Therefore justification as taught in the gospel implies salvation from the punishment of sin that has been committed.

IV. The scriptures clearly teach that some have been saved from the punishment they deserved.

Ezra ix. 13. "And after all that has come upon us for our evil deeds, and for our great trespass, seeing that thou, our God, hast punished us less than our iniquities deserve, and hast given us such deliverance as this." The text is as plain as words can make the sentiment we advocate. If being punished less than we deserve, does not imply salvation from deserved punishment, we have yet to learn the meaning of language.

Exo. xxxii. 9, 10, 11, 12, 14. "And the Lord said unto Moses, I have seen this people, and, behold, it is a stiffnecked people: Now therefore let me alone, that my wrath may wax hot against them, and that I may consume them. And Moses besought the Lord his God, and said, Lord, why doth thy wrath wax hot against thy people," &c. "Turn from thy fierce wrath, and repent of this evil against thy people. And the Lord repented of the evil which he thought to do unto his people." Here God is represented as threatening his people with an overthrow, and as turning away from the evil which he thought to do, at the intercession of Moses. The evil, with which God threatened them, was a punishment for the sin of idolatry, in making and worshipping a golden calf. Now, this threatened punishment was just, or it was not; if it was just, then God saved the rebellious Israelites from a just punishment, for he turned away from the evil which he thought to do unto them, and did it not; and if the threatened punishment was not just, then God once thought to do an unjust evil to his people; therefore, it must be admitted that God did save the people from a just punishment, in this case, since it cannot be admitted that he threatened and thought to do that which was not just.

The divine clemency, exercised towards condemned and devoted Nineveh, is another instance of salvation from just punishment. God threatened Nineveh with an overthrow in forty days, and yet, on their repentance, it is said, Jonah iii. 10. "And God saw their works, that they turned from their evil way; and God repented of the evil that he had said that he would do unto them; and he did it not." The remarks which have just been made, on the case of the idolatrous Israelites, will apply with equal force to the preservation of Nineveh. God either saved the people of Nineveh from a *just* punishment, or else he threatened them with an *unjust* punishment. It will not be a sufficient reply to this, to say that the punishment, with which they were threatened, would have been just had they not repented, but in view of the change which took place in their moral character, it was not just, and therefore was not inflicted; for this would be to suppose that the threatened overthrow was intended as a punishment for their sins which they had not committed, but which they would have committed in future time, which is false.

1. They were threatened directly for what they had already done. The Lord said unto Jonah, Chap. i. 2. "Arise, go to Nineveh, that great city, and cry against it; for their wickedness *is come up before me.*" God here speaks of their wickedness in the present tense, *is come up*, and not in the future, *will* or *will have come up*. God did not command Jonah to cry against them because they were about to be very wicked, but because their wickedness had already come up before him.

2. Jonah attributes the preservation of Nineveh to the grace, mercy, and great kindness of God. Chap. iv. 2. "I

knew that thou art a gracious God, merciful, slow to anger, and of great kindness, and repentest thee of the evil." Now, on the supposition that the Ninevites did not deserve the threatened overthrow in view of their reform, wherein do the grace, mercy, and great kindness of God appear in their preservation? This view represents God as being gracious, merciful and great in kindness, merely because he did not inflict an unjust punishment, which is too absurd to be indulged for a moment. It is clear then that the punishment, with which Nineveh was threatened, was just, in view of what they had already done; and if so, it is conclusive that God saved them from a just punishment. It is unnecessary to multiply examples of this character, for were we to attempt to bring forward all that might be adduced, it would require a comment on a great portion of the divine administration, as recorded in the Bible. In every case in which God is said to be entreated, and turn away from doing a threatened evil, to be slow to anger, to turn away his wrath, &c. &c. salvation from a just punishment is implied; and these instances are frequent, as is declared in a text which has already been quoted. Ps. lxxviii. 38. "But he being full of compassion forgave them their iniquity, and destroyed them not, yea many a time turned he his anger away and did not stir up *all* his wrath."

V. In support of the theory of salvation from the punishment of sin, we will adduce a few passages of scripture, which, we think, clearly imply the doctrine in question. These scriptures are various, some being introduced by way of explanation and others in the form of promises.

Ezek. xviii. 21, 22. "But if the wicked will turn from all his sins that he hath committed, and keep all my statutes, and do that which is lawful and right, he shall surely live, he shall not die. All his transgressions that he hath committed, they shall not be mentioned unto him." We have nearly the same language in chap, xxxiii. 14, 16. "When I say to the wicked, thou shalt surely die; if he turn from his sin, and do that which is lawful and right, none of his sins that he hath committed shall be mentioned unto him." These texts most clearly assert that past sins shall not be mentioned to the sinner on condition of his reformation. Now, by this assurance, that past sins shall not be mentioned, nothing can be meant less than that God proposes to remit the punishment of past sins, if the sinner will repent and reform. What does God mean, when he says, "none of his sins that he hath committed shall be mentioned unto him," if it is not that he shall be exempt from suffering the punishment they deserve? If it be said that past sins are intended, for which the sinner has already been punished, we reply, that this would make God threaten the sinner with another punishment, for sins for which he had already been punished all he deserved, which is manifestly absurd. When God says to the sinner, that all his transgressions that he hath committed shall not be mentioned unto him, if he turn from his sin, it most clearly implies that they *shall* be mentioned if he does not turn; hence to suppose that reference is had to sins for which punishment has been already inflicted, would be to make God threaten a double punishment. If it be said that in the expression, "none of his sins shall be mentioned unto him," no reference is had to punishment, or to release from punishment, we repeat the question asked above, what does God mean by this expression? Is it said that the meaning is that the sinner shall not be reproached or upbraided with his sin? We answer, to be reproached and upbraided with sin, is a punishment itself, to some extent, especially if God reproach us with our sins. This throws it back on the former ground, so that if sins are intended for which the sinner has been already punished, God is made to threaten him with a second punishment for the same offence; and if sins are intended, for which the offender has not been punished, then, God promises to save from the punishment due to past sins, if the sinner will repent and reform. When God says, "none of his sins which he hath committed shall be mentioned unto him," he, no doubt, holds out some advantage to be possessed by the returning sinner; and this advantage is negative, or the advantage of exemption from some inconvenience, evil, or malediction, growing out of sin: and as it relates exclusively to sins which have been already committed, such exemption is most clearly salvation from punishment. Give it any exposition of which it is capable, and still, if it mean any thing, it means all for which we have contended. Deny salvation from punishment, after sin has been committed, and when God says of the sinner, none of his sins which he hath committed shall be mentioned unto him, he, in effect, says just nothing at all.

The parable of the barren fig tree is full in proof of the point in question. Luke xiii. 6, 7, 8, 9. "A certain man had a fig-tree planted in his vineyard, and he came and sought fruit thereon, and found none. Then said he unto the dresser of his vineyard, behold, these three years I come seeking fruit on this fig-tree and find none, cut it down, why cumbereth it the ground? And he answering said unto him, Lord, let it alone this year also, till I shall dig about it, and dung it: And if it bear fruit, well; and if not, then after that thou shalt cut it down." It is not necessary to enter into a particular examination of this parable, in all its minute bearings, to discover that it contains the doctrine of salvation from just punishment. It was, no doubt, intended to illustrate the dealings of God with men; hence, by the owner of this vineyard, we are to understand God, and by the fig-tree, moral accountable beings. Taking this view, the doctrine in question appears plain upon the very surface of the text.

1. The moral beings represented by the fig-tree, are

guilty, and deserve to be punished, as a fruitless tree should be removed as a cumbrance from the soil.

2. The proposition to spare the fruitless tree, for another trial, saying, "if it bear fruit, well; if not, then after that thou shalt cut it down," clearly supposes that, on condition of its bearing fruit in future, it was to be exempt from the punishment it deserved for its former barrenness, which implies salvation from just punishment. Keeping in view, that what is said of the fig-tree relates to moral beings, and we see, if the fig-tree did not deserve to be cut down, then God threatens an unjust punishment; and if it did deserve to be cut down, then, a proposition is made to save from just punishment: and as no one dare assert the former, the latter must be true.

This class of scripture proofs might be multiplied to almost any extent, but we must forbear, having said enough to furnish the reader with a train of thought, which he will please to carry out in his own mind, as he reads those numerous passages, which like the above, imply salvation from the punishment of sin.

VI. Salvation from sin, which the scriptures teach, and which universalists must admit, most clearly implies salvation from the punishment it deserves. It was said of Jesus Christ before he was born, Matt. i. 21, "Thou shalt call his name Jesus, for he shall save his people from their sins." This must relate to sin that has an existence, for it has already been remarked that men cannot be saved from sin which is never committed. Men may be saved from the commission of sin; but that is very different from being saved from sin itself. Is it said that salvation from the commission of sin is all that is meant, in the above text? We reply, that in this sense the text is not true. The text declares that "he shall save his people from their sins." Now, we ask of what people this is true, if it means salvation from the commission of sin? It can be true of no people, unless a people can be found who have never committed sin, which cannot be, for "all have sinned and come short of the glory of God." No man, who has, or shall hereafter commit sin, can be said to be saved from sin; if by salvation the non-commission of sin be meant. It is clear then that Christ saves his people from sins which have been committed, and this we maintain, implies salvation from the punishment it deserves. But universalists, to avoid the force of this conclusion, have sometimes attempted to make a distinction between salvation from sin; and salvation from the punishment it deserves. To this absurd distinction we object, and will attempt to refute it. We speak exclusively of actual sin, consisting in the transgression of the law. Now, we say, after sin has been committed, it admits of no salvation, except from its guilt and punishment. Men cannot be saved from the act of sin after it has been committed; an act once performed can never be recalled: the consequences of the act are all that admit of salvation, and salvation from these imply salvation from the guilt and punishment of sin.

But another view of the subject will show, equally clear, that salvation from sin, implies salvation from the punishment it deserves. Let it be noted,

1. That no man can be saved from sin, or be in a state of salvation, while he is suffering punishment as a sinner, under the sentence of God's righteous law. This is so self-evident as hardly to need confirmation. To suppose that a man can be in a state of salvation from sin, while he is suffering as a sinner, would be to suppose that he was innocent, free from sin, and a sinner, guilty and deserving punishment at the same time; which is too trifling to occupy further attention.

2. No man can be punished for his sin after he is saved from it; for as salvation implies a restoration to the favour and image of God, to suppose that the saved are still li-

able to punishment, would be to suppose that the innocent who are conformed to the divine will and likeness, are proper subjects of punishment

Now as no man can be saved from sin while he is yet liable to punishment, and as no man can be punished when he is saved from sin, it is clear that salvation from sin and salvation from the punishment of sin, are inseparably connected, and that they reciprocally imply each other.

VII. If there is no salvation from the punishment of sin, it must follow that God is limited as to the time of salvation, in opposition to those declarations of his word, in which he represents himself as able and willing to save at any time, and at all times, when the sinner will comply with the conditions of salvation. To say that a man is punished for his sins, supposes a time in which he endures such punishment. Now as no one will contend that the sinner can be saved while he is in a state of suffering for his sins, it follows that God himself cannot save the sinner until the expiration of the period necessary to punish him for all his past sins, without saving him from the punishment he deserves; therefore if there is no salvation from the punishment of sin, God is limited in the time of salvation. The sinner may repent, and weep, and pray, and plead the promises of the gospel, believing in Christ, and still, omnipotence itself can afford no relief until the expiration of a certain period, necessary for the full punishment of his past sins. This is opposed to the general tenor of the gospel, and too absurd to be indulged for a moment.

VIII. To deny salvation from punishment, must destroy the idea of salvation itself, and involve the sinner in a dilemma which must render his continuance in sin and misery, eternally unavoidable.

Salvation implies a time of salvation, in which it is

enjoyed, and punishment supposes a time of punishment, in which it is endured. Now as salvation and punishment are both states which imply lapse of time, it must follow that if sinners are saved and punished too, they must be saved before they are punished, at the time they are punished, or after they are punished; therefore, if it can be shown that sinners cannot be saved and then punished, that they cannot be saved at, or during the time in which they are punished, and that they cannot be saved after they have received all the punishment they deserve, the conclusion will be irresistible that if they are punished all they deserve, they can never be saved.

1. The sinner cannot be saved and then punished. If the dinner can be first saved and then punished, it follows that salvation is no preventive of damnation, or security against it; and if so, universal salvation, if proved, would constitute no objection to the doctrine of endless punishment, since punishment may exist after salvation has taken effect.

2. The sinner cannot be saved and punished at the same time. If the sinner be saved and punished at the same time, then salvation and damnation are made to meet, at the same time, in the same subject, and exist together. Salvation in such case, as before remarked, can be no security against damnation, and damnation, in turn, can be no preventive of salvation; universal salvation becomes consistent with universal damnation. Now, if this be all true, it may yet appear that if all men should be saved, they may notwithstanding be punished endlessly for their sins.

3. The sinner cannot receive all the punishment he deserves first, and then be saved. As this point is the nucleus around which universalists must rally, if they think of saving their cause, it shall receive particular attention.

That sinners cannot be punished all they deserve,

and then be saved, must appear from the following considerations:

1. The sinner cannot receive all the punishment he deserves until a space of time shall have elapsed, after he shall have ceased to commit sin, and he can never cease to commit sin while he is in a state of condemnation and punishment; he cannot, therefore, receive all the punishment he deserves prior to his being saved. It cannot be denied that faith is essential to salvation, for it is written, Mark xvi. 16. "He that believeth and is baptised shall be saved, and he that believeth not shall be damned." This clearly proves that no unbeliever can be saved. But to evade the force of this, in proof of endless punishment, universalists generally explain the above text by John iii. 18. which says, "He that believeth on him is not condemned, but he that believeth not is condemned already." By this they endeavor to prove that in the expression, "he that believeth not shall be damned," nothing is meant, more than that the unbeliever will be condemned, here in this life, while he remains in unbelief, without any reference to a future state. This we will admit, at present, for the sake of the argument, and try them by their own exposition. It is agreed, then, that unbelief is a sin, for which the unbeliever deserves to be damned, and must be damned and punished so long as he remains an unbeliever, and no longer. From this it must follow, that the moment faith is exercised, the sinner must be released from condemnation and punishment. We ask then, can the sinner believe while he is yet receiving punishment for his past unbelief? Most certainly not, if there is no salvation from punishment; for as the sinner can be condemned and punished no longer than he remains an unbeliever, to say that he can believe at any time prior to his having received all the punishment he deserves, would be to say that he might be saved from just punishment; which is the point for which we contend. If the sinner,

then, cannot believe before he has received all the punishment he deserves, we ask, can he receive all the punishment he deserves before he believes? Assuredly not; for unbelief is sin, for which the sinner must be damned and punished, and we have already remarked that punishment supposes a time of punishment, in which it is endured, and this time of punishment must elapse after the commission of the sin, for a man cannot be punished before he commits the sin for which he is punished. Taking this view, it must be clear that, at the point of time when the sinner believes, he will still deserve punishment for his last unbelief, he cannot, therefore, receive all the punishment he deserves before he believes. It is evident then, that the sinner cannot believe before he receives all the punishment he deserves, without being saved from such punishment, while it is equally apparent that he cannot receive all the punishment he deserves until after he does believe; therefore, the conclusion is irresistible that the sinner must remain in sin and misery for ever, or else be saved from the punishment he deserves. As it is perfectly clear, that punishment must be subsequent to the commission of the sin for which it is inflicted, it follows that while the sinner fails of his entire duty, he will deserve punishment which must be still future; hence, he must first become conformed to the perfect law of righteousness, and then, after that, suffer all the punishment he deserves for his past delinquency, before he can have suffered all the punishment due to his sins. We maintain that this is impossible; for, while the sinner is in a state of condemnation and punishment, he cannot be thus conformed to the law of righteousness, for it is manifestly absurd to suppose that a man can be holy, living without the commission of sin, serving God with all his powers and loving him with all his heart, and that he is, at the same time, a sinner, guilty, deserving punishment, and is actually suffering under the divine displeasure. To state the point clearly, suppose a sinner hears the gospel to day, and rejects it in unbelief; for this conduct he deserves to be punished longer or shorter; the length of his term of punishment can make no difference with this argument, so long as it is acknowledged to be limited. Suppose, then, for the sake of the argument, that this unbeliever for rejecting the gospel to day, deserves to be punished in some way, it matters not how, twenty-four hours; now, while be is enduring this twenty-four hours' punishment, does he not come short of the divine requisition? Most certainly he does, unless man be capable of turning his powers to a two-fold account; that of suffering for the past, and obeying for the present, all at the same time. This we think is manifestly absurd; for it implies that man is capable of doing more, during any given period of time, than the perfect law of his creator requires. If while the sinner suffers the supposed twenty-four hours' punishment, he answers the claims of the divine law, by obeying for the same time in which he suffers for the past, then he answers the claims of the divine law, for a given period, in just half that period; that is, in twenty- four hours he discharges the entire claim of the law for forty-eight hours, by suffering for one twenty-four hours' delinquency, and by obeying for another twenty-four hours, during which he suffers. Now, if this be true, it follows that man can discharge the claims which his creator has upon his, entire existence, in just half the time during which he enjoys existence; which is too absurd to need farther refutation. If, then, the sinner must come short of the divine claim, during the time in which he suffers for the past, it must follow, that at the expiration of the twenty-four hours, above supposed, he must deserve just as much punishment as he did at its commencement; therefore, the sinner can never suffer all the punishment he deserves, preparatory for salvation, but if he is ever saved his salvation must commence with the remission of the punishment which he at that time may deserve. The following very appropriate remarks, are extracted from Dr. A. Clark's Sermon, entitled "SALVATION BY FAITH."

"We have already seen that every intelligent being owes the full exercise of all its powers to its Creator, through the whole extent of its being, and if such creature do not love and serve God with all its heart, soul, mind and strength, through the whole compass of its existence it fails in its duty, and sins against the law of its creation. Now, it cannot be said, that beings in a state of penal sufferings, under the wrath and displeasure of God, (for if they suffer penally they must be under that displeasure,) can either love or serve him. Their sufferings are in consequence of their crimes, and can form no part of their obedience. Therefore all the ages in which they suffer, are ages spent in sinning against this first essential law of their creation; and must necessarily increase the aggregate of their demerit, and lay the eternally successive necessity of continuance in that place and state of torment," *Clark's Ser*, vol. 3. p. 199. These remarks show that a sinner can never arrive at a point when he will have suffered all the punishment he deserves, therefore a man cannot first suffer all the punishment he deserves and then be saved.

There is no way to evade the force of this conclusion, unless it can be shown that sin deserves no punishment, which extends, in duration, beyond the time occupied in committing the offence; and to take this ground would be not only ridiculous in its consequences, but it would suppose that many offences receive no punishment at all, which is to desert the question in debate; for if sin deserves no punishment it is worse than trifling to contend that the sinner must receive all the punishment he deserves on the one hand, or that the gospel provides for the salvation of sinners from the punishment of sin on the other hand.

Though we think the above fully settles the question, yet we will add,

2. If it were possible for man to suffer all that his sins deserve, he would then stand in no need of salvation, in any consistent sense of the term. From what can men be saved, after they have suffered all the punishment they deserve? They cannot be saved from punishment, for this would prove the point for which we have contended; and not only so, but there can be no danger or possibility of their suffering more than they deserve. They cannot be saved from the commission of sin, for they must first cease to commit sin before they can receive all the punishment they deserve. They cannot be saved from the love of sin, as universalists sometimes assert, for as we are required to love God with all the heart, to love sin is coming short of the divine command, and must be sin itself, and consequently deserving of punishment. Now as men deserve punishment for loving sin, they must be saved from the love of sin before they can receive all the punishment they deserve. They cannot be saved from death, for salvation does not secure us from the death of the body; nor can the resurrection be resorted to as salvation, possible after the penalty of the law has been endured, for we have shown in Chap. I. that death itself, is a part of the curse which the law inflicts for sin, and hence it follows, that men cannot be said to have received all the punishment sin deserves, while death holds its dominion over the body. Not only so, but if the resurrection be resorted to as salvation, it will follow on the above principle, that it is salvation from just punishment, which is the very thing for which we contend. They cannot be saved from hell, for this would imply that they deserve to go to hell, which cannot be true if they have already suffered all that they deserve. They cannot be saved from annihilation, unless it be admitted that they deserve it, or are in danger of being annihilated; and if this be admitted, the point in

dispute is given up. We repeat the question, From what can men be saved after they have received all the punishment they deserve? We read, Matt. xviii, 11, "The son of man is come to save that which was lost." But in what sense will men be lost, when they shall have suffered all the punishment they deserve? When the last thunderbolt of wrath divine shall have spent its force, and the storm of vengeance shall have gone by, will men still be lost? When the consequences of man's own misconduct shall have entirely subsided will he still be lost so as to need salvation? As well might it be said that man was created lost! That he came lost from the hands of his divine author! Is it said that salvation consists in the joys of heaven, and that these are bestowed after the sinner has suffered all the punishment he deserves? We reply,

1. Mere accession of good does not constitute gospel salvation. Salvation implies deliverance from some positive evil to which we are exposed, as well as accession of good. The scriptures uniformly use the words save and salvation in this sense. This also is the sense in which these words are used in common conversation; when we have rescued a man from imminent danger, we say we have saved him: but whoever heard the term salvation, applied to a man in comfortable circumstances, on the accession of an estate?

2. Gospel salvation is something attainable, at least in part, in this life; and therefore, it cannot exist exclusively in being admitted to the society of the blest in the future world. Tit. iii, 5. "According to his mercy he saved us by the washing of regeneration, and renewing of the Holy Ghost." 2 Tim. i. 9. "Who hath saved us, and called us with a holy calling." These texts speak of our being saved in this life; for they spake at the time in which they were written, to the living, concerning what had been done for them. But there is no necessity of proof on this point, for universalists contend that all those texts

which speak of a conditional salvation, such as "he that believeth shall be saved," &c. &c. have exclusive reference to this world; and if so, salvation cannot consist in the bliss of a future world.

3. Salvation consisting in the joys of heaven after suffering all the punishment our sins deserve, could not be by Jesus Christ; and, consequently, Jesus Christ could not be the Saviour of such. Suppose a man to live and die in sin and to suffer all the punishment his sin deserves, in this world or the world to come, and then be taken to heaven, in what sense could his salvation be attributed to Jesus Christ? He certainly has not saved him by his gospel; for that, the supposed individual rejected; its precepts he disobeyed, its promises he disbelieved, and its threatenings he disregarded, and bore, in his own person all the evil they imply. Will it be said as a last alternative, that a future state of bliss is the result of Christ's labour of love in our behalf? That though he saves us from no punishment; yet he has procured eternal happiness for us? The question returns, how has he done this for us? It is not by any influence which his life, death, or his truth, produces on the sinner himself, in those cases in which men reject the gospel and die in sin and unbelief, as we have just seen; and if it is by purchase that he has procured eternal happiness for us, it implies the doctrine in question; for, if Christ has purchased eternal life for us, we could not have deserved it on principles of justice, and if we did not deserve eternal happiness, we must have deserved eternal misery, or eternal annihilation; and if we deserved either of these, then Christ, by purchasing eternal happiness for us, has saved us from a just punishment, by saving us from eternal misery, or eternal annihilation, which we deserved. If Christ has purchased eternal happiness for us, then God would not have bestowed it without such purchase, and if God had not bestowed on us eternal happiness, he must have made us eternally

miserable, or else annihilated us for ever, for we can have no conception of any other state. Again, when sinners shall have suffered all that they deserve, there will be nothing to hinder their free access to the Father of Spirits; no sin, no guilt, no punishment can longer gather between them and the fountain of all true happiness, which is God. There can then be nothing to hinder the goodness of the Father from flowing directly to them in one eternal stream of bliss. Such beings can need no Redeemer, no Intercessor, no Mediator, no Saviour, any more than the Angels that shout around the throne. It is, then, clear that if salvation consists merely in the gift of happiness, *after we have suffered all that we deserve*, we cannot be dependent on Jesus Christ for salvation!

We think we have now fully shown that sinners cannot be punished all they deserve and then be saved.

The argument, which we will now close, stands thus:

1. Sinners cannot *be saved first* and *then punished* for their sins.

2. Sinners cannot be *saved* and *punished* for their sins at the same time.

3. Sinners cannot be saved *after* they *have been punished* all that their sins deserve; therefore, if sinners are *punished all that their sins deserve*, they can *never be saved*. Nothing can be more clear than this conclusion, if the propositions from whence it is deduced, have been sustained, and we trust that they have. If men are punished, there must be a *time when* they receive their punishment; and if they cannot be saved *before* this time of punishment, *at* or *during* this time of punishment, nor yet *after* this time of punishment it is clear that there is no time in which they can be saved. Universalists therefore, must either give up the notion, that every man is punished all his sin deserves, or else erase from their creed the expression, *"universal salvation"* and write in lieu thereof, UNIVERSAL DAMNATION.

V
On the Punishment of Sin in a Future State

IT IS, DOUBTLESS, GENERALLY understood that there are two classes of universalists, distinguished from each other by a difference of belief respecting the time when sinners receive their punishment; one maintaining that all punishment is confined to this life, while the other class, commonly called Universal Restorationers, admit that those who die in sin and unbelief will be punished after death. But while they differ in this respect, they both agree in maintaining the certain and final salvation of all men, and in controversy with those who believe in the doctrine of endless punishment, they generally merge this difference, and refuse to take ground on the question of future punishment. Their reasons for this course are obvious; each theory has its difficulties, which they can avoid only by refusing to avow or deny either. If the doctrine of future punishment is denied; so many absurdities are involved, and so many and clear are the declarations of scripture to the contrary, that but few dare venture the entire cause of universalism on the supposition that there is no punishment after death, without holding in reserve the doctrine of restoration from hell, through which to escape, should it prove true that sinners will be punished in a future state. On the other hand, if the doctrine of future punishment be admitted, the circumstances which must attend punishment in a future state, unfavorable to a moral reform in hell, press so hard upon the theory, that it is very rarely the case that men, believing in universal salvation, will unreservedly rest their cause on a redemption from hell in a future world. Under these circumstances, when a universalist is asked by an opponent, if he believes in punishment after death or not, he is as much put to it for an answer as the Pharisees were when Christ asked them if the baptism of John was from heaven or of men.

These circumstances render it necessary to take a separate and distinct view of these points. It is true that sinners are exposed to punishment after death, or it is false; and whether it be true or false, has a very important bearing on the main question at issue; and for universalists who hold out the hope of final salvation to all men, to evade so important a point, and refuse to say whether they believe that sinners are liable to punishment after death or not, not only betrays a fear to meet the objections which may be urged against their theory, when it is definitely stated, but is actually trifling with man's dearest interest. As they contend that sinners must suffer all the punishment their sins deserve without *possibility of escape*, it is a matter of vast importance to know the extent of divine punishment. If sinners receive all their punishment in this life, why should they be tormented with the fearful apprehensions of a future hell, as restorationers teach? And if they do not suffer all they deserve in this life, but are liable to punishment in the future world, it is awful in the extreme to flatter themselves with the hope of entering upon a state of perfect bliss at death, as universalists teach! Not only so, but it is necessary to settle the question, whether or not sinners are liable to punishment after death, that we may be enabled to come to a more certain conclusion on the question of endless punishment. If our opponents will take the field and maintain the position that there is no punishment awaiting sinners in a future world, it will follow of course that the doctrine of endless punishment is false; but if we can prove that sinners will be punished after death, it will give us the advantage of all those circumstances, unfavorable to a moral reform, attendant on punishment in a future state, in proof of endless punishment. Those who do not believe in any punishment after death are not prepared to appreciate arguments in proof of endless punishment, until the position they occupy is shown to be untenable. When arguments are advanced in favour of endless punishment and proof texts adduced, it is common with universalists to dispose of the whole by saying, "it has not yet been proved that these texts relate to a future state." Now, this point we propose settling at once, by proving that sinners are liable to punishment after death, from which it will follow that every text relates to a future state which speaks of the final punishment of the wicked.

I. All universalists hold principles which, if carried out, go to confirm the doctrine which asserts that sinners will be punished in a future state. They contend that the object of all divine punishment is to reform the sufferer. This appears to be a fundamental principle in their theory; it is advanced by every writer and reiterated by every pulpit declaimer on the subject of universalism. So common is this sentiment that it is unnecessary to quote authority. If however, universalists will disavow the corrective nature and design of all divine punishment they will escape the force of the argument we are about to draw from it in proof of future punishment; but until this be done, the argument must be fatal to their theory. Let it be understood, we do not admit that all punishment is corrective; but simply propose showing that as universalists contend that it is, they must admit the doctrine of future punishment, to be consistent with themselves.

If all divine punishment be designed to reform the sufferer, as universalists contend, one of three consequences must follow, viz. every sinner must be *reformed in this life*, or punishment must *fail to effect the reformation of the sinner*, for which it is designed, or else it must be *continued in a future state*, until it effect there what it fails to accomplish in this world.

1. All sinners are not reformed in this life, as scripture and matter of fact abundantly declare. It is said Prov. xiv. 32. "The wicked is driven away in his wickedness, but the righteous hath hope in his death." If then the wicked are driven away in their wickedness, in opposition to the hopeful death of the righteous, it is clear that they are not reformed and saved from their sins before death. Indeed it cannot be denied that some men sin on life's most extended verge, and blaspheme with their last breath; it is certain, therefore, that all men are not reformed in this life.

2. Will it be said that punishment fails to effect its designed object, in those cases in which men are not reformed in this life? We answer, such a concession must be fatal to the argument drawn from the corrective design of punishment; for what does it avail to contend that punishment is designed to reform the sinner, if it be admitted, at the same time, that it may fail to produce the designed effect? If it be admitted that God does inflict punishment, which does not reform the sufferer, the fact that endless punishment cannot reform its subjects, forms no argument against it. Not only so, but if it be contended that punishment be de-

signed to reform the sinner, and admitted at the same time, that it may fail to effect this design, it must follow that the means which God employs to reform sinners fail of their object. Now, if sinners can and do resist and render ineffectual the means which God employs to bring them to repentance and salvation, the final salvation of all men, to say the least, must be doubtful.

3. As universalists contend that all punishment is designed to reform the sinner, and as it is fatal to their cause to admit that it may fail in its design, they must allow that it will be continued in a future state, since it is manifest that it does not effect its intended object in this life. There is no way to escape the force of this conclusion. There are three alternatives between which they may choose, viz. they may admit that all punishment is not designed to reform the sufferer, or they may hold on to the corrective design of punishment and admit that it sometimes fails to effect its intended object; or they may contend that it will effect the reformation of the sinner, and admit that for this purpose it will be continued in a future state. Now, as it would be fatal to universalism, to assent to either of the two former positions, the conclusion is that universalists, in order to be consistent with themselves must allow that sinners will be punished in a future state.

II. There are some sins which will not admit of punishment in this life. In all cases where life is ended in sin, the subject cannot receive all the punishment he deserves before death, and therefore must be punished in a future state.

When we look into this world of wickedness and death, we see one man die in a drunken fit; another fall by the hand of his intended victim whom he was about to murder and rob—falling with the instrument of death in his hand, and murder in his heart; another has his head shot off in the field of battle; another is struck dead by lightning from the clouds, when in the act of blaspheming the name of God; and another perishes by his own hand—blowing out his own brains, and sending his soul into the future world, "as sudden as the spark from the smitten steel," stained with his own blood. Nothing can be more clear, than that sinners, dying under the above circumstances, cannot receive their full punishment in this world. If sinners are punished all they deserve in this life, under these circumstances, at what time do they receive it, and in what does it consist? Is it said that it is inflicted, prior to the commission of the crime? The notion is too absurd to be indulged for a moment.

1. If sin be punished before it is committed, then the innocent receive the punishment: before sin is committed man is innocent; he is then punished, if the punishment is prior to the sin for which it is inflicted; after that he commits sin; he is then guilty and receives no punishment on the above principles.

2. If sin be punished before it is committed, it must follow that sinners do not render themselves liable to punishment, by the commission of their crimes. On this principle, when a man has an opportunity to commit sin, and is disposed to do it, he may take it for granted that the punishment is past and commit the act with impunity.

Will it then be said that sin is punished at the time it is committed? This would imply that sin deserves no more punishment than is endured while the sinner is engaged in the crime, which in some of the above supposed cases can be but a moment. The absurdity of such a notion we have already shown in a preceding chapter, (see Chap. IV. Argument viii.) to which we will here add.

1. To say that sin receives its punishment at the time of its commission, so that it is fully punished by the time the act is finished, is to encourage sin. Sin is often committed with no other object than the gratification which the act itself affords; now, if the punish-

ment is received at the same time, it must be overbalanced by the gratification, making the pleasure of sin greater than its punishment; thus, the scale must preponderate in favor of sin.

2. The above notion is contradicted by plain matter of fact. Did Cain receive all the punishment his wicked murder deserved while he was slaying his righteous brother; or was he punished after the act was committed? The same inquiry might be made of every case of divine punishment recorded in the Bible. The same inquiry also may be made of every penalty inflicted by courts of justice, at the present day. If theft be punished all it deserves while the thief is in the act of stealing, imprisonment for the same act must be over and above justice.

But if sin receives all its punishment while the sinner is committing the act, in what does the punishment of sin consist? Suppose a man takes his own life by blowing out his own brains in an instant, or is shot dead in the act of attempting to kill another, does his punishment consist in the pain he endures? This cannot be.

1. This would make the punishment of murder consist in the pang of an instant, of which we can scarcely have any perception. Murder, in such case, is punished with less smart than good parents often inflict on their children for a much less offence.

2. The pain of dying in such case cannot be greater than men generally endure in death, whether they save life or take it; for all must die, and generally suffer more than the man whose existence is ended in an instant as above supposed.

3. To suppose that the punishment of suicide consists in the pain of dying, would be to suppose that the man punishes himself for his own sin, and that the act which constitutes the sin, and the act which inflicts the punishment are the same. From this, one of two fatal conse-

quences must follow, viz. as the same act produces both the sin and the punishment, it must follow that God is the author of the sin, or else that he is not the author of the punishment. Now if it be said that God is the author of both the sin and the punishment, then he punishes for that of which he is the author; and if it be said that God is not the author of the punishment, then the sin is not punished by God, and the pain of dying is proved not to be the punishment of suicide.

Will it be said that the punishment of suicide, or the punishment of a man who is shot dead in an attempt to murder another, consists in the loss of life? If so we reply,

1. The loss of life cannot be greater to the highway robber, or to the poor wretch, who is so tired of life as to commit suicide, than it was to righteous Abel or St. Stephen. The loss of life must be as great to the man who loses it in attempting to save the life of another, as it is to the man who loses it in an attempt to kill another.

2. On the supposition that there is no punishment after death the loss of life is, in fact, no loss, but a great gain, just in proportion as heaven is to be preferred to earth!

3. To suppose that the punishment of suicide consists in the loss of life, confounds sin with its punishment, and destroys all distinction between them. Suppose a man to hang himself, in what does the sin consist? It must be acknowledged that the sin consists in the sacrifice of life, while it is said that the punishment consists in the loss of life, which amounts to the same thing: a man sins by hanging himself, and he is punished for it by hanging; or a man is guilty for the loss of life, and he is punished by the loss of life, for which he is guilty. It must be clear that this makes sin and its punishment the same; the sin consists in the punishment and the punishment consists in the sin. Now, if this be granted, there are some sins for which many persons would esteem it a privilege to be punished.

It must appear conclusive from the above reasoning, that there are many sins which are not, and which cannot be punished in this life; they will therefore be punished in a future state.

III. To suppose that sin receives its full punishment in this world, must defeat every object of punishment which can be considered worthy the divine administration. If the full penalty of the law be inflicted, and endured by the offender in this life, it cannot be known what the punishment of sin is, how much of it the transgressor must endure, on whom the weight of the divine penalty falls, nor for what purpose it is inflicted.

1. If sinners are punished in this life all their sins deserve, it cannot be known in what their punishment consists. Can universalists tell in what the sinner receives his reward? If they can, they will please inform us in what way transgressors suffer for their impiety. Do different sins receive the same punishment, in kind? Or are profane swearers punished in one way and liars in another? Do the same acts of transgression always receive the same punishment, in kind, or are the violations of the same command punished sometimes in one way and sometimes in another? There is no suffering which sinners endure in this life, that we can recognize as the full penalty of the law. The punishment cannot consist in the misfortunes, sufferings, and death common to human beings; for these evils would overtake us if we were to refrain from sin and serve God with all our powers: good men suffer and die as well as bad men. The punishment of sin cannot consist in the penalties inflicted by the law of the land; for the laws enacted by men are sometimes unjust and oppressive, punishing virtue and rewarding vice. Different governments annex different penalties to the same prohibition, and all often change, while many sins are beyond the reach of the best civil authorities. Nor can the punishment of sin consist in mental anguish, or re-

morse of conscience. If the punishment of sin consisted in guilt of conscience, it would appear that the moral sensibility of the soul must be waked up in proportion to its progress in sin and guilt, which is not the case. Progress in sin is attended with greater and greater insensibility until every moral feeling of the soul is so blunted that the sinner can sport in the midst of' those scenes of enormity, which would have shocked his soul and struck him dumb in the commencement of his vicious career. The man of general good life and upright intentions, feels much more distress at the slightest deviation from moral rectitude than the most abandoned libertine careering in his licentious course, who has given himself up to work all manner of filthiness with greediness. The first deviation from probity is attended by a keen sense of guilt; conscience is on the alert. On a second offence conscience feels less, and so, until she is lulled to sleep, and sin is punished with little or no remorse. With this view the testimony of scripture accords. We read of some who have "their conscience seared as with a hot iron," 1 Tim. iv, 2. We read of others, "who being past feeling, have given themselves over unto laciviousness to work all manner of uncleanness with greediness," Eph. iv. 9.

2. On the supposition that the sinner receives his full punishment in this life, it cannot be known how great, or how small an evil the punishment of sin is. We may tell sinners that for their transgression they must be punished, and that except they repent they will perish, but how much they must suffer we cannot inform them; we cannot threaten them with an hour's punishment, for the worst of crimes; for we know not that they will live an hour. The law of God does not inform its subjects how much they must suffer if they incur its penalty, if there is no punishment after death. The sinner knows he cannot suffer long, but does not know that he shall suffer another day or hour; for the law,

with all its threatened penalties, does not give assurance that we shall survive that length of time; therefore God's law does not *positively* threaten the sinner with an hour's punishment, unless it threaten punishment after death. How long the sinner must suffer for his sin is therefore as uncertain as the day of his death; and more so, for while it is asserted that punishment shall not exist after death, it is not contended that the sinner will certainly be punished up to that period.

3. It cannot be known who suffer for sin, if its punishment be all endured in this life. We cannot know who are the subjects of divine punishment, by the sins of which those around us are guilty; for some commit their deeds in darkness, and others conceal the heart of a hypocrite under an external appearance of sanctity. Nor can we discover who are the objects of divine punishment by the suffering we see men endure, for there is no visible suffering endured by the wicked to which the righteous are not exposed, and sometimes actually endure. It is clear then that we cannot know in this world who suffer for their sins.

4. If sin receive its full punishment in this world, we can see no important object to be secured by it; no object worthy of the divine administration. It cannot be to make an exhibition of the divine justice, nor to vindicate the divine law and government; for no exhibition is made of the punishment, inflicted, nor of the subjects on whom it falls. It cannot be to make the sufferer an example to others; for neither the sufferers nor the punishment they endure is known as above stated. Nor can punishment be designed to reclaim the sufferer if it be confined to this world; for if there is no punishment after death, all will, of necessity, be reformed when they die; hence, if reformation be the end of punishment, such reformation must be confined to this life. To say men are punished in this life to re-

form them after death, would be to admit that they will be sinners in a future state, and consequently subject to punishment. If punishment, then, is designed to reform the sinner, it must reform him in this world, or be continued after death, or fail of its design, as we have shown in a preceding argument. Now, it is notorious, that all sinners are not reformed in this life; some sin and blaspheme with their last breath. This leaves no motive to punish the sinner for sins committed just as he is leaving the world; for, as the reformation which punishment is designed to effect has exclusive reference to this life, it can be of little consequence just as the sinner is entering eternity. To punish a dying sinner to reform him, with exclusive reference to this world, when in a week, a day or an hour, he will certainly be conveyed by death where his sin cannot follow him, and where he will need no reform, looks to us to be unworthy of the divine administration.

That punishment is not designed to reform, and that it does not result in reformation, on the supposition that it is confined to this life, is farther evident from the fact, that sinners themselves do not always know when they are punished, or that they are punished at all for sin in this life. We are liable to suffering here whether we sin or not; and who can tell which of his trials and sufferings are to punish him for his sins, and which are his natural inheritance, as a citizen of this world of sorrow? Not only so, but some have lived and died in a belief that God never punishes sin, in this world or in the world to come. Such persons are not only without reformation by their punishment, but on the supposition that sin is fully punished in this world, they receive the whole penalty of Jehovah's law without knowing that they are punished for sin.

It is clear then, if sinners be punished in this life all they deserve, their punishment cannot be designed to display the divine justice, nor to vindicate the divine government and authority. It cannot be to make the punished an example to others, nor can it be to reform the sufferer; to which we add, it therefore can reflect no glory upon the divine attributes, nor upon the divine administration. It must therefore follow that sinners go unpunished, or endure a punishment which can answer no important end to the punished, to others, nor to the divine government, or else they must be punished in a future state; and to us the latter appears most consistent.

IV. It does not appear that wicked men suffer more in this life than many of the most pious.

We have shown in a preceding argument that it cannot be known in what the punishment of sin consists, nor on whom it is inflicted, if it be confined to this world. This certainly goes far towards proving that the wicked do not suffer more in this life than those whom the scriptures denominate righteous; for if we cannot know what, and how much punishment the sinner endures in this life, we think it must be difficult to prove that he suffers more than the good man, around whom wants and sorrows often gather, and storms of adversity and persecution howl. But we will not rest the argument on a supposed impossibility of proving that sinners do always suffer more in this life than the righteous, but will attempt to show that they do not. The righteous have sometimes endured all that men are capable of suffering in the flesh. They have endured cold and hunger, nakedness, famine, prisons, racks, fire, and sword. Many devoted christians have closed their eyes amid the hellish tortures of an inquisition. Now we ask, what more than all these have wicked men suffered? Some, it is true, have endured the same or similar trials; but many others who have been very wicked have endured none of them, but have walked through life in paths perpetually cheered by the sunshine of prosperity. Do universalists say that sinners suffer from a guilty conscience, what is paramount to all those evils which sometimes all in the path of the righteous? We reply,

1. That this is what can never be proved.

2. It is what the sinner will not himself admit. What sinner will say that he suffers more than would equal the afflictions of Job, the trials of Jeremiah, or the labours and sufferings of Paul?

3. It is what we think no man of sober thought will believe. Who will believe that the wicked men of their acquaintance, who are surrounded by all the good things of this world, and appear sportfully merry, actually suffer more than the devoted christian, whose sighs escape from his dungeon through iron grates, or whose groans tell the deadly work of the instrument of torture? If it be said that the righteous have the support of religion amid all these trials, it is granted; but we add,

1. The wicked have many blessings, such as health, peace, and plenty, of which many of the godly have not been permitted to taste; and these mercies must serve much to mitigate their sorrow, admitting that they are punished here.

2. The righteous, amid all the supports which religion affords, endure much mental distress to which the ungodly are strangers; the best men often sorrow and weep, while wicked men rejoice. Hear the Prophet exclaim, "O that my head were waters, and mine eyes a fountain of tears, that I might weep day and night." Hear an Apostle declare," I have great heaviness and continual sorrow in my heart." Consider that these are exercises which sinners never feel, and we think it will appear that wicked men do not always suffer more in this life than good men. Indeed if the tears or both were numbered, we have no doubt it would appear that the man of God sheds the most. This argument may be thus stated: If sinners are punished in this life all their sins deserve, they must suf-

fer more than the righteous. But sinners do not always suffer more in this life than the righteous, therefore they are not punished in this life all their sins deserve, and consequently must be punished in a future state.

V. If there is no punishment after death, it must follow that the piety of the pious, and the wickedness of the wicked can affect them only in this life; all the consequences of virtue and vice, here, must cease at death. To say that the virtue of good men, or the vice of bad men, will affect them after death, would be to admit the doctrine of future punishment. Taking this view of the subject, it is obvious that to deny future punishment is to dispossess religion, at least, of most of its motive influence with which it addresses itself to the better interests of mankind.

1. The pious have no object to secure by their fidelity in religion, only what they enjoy in this life. Suppose then, as universalists must, to be consistent with their own theory, that prophets, apostles, confessors and martyrs, knew that their profession of the truth which brought upon them the contempt of the world, the frown of kings, and prepared the rack to torture them, and the fiery fagot to burn them; suppose, we say, that they knew the benefits of their profession would last no longer than the sufferings which they endured for its sake, and can any one believe that they would have braved all the storm of persecution that fell upon them with such undying fortitude as marked their career? Would Moses have chosen to suffer affliction with the people of God on earth, if he had believed that he could enjoy the splendour of the Egyptian throne and heaven too? Would Paul have endured what he did for the sake of the gospel, had he believed that himself and all others would be just as well off at death without the gospel as with it? Would he have warned every one, night and day, with tears, if he had known that all distinction between the righteous and the

wicked would cease at death? We see then that the course pursued by the prophets, apostles, and fathers, was such as would not have resulted from a belief that the conduct of the present life has nothing to do with our future destiny. Had they believed that their perseverance in the truth would not benefit them after death, their blood would never have stained the ground, nor would Nero's garden have been lighted with their funeral piles. If it be said that religion yields a present comfort to the believer sufficient to support him under all these trials, we make our appeal to the christian world, and ask what christian there is who will say that he enjoys comfort enough in religion, aside from any hope or fear respecting a future state, to support him in the dungeon, loaded with chains, or to carry him to the stake? There is comfort in religion, and joy in believing, we admit; but take away that joy which springs from a hope that takes hold on a future reward, and remove that faith which connects present fidelity with future happiness, and what remains will be dissipated at the first motion of the wheel, or at the first touch of the fiery fagot.

2. The wicked have nothing to fear in consequence of their sins, only what befalls them in this life. This certainly leaves sinners with as little to fear, in view of their wickedness, as we have seen the righteous have to hope in consequence of their piety. Some men who are notoriously wicked pass through life as smoothly as the devoted christian, or the zealous minister, who, like Paul, warns all, night and day, with tears. If it be said that sinners suffer some unseen punishment, which is designed to operate as a restraint upon them to deter them from transgression, we answer, the absurdity of such a hypothesis has already been shown; in addition to which we here make our appeal to the sinner himself, and ask him what he has suffered as a punishment for sin, calculated to restrain him in future? It must be seen then that to deny

future punishment, is to remove all the terror from the divine law, by nullifying its threatened penalty, and leave the sinner to act without fear of punishment. Is it said that those who deny punishment after death, assert, that if men sin they must be punished for it in this life, and that there is no possibility of escaping it by repentance and faith? We reply, that sinners have no reason much to fear a mundane hell; for that sentiment which denies a future hell, teaches them that they have been in hell ever since they began to sin; and having found it supportable, and in general quite comfortable, they can have but little to fear for the future.

VI. The descriptions given of the punishment of the wicked by the pen of inspiration) are such as to preclude the idea of any thing which sinners generally suffer in this life; and if so, such descriptions must refer to punishment in a future state. Rom. i. 18. "The wrath of God is revealed from heaven against all ungodliness and unrighteousness of men." Rom. ii. 8, 9. "Indignation and wrath, tribulation and anguish upon every soul that doeth evil." 2. Thess. i. 7, 8. "When the Lord Jesus shall be revealed from heaven in flaming fire, taking vengeance on them that know not God." Rev. xxi. 8. "But the fearful and unbelieving, and the abominable, and murderers, and whoremongers, and sorcerers, and idolaters, and all liars, shall have their part in the lake which burneth with fire and brimstone." Rev. xx. 15. "And whosoever was not found written in the book of life was cast into the lake of fire." Matt. xxii. 13. "Then said the king to the servants, bind him hand and foot, and take him away, and cast him into outer darkness." Matt. xxv. 30. "And cast ye the unprofitable servant into outer darkness: there shall be weeping and gnashing of teeth." Now who can suppose that these descriptions belong to punishment happening to sinners, generally, in this life? Indignation and wrath, wrath of God revealed from heaven, Christ revealed from heaven in flaming fire, taking vengeance, cast into a lake that burneth with fire and brimstone, cast into outer darkness where is weeping and gashing of teeth, &c. such expressions are too high wrought to come from the pen of the most impassioned poet, if he were describing the suffering common to sinners in this life. Let it be remarked that some of the above texts speak of all sinners, as "every soul of man that doeth evil," "all liars," &c. What would be thought of a writer who, in attempting to describe the punishment which all liars receive in this life, should assert that they have their part in the lake that burneth with fire and brimstone? Would liars themselves believe such statements? And can any one believe that the Holy Ghost ever dictated descriptions so far from sober fact? And yet we must admit it, or else admit that the Bible threatens sinners with a punishment which they do not receive in this world. If then the descriptions which are given in the Bible of the punishment of the wicked cannot be consistently applied to any thing happening to sinners generally in this life, it must follow that these descriptions belong to punishment in a future state.

VII. The scriptures associate with the punishment of the wicked, the idea of a place or locality in a manner that forbids the supposition that it is endured in this life. Hell is referred to as a place of punishment, not in this world, but in a future state. Psa. ix. 17. "The wicked shall be turned into hell and all the nations that forget God." Luke xvi. 23. "And in hell he lifted up his eyes being in torments." Mark ix. 43. "It is better for thee to enter into life maimed than having two hands to go into hell." 2 Pet. xi. 4. "For if God spared not the angels that sinned, but cast them down to hell, and delivered them into chains of darkness to be reserved unto judgment." Rev. xx. 10. "The devil that deceived them was cast into the lake of fire and brimstone, where the beasts [sic] and the false prophets [sic] are." The above quotations clearly imply a local hell. "Shall be turned into hell, to go into hell, in hell he lifted up his eyes," &c. are expressions which involve the idea of a place; and if there is not a place of punishment such expressions are words without meaning. If the trials and sufferings of this life make up the sinner's punishment, it could not be said, "the wicked shall be turned into hell," for in such case the wicked are already in hell, and it would be strange indeed to threaten a man with being cast into a pit in which he had already fallen. If the worm that dieth not and the fire that is not quenched are nothing, more than remorse of conscience here in this life, the wicked are not "turned into hell," do not "go into hell," but hell is turned into the wicked, and the rich man instead of lifting up his eyes in hell, must have lifted them up having hell within himself. The casting down of the angels that sinned into hell, in chains of darkness, and the casting of the devil into the lake that burneth with fire and brimstone, where the beast and the false prophets are, so clearly imply a place of punishment that farther remarks are unnecessary. We ask then, is there any such place as hell in which sinners are now punished in this life? It is presumed that no one will contend for the existence of a local hell in this world in which sinners *are now punished*. We say then there is a place called hell, in which sinners are or will be punished. There is no hell in this world) in which sinners are punished, therefore hell must be in a future state, and consequently, the punishment of the wicked must be in a future state also. This argument must prove conclusive to the entire overthrow of modem universalism, if the existence of a hell as a place of punishment be proved. Of this universalists themselves are aware; hence, every possible effort has been made to annihilate this gulf of perdition, or to metamorphose it into the grave, or into a valley near Jerusalem, whither the filth of the city used to be conveyed and burned. This point has been considered of such great importance that Mr. Balfour has written an entire volume on the word hell, in which he labours to disprove the common notion that hell is a place of punishment in the future world. We cannot, within the compass of our intended limits, review Mr. B's laboured work on this subject, nor do we think it necessary, believing that the question can be settled in a few pages, at much less expense both to the writer and reader. To show the ground taken by universalists on the subject of hell, the reader is here presented with the following extract from Mr. Morse's reply to Rev. Joel Parker. On pages, 17, 18, 19 and 20, the author holds the following language: "He" (Mr. Parker) "took it for granted that *hell* is in a future state of being—he has furnished no proof of it—Christ never taught that hell is beyond the grave.— David says, 'thou hast delivered my soul from the lowest hell.' Was David in this world or the next when he used that language?

"There are four different words in the original languages which are rendered hell in our English Bibles in common use, viz. *sheol, hades, tartarus* and *gehenna*. Critics now generally agree that neither *sheol, hades*, nor *tartarus* was ever used by any sacred writer to communicate an idea of endless suffering—and therefore should not have been translated hell. Concerning the word gehenna Dr. Campbell says, 'It is originally a compound of the two Hebrew words *ge, Hinnom*; the valley of Hinnom *a place near Jerusalem* of which we hear first in the Book of Joshua 15, 8. It was there that the cruel sacrifices of children were made by fire to Moloch, the Ammonitish idol, 2 Chron. 23, 5.' The Dr's opinion that *gehenna* is used in the New Testament to denote the place of future punishment is entirely without evidence. Parkhurst speaking of *gehenna* says, it is 'a corruption of two Hebrew words *ge* a valley, and *Hinnom* the name of a person who was once the possessor of it. This valley of Hinnom lay near Jerusalem, and had been the place of those abominable sacrifices, in which the idolatrous Jews burned their children alive to Moloch, Baal, or the Sun. A particular place in this valley was called tophet,' &c. He also says, 'a gehenna of fire. Matt. 5. 22. does I apprehend, in its outward and *primary* sense, relate to that dreadful doom of being burnt alive in the valley of Hinnom.' Cruden says, 'it is thought that *tophet* was the butchery, or place of slaughter at Jerusalem, lying to the south of the city, in the valley of the children of Hinnom; it is also said, that a constant fire used to be kept there for burning the carcases [sic] and other filthiness, that was brought thither from the city. It was in the same place that they cast away the ashes and remains of the images of false Gods, when they demolished their altars, and broke down their statues.' Isa. says 30. 33. "For tophet is ordained of old; yea for the king it is prepared; he hath made it deep and large. The pile thereof is fire and much wood; the breath of the Lord like a stream of brimstone doth kindle it.' Cruden further says, 'others think the name of tophet is given to the valley of Hinnom, because of the sacrifices that were offered there to the god Moloch, by beat of drum, which in Hebrew is called *toph*. It was in this manner that those sacrifices were offered. The statue of Moloch was of brass, hollow within, and its arms extended, and stooping a little forward. They lighted a great fire within the statue, and another before it: they put upon its arms the child they intended to sacrifice, which soon fell into the fire at the foot of the statue, putting forth cries, as may easily be imagined. To stifle the noise of their cries, and howlings, they made a great rattling of drums and other instruments, that the spectators might not be moved with compassion at the clamours of these miserable victims.' Calmet gives a similar account of Tophet, the valley of Hinnom and the horrid, cruelties practiced in the worship of the idol Moloch. We have positive proof that gehenna, or the valley of the son of Hinnom is in this world, in the book of Joshua 15. 8. 'And the border went up by the *valley of the son of Hinnom* unto the south side of the Jebusite, the same is Jerusalem.' For further confirmation of this important truth, see the 7th and 9th chapters of the prophecy of Jeremiah. The word *gehenna* is found in the New Testament twelve times only, it was always addressed to the Jews. Nothing is said of *gehenna* to the Gentiles. This word is found Matt. 5. 22-30; Matt. 18. 9; Mark 9. 43-47; Luke 12. 6; Matt. 10. 23; Matt. 23. 15, 33; and James 3. 6."

The above extract, we think, contains a brief view of what universalists generally believe concerning hell. The substance of the whole is, that there is no place of punishment in the future world, called hell. It is said plainly, "Christ never taught that hell is beyond the grave." To sustain this position two grounds are taken, viz. first, the words sheol, hades, and tartarus are improperly translated hell; and secondly, the word gehenna is expressive of a place in the valley of Hinnom, near Jerusalem, where a fire was kept for the purpose of burning the filth of the city, &c. Now, on both these points we join issue. We will first notice Mr. M's brief method of disposing of three of the words rendered hell. He says, "Critics now generally agree that neither the words sheol, hades, nor tartarus was ever used by any sacred writer to communicate an idea of endless suffering—and therefore should not have been translated hell." Now, to this dexterous method of disposing of so weighty a matter we offer the following reply:

1. When Mr. M. says that "Critics generally agree that neither *sheol, hades,* nor *tartarus* was ever used by any sacred writer to communicate an idea of endless suffering—and therefore should not have been translated hell," he, in effect, admits that the word which is properly translated hell, must have been used by sacred writers "to communicate an idea of endless suffering." It is too plain to

be overlooked, that if as Mr. M. states, these words ought not to be translated hell, *because they were not used by sacred writers to communicate an idea of endless suffering*, then, any word which may be properly rendered hell, must communicate an idea of endless suffering. Now as he has told us in the above extract, that there are but four words in the original languages which are rendered hell, three of which he says should not be so rendered, because they were not used by the sacred writers to communicate an idea of endless suffering; it follows that the fourth word, which is *gehenna*, to the translation of which he makes no objection, must have been used by the sacred writers to communicate an idea of endless suffering. This testimony in favor of future and endless punishment, though from a universalist, is good as far as it goes. But the reader will please to bear in mind, that the question in this place is not whether hell is a place of endless suffering, but whether or not there be any such place as hell, where sinners will be punished after death.

2. When Mr. M. says that critics are generally agreed that the words *sheol, hades,* and *tartarus* are never used by the sacred writers to communicate an idea of endless suffering, he states what we think can never be shown, unless "critics generally" have thus far escaped our observation. Had he stated that critics generally agree that these words are not *always* used to communicate an idea of endless suffering, or a place of future punishment, he would have come nearer the truth; but that critics are agreed that they are never used in this sense we deny. On the word *sheol,* of the Old Testament, which is sometimes rendered *grave,* sometimes *pity,* and sometimes *hell,* Dr. A. Clark has made the following remark in his notes on Job vii. 10. "The word which we, properly enough, translate *grave,* here signifies also the *state of the dead, hades;* and sometimes any *deep pit,* or even *hell* itself." On Job xxiv.

19, the Dr. remarks again, "I have elsewhere shown that *sheol* signifies not only *hell* and the *grave* but any *deep pit.*" On Samuel ii. 6, the same critic remarks thus: "The Hebrew word *sheol* which we translate *grave* seems to have the same meaning in the Old Testament with *hades* in the New, which is the word generally used by the Septuagint for the other. It means the *grave*, the *state* of the dead, and the *invisible place* or place of *separate spirits.*"

Mr. Henry remarks on Psa. ix. 17. "In the other world the wicked shall be turned into hell."

Again, on Psa. xlix. 15, he paraphrases thus: "God shall redeem my soul from the *sheol* of hell the wrath to come, that pit of destruction into which the wicked shall be cast."

Again, on the expression "Hell, (*sheol*) and destruction are before the Lord," Prov. xv. 11. Mr. Henry remarks thus: "The place of the damned, in particular, and all their torments which are inexpressible, the state of separate souls generally and all their circumstances, are under God's eye."

Mr. Cruden says, "This word *sheol* is sometimes put for *hell*, the place where the wicked are damned or tormented."

We trust we have now shown that critics do not generally agree that the word *sheol* is never used to communicate an idea of endless suffering, or what is more properly the question in this place, punishment in the future state. But before we dismiss this word we will offer a few remarks which may serve to convince the plain reader, without any reference to critics, that it is properly translated by our English word, *hell*. From the above authorities it appears that the word *sheol* signifies the grave or any deep pit or cavity in the earth; that it also signifies the state of the dead in general, and sometimes hell, or a place of future punishment. Now we maintain the correctness of the latter application in certain cases, from the fact that some of the instances in which it occurs, the connection will not admit of either the former renderings. Job xi. 8. "It is high as heaven what canst thou do; deeper than hell what canst thou know." The subject of discourse in this text is the unsearchableness of God. The preceding verse inquires, "Canst thou by searching find out God? Canst thou find out the Almighty to perfection? It is as high as heaven it is as deep as hell." The simple meaning is, that man can no more find out God than he can scan *heaven* and explore *hell*. Now, understand hell to refer to the future world and the comparison is not only correct, but is awfully sublime! As hell, (*sheol*) is in the yet unseen and unknown world; in the bosom of undeveloped eternity—remote from the light of time and the scrutiny of man, so God is unsearchable. But suppose *hell* to be in this world; that in this text, it is the grave or some dark cavity or pit in the earth, and the text is not only stripped of its sublimity, but of its common sense also. Men are capable of exploring subterraneous caverns, and graves are the work of mens' hands, and they are capable of opening vaults and charnel-houses, and marble tombs, and of exposing the mouldering dead, and the darkness of the grave, to the gaze of the noon-tide sun-beams; hence, there is no force nor sense in the text if its object be to assert that the mystery of the divine nature is as deep as the grave.

Psa. ix. 14. "The wicked shall be turned into hell." It cannot be denied that this text distinguishes the wicked from the righteous by the punishment they endure; hence, being "turned into hell," distinguishes the wicked from the righteous, who consequently cannot be turned into hell. Now, we ask by what English term the word *sheol* should be rendered, if not by the word hell? By what other term could it be consistently rendered, and have the text still distinguish the wicked by the punishment they endure? It will not answer to render it *grave*, for then it would express nothing peculiar to the wicked; it would affirm nothing which might not be affirmed of the righteous: the righteous are turned into the grave as well as the wicked. Nor will it obviate the difficulty to render it *pit*; for if by this term any thing is meant less than *hell*, it is not true of the wicked any more than of the righteous.

Psa. cxxix. 8. "If I ascend up to heaven thou art there: If I make my bed in hell thou art there." The Psalmist is here treating of the divine omnipresence, showing that God is every where present, filling all in all. With a warmth perfectly becoming the inspiring character of his subject, he exclaims, "Whither shall I go from thy spirit? Or whither shall I flee from thy presence? If I ascend up to heaven, thou art there: if I make my bed in hell, thou art there." Now, suppose *hell* to mean no more than the grave, or some pit or cavern in the earth, and the sublimity, beauty and propriety of these high wrought strains disappear.

Such an exposition destroys the parallel between heaven and hell: "If I ascend up to *heaven* thou art there; if I make my bed in hell thou art there." Here heaven and hell are referred to, as places of equal distance in opposite directions, to illustrate the divine omnipresence, by affirming that God is alike in the one and in the other. If the grave be understood, it forms no parallel to heaven, which must be in a future world, if it is to be the eternal abode of all souls, as universalists contend. But should heaven be understood, in this place, to mean no more than the starry regions, still the narrow limits of the grave, which are formed by man, and by him may be explored, form but a poor illustration of the divine omnipresence, in contrast with the heavens, where the Almighty's goings are marked by the sweep of revolving worlds.

We have now done with the Hebrew word *sheol*, which our translators have rendered hell, in some instances, and in others *graves* and *pit*. Other quotations, it is true, might be added to the above, but probably enough has been said, and our intended limits forbid to say more.

But Mr. Morse also asserts that critics are generally agreed that the word *"hades* was never used by any sacred writer to communicate an idea of endless suffering."* Let us then listen for a moment to the voice of some of the critics and compare their language with the above declaration.

Mr. Groves, in his Greek and English Dictionary, gives the following exposition of the term in question. "Hades" (from *a*, negative, and *eido*, to see) a dark, obscure place; a place unseen or not to be seen by mortals; the receptacle or region of the dead. According to the christian doctrine, *the invisible place of spirits, the unseen place of souls; the place of the dead* generally, but vulgarly *a place of torment; the abode of the damned.* With the above, accord the remarks of Dr. A. Clark. In his note on Matt. xi. 23, he has given the following criticism: "The original word is *hades*, from *a, not*, and *ideim, to see*—the invisible receptacle or mansion of the dead, answering to *sheol* in Hebrew, implying often, 1st, the grave, 2ndly, the state of *separate souls* or *unseen* world of spirits, whether of *torment* or *in general*." Again, on Acts ii. 27, the Dr. remarks thus: *"Thou wilt not leave my soul in hell; in hades,* that is, the state of *separate spirits,* or the state of the *dead.* Hades was a general term among the Greek writers by which they expressed this state: and this HADES was *tartarus* to the *wicked,* and *elysium* to the good." To the above we will add the testimony of a more modern critic still. Dr. Chapman, of the Protestant Episcopal Church, in his sermon on *"Hades,"* has given the following criticism; the object of which is to explain and defend that article of the Church which asserts that Christ descended into hell. Of Christ he says: "He indeed descended into hell; but we are to remember that this sentence concludes with a word of Saxon derivation. A word, that, instead of implying, as it now does, the reverse of heaven, originally imported no more than the *inferi* of the Latins and the *hades* of the Greeks; that is, in our English tongue, the place of departed spirits. The same observation applies to no less than eleven passages of the New Testament, wherever indeed the original word is *hades*, and not *gehenna*, both of which are translated hell; but while the latter indicates the place of eternal misery, the former merely denotes the intermediate state of the soul after death, and prior to the general judgment. It includes the elysium and the tartarus of the poets, and is sufficiently delineated in the parable of the rich man and Lazarus to convince us that it is divided into two separate mansions; the one being a common receptacle for the souls of the righteous; the other for the ungodly and sinner." We might multiply the list of critics, but we forbear. From what has been said it appears that *hades*, (*hell*,) is used to express the place of departed spirits; a place of misery or happiness according to the moral character of the subject. And what goes far towards confirming this exposition is, it is in perfect accordance with the opinions held by the Jews as appears from Josephus. The following extract is taken from his "discourse to the Greeks concerning *hades*."

"Now as to *hades*, wherein the souls of the righteous and unrighteous are detained, it is necessary to speak of it. *Hades* is a place in the world not regularly finished; a *subterraneous* region, wherein the light of this world does not shine; from this circumstance, that in this region the light does not shine, it cannot but be there must be in it perpetual *darkness*. This region is allotted as a place of custody for souls, in which angels are appointed as guardians to them, who distribute to them *temporary punishments*, agreeable to every one's behaviour and manners.

In this region there is a certain place set apart as a *lake of unquenchable fire*; whereinto we suppose no one hath hitherto been cast; but it is prepared for a day aforedetermined by God, in which one righteous sentence shall deservedly be passed upon all men; when the unjust, and those that have been disobedient to God, and have given honor to such idols as have been the vain operations of the hands of men, as to God himself, shall be adjudged to this *everlasting punishment,* as having been the causes of defilement; while the just shall obtain an *incorruptible* and never-fading *kingdom.* These are now, indeed, confined in *hades* but not in the same place wherein the just are confined.

"For there is one descent into this region, at whose *gate* we believe there stands an archangel with a host; which *gate* when those pass through that are conducted down by the angels appointed over souls, they do not go the same way, but the just are guided to the *right hand,* and are led with hymns, sung by the *angels* appointed over that place, unto a region of light.

"But as to the unjust, they are dragged by force to the *left hand* by the angels, allotted for punishment, no longer going with a good will, but as prisoners driven by violence; to whom are sent the angels appointed over them to reproach them, and threaten them with their terrible looks, and to thrust them still downward."

But there is a third word in the original, rendered *hell* in the English Bibles in common use, which is *tartarus.* Concerning this, Mr. Morse also affirms that "critics are now generally agreed that" it was "never used by any sacred writer to communicate an idea of endless suffering." This statement, we think, will appear just as true in relation to this word, as it has proved to be of the two former, and no more so. The word *tartarus* is found but once in the scriptures, which is 2 Peter ii. 4. "For if God spared not the angels that sinned, but cast them down to hell, *tartarus,* and delivered then into chains of darkness to be reserved unto judgment." We will now hear what critics say concerning this word. The word is thus defined in Groves' Greek and English Dictionary. *"The infernal regions, hell of the poets, a dark place, prison, dungeon, jail, the bottomless pit, hell."* It is worthy of remark that there is not one of the above definitions, which does not, when applied to the fallen angels, imply a hell in the common acceptation of the term. In the text above quoted the word is used in the participial form, *tartarosos*; which denotes the act of throwing, or casting into, *tartarus*. The following is from the pen of Dr. Mc Knight, as quoted by Mr. Benson, in his note on the text in question. "The word *tartarus* is not found in the 70, nor any where in the New Testament but here; its meaning therefore must be sought for among the Greeks. Homer represents *tartarus*, Iliad, viii. page 13, as a deep place under the earth, where there are iron gates and a brazen entrance. It is derived from a word expressive of terror, and signifies the doleful prison where wicked spirits are reserved until they shall be brought out to public condemnation and execution.

"Hesiod speaks of *tartarus* as a place far under ground, where the Titans are bound with chains of thick darkness. Wherefore, seeing the Greeks named the place where they supposed the Titans, the enemies of the gods were confined, *tartarus*, it was natural for Peter, when writing in the Greek language concerning confining the evil angels in the place where they were shut up, to call it *tartarus*; although his idea of *tartarus* was different from that of the Greeks.

Perfectly in accordance with the above, is the following extract from Dr. A. Clark's note on the same text. The Dr. says, "as the word *tartarus* is not found in the *New Testament*, nor does it appear in the Septuagint, we must have recourse to the Greek writers for its meaning; and in order to know what was the precise intention of the Apostle by this expression, we must inquire what is the accurate import of the word *tartarus*. Now, it appears from a passage of Lucian, that by *tartarus* was meant, in a *physical* sense, *the bounds* or *verge of this material system*; for addressing himself to *Eros, Cupid,* or *Love,* he says, 'Thou formest the universe, from its confused and chaotic state, and after separating and dispersing the circumfused chaos in which, as in one common sepulchre, the whole world lay buried, thou drove it to the confines of outer *tartarus,*

> Where iron gates and bars of solid brass.
> Kept in durance irrefrangible;
> And its return prohibit.

"The ancient Greeks appear to have received by tradition, an account of the punishment of the fallen angels, and of bad men after death; and their poets did, in conformity, I presume, with that account, make *tartarus* the place where the giants who rebelled against Jupiter, and the souls of the wicked were confined. 'Here,' said Hesiod, 'the rebellious Titans were bound in penal chains,

> As far beneath the earth, as earth from heaven,
> For such the distance thence to *tartarus*.

Which description will very well agree with the proper sense of *tartarus*; if we take the earth for the centre of the material system, and reckon from our zenith, or the extremity of the heavens that is over our heads. But as the Greeks imagined the earth to be of a boundless depth; so it must not be dissembled that their poets speak of tartarus as *a vast pit,* or *gulf in the bowels of it.* Thus, Hesiod,

> 'Black tartarus in earth's spacious womb.'

And Homer, Iliad viii. line 13, &c. introduces Jupiter

threatening any of the gods who should presume to assist either the Greeks or the Trojans, that he should either come back wounded to heaven, or be sent to *tartarus*,

> 'Or far, O far from steep Olympus thrown,
> Low in the deep *tartarean* gulf shall groan.
> That gulf which iron gates and brazen ground
> *Within the earth* inexorable bound;
> As deep beneath the infernal centre hurled
> As from that centre to the etherial world.'

"On the whole then, *tartaron* in St. Peter, is the same as *riptein es tartaron, to throw into tartarus*, in *Homer*; only rectifying the poet's mistake of *tartarus* being in the bowels of the earth, and recurring to the original sense of that word above explained; which, when applied to *spirits* must be interpreted *spiritually:* and thus *tartarosos*, will import, that God cast the apostate angels out of his presence, *into that blackness of darkness*, (2 Peter ii. 17. Jude, ver. 13.) where they will be forever banished *from the light of his countenance*, and from the *beatifying influence of the ever blessed Three*; as truly as a person plunged into the *torpid boundary of this created system* would be from the *light* of the sun, and the *benign* operations of the material heavens."

We have now done with the words, *sheol, hades,* and *tartarus,* which are rendered hell in the scriptures; and though we have dealt sparingly in criticism, not having introduced but a small portion of the testimony which might be brought forward, yet enough has been said to enable the reader to judge with what correctness it has been asserted that "critics now generally agree that neither *sheol, hades,* nor *tartarus,* was ever used by any sacred writer to communicate an idea of endless suffering, and therefore should not have been translated hell." We do not, however, pretend to have proved that these words were used "to communicate an idea of *endless* suffering," but that they were used to express suffering or punishment, *in the future state, after death,* which is as clearly denied, in the above extract, as the doctrine of endless punishment.

We will now consider the fourth and last term rendered hell, which is *gehenna*. Universalists, we believe, do not object so much to the translation of this word, as they do to the idea attached to the English term *hell,* by which it is rendered. As this is the word generally employed by the Saviour in those discourses in which the term hell occurs in the English translation of the scriptures, and as Mr. Morse says in the extract, which has been made from his reply to Mr. Parker, "Christ never taught that hell is beyond the grave," he is understood to deny that this word, as used in the gospel relates to a future state; and if we understand his mode of argumentation, he intends to offer three reasons in support of his position, founded on the derivation of the word itself, its unfrequent occurrence in the New Testament, and the circumstance that it was always addressed to the Jews, but never to the gentiles. These reasons shall now receive due attention.

We will first notice what is said on the derivation of the word. Mr. Morse quotes from several criticks, to prove that the word *gehenna* was originally applied to the valley of Hinnom, a place near Jerusalem, where the Israelites caused their children to pass through the fire to Moloch, and where a fire was afterwards kept constantly burning to consume the carcases and other filth that were brought thither from the city. This he appears to consider conclusive evidence that *gehenna* cannot be employed to express a future hell; for he says: "We have positive proof that *gehenna,* or the valley of the son of Hinnom, is in this world." To this we reply, that the conclusion does not follow from the premises; the question is not what was the origin of the term *gehenna*, but in what sense Christ employed it in his discourses.

1. The origin or primary sense of a word does not determine its popular sense in after times. A few examples will satisfy the candid reader of this fact. If, as Mr. Morse supposes, because the word *gehenna* was originally the name of a place in this world, the valley of the son of Hinnom, it cannot have been used to express a place of punishment in the future world, by the same mode of reasoning we might disprove the reality of a future state. The Greek word *psuche*, which is rendered *soul*, in the scriptures, is derived from *psucho*, which signifies *to breathe*; hence, *psuche, soul*, literally signifies the breath, and therefore cannot, according to Mr. M's reasoning, signify the immortal spirit. The Greek word *ouranos*, rendered *heaven*, is derived from *oros* which signifies *the end* or *boundary* of a thing or place, or from *horao, to see*; hence, *ouranos, heaven*, literally signifies the atmosphere or region of the stars and therefore cannot if Mr. M. reasons well, be applied to a future state of happiness. "We have the most positive proof that" heaven "is in this world," for we read of the fowls of heaven, the dew of heaven, the clouds of heaven, &c. The English word *hell*, is now used by common consent, to express a place of future punishment. Universalists themselves will not deny that this is now the common acceptation of the term, though they do not believe in the existence of such a place; but such was not the primitive signification of this word. It is of Saxon origin, and is derived from *helam* which signified to cover or hide; hence, the slating of houses and the covers of books were called *heling*. See Dr. A. Clark's note on Matt. xi. 23. Now should this book after surviving a thousand years, be translated into another language, and should a controversy occur concerning the word *hell*, reference to the root and primitive use of this term, it might be shown that no reference is had to a future state, just as

conclusively as Mr. M. proves that Christ did not teach a hell beyond the grave, in the use of the word *gehenna*, because this term in its literal sense was applied by the primitive Hebrews to the valley of Hinnom.

2. Mr. M's critics, whom he has introduced to prove that the word *gehenna* was the name of a place near Jerusalem, are all against him respecting the sense in which Christ employed this term; he is under the necessity therefore of impeaching his own witnesses. After introducing what Dr. Campbell says on the subject of the origin of the word *gehenna*, lest the Dr's testimony should prove too much for the good of his cause he adds: "The Dr's opinion that *gehenna* is used in the New Testament to denote the place of future punishment is entirely without foundation." This is a full concession that so far as Dr. Campbell's criticism and opinion go, when taken as a whole, they are against universalism; hence, Mr. M. after forcing the Dr. into court, found it necessary to impeach him and close his mouth before he had half finished his testimony. Mr. Cruden, whom Mr. M. has also introduced on this point, likewise understood *gehenna*, as used by the Saviour, to refer to punishment in the future world. He says, "the wicked *in hell* not only undergo the punishment of sense, but also that of loss, which is a separation from God, a privation of his sight and of the beatific vision. Add to these the eternity of their misery, which, above all considerations, makes it intolerable: their worm dieth not and their fire is not quenched, Mark 9. 48." This clearly proves that the very critics, on whose testimony Mr. M. relies to prove that *gehenna* primarily related to the valley of Hinnom, considered this circumstance perfectly consistent with its application to the place of the damned in the future world, by our Lord. But to these witnesses other names may be added. Mr. Groves, in his Greek and English Dictionary gives the following exposition of the term *gehenna*. He says, "it is from He-

brew, the valley of Hinnom, and signifies *hell, hell fire, torments of hell.* " Dr. Clark remarks on Matt. v. 22. "From the circumstance of this valley," (the valley of Hinnom) "having been the scene of those *infernal sacrifices,* the Jews in our Saviour's time used the word for *hell,* the *place of the damned.* See the word applied in this sense by the *Targum,* on Ruth ii. 12. Psal. cxl. 12. Gen. iii. 24. xv. 17." On Isa. xxx. 33, the same critic remarks thus: "Tophet is a valley very near to Jerusalem, to the south east, called also the valley of Hinnom or *gehenna* where the Canaanites, and afterwards the Israelites, sacrificed their children by making them pass through the fire, that is, by burning them in the fire to Moloch, as some suppose. It is therefore used for a place of punishment by fire, and by our blessed Saviour in the gospel, for hell fire, as the Jews themselves had applied it."

The following pointed remarks are extracted from Hawe's Letters. "But there is another term used to denote future punishment much more definite than the two just considered, (*sheol,* and *hades.*) I refer to *gehenna.* This word, I know, has been frittered away by universalists to mean only a valley in the vicinity of Jerusalem. But how was it used by our Saviour, and how was it understood by the Jews who heard his discourses? I answer, the Saviour always used this term to denote the place of future punishment, and that it was uniformly understood in this sense by the Jews of his time. It is a word peculiar to the Jews; and was employed by them, some time before the coming of Christ, to denote that part of *sheol* which was the habitation of the wicked after death. This is proved by the fact of its familiar use in the New Testament, and by the fact of its being found in its apocryphal books and Jewish Targums; some of which were written before the time of our Saviour. These Targums were translations and interpretations of the scriptures; and in remarking upon various passages of the old Testament, use the word *gehenna*, and expressly explain it to mean the place of punishment for the wicked. If then our Saviour did not use this word in a totally different sense, from that in which it was used by the persons whom he addressed, he must have employed it to denote the place of future punishment."

3. What fully confirms this point, is, the connection in which the word *gehenna* is uniformly used by Christ in the New Testament. A few examples will be sufficient. Matt. xviii. 9. "If thine eye offend thee, pluck it out and cast it from thee; it is better for thee to enter into life with one eye, rather than having two eyes to be cast into (*gehenna*) hell fire." Christ here clearly speaks of being cast into hell, *gehenna*, as an evil to which men may become liable by their conduct, and which they are to avoid. The question then is, did Jesus Christ, in this text, warn men against being literally cast into the fire which was kept burning in the valley of Hinnom to consume the filth of the city? We think not, for the following reasons:

1. There is no evidence that criminals were executed in the days of our Savior or at any subsequent period by being burnt in the valley of Hinnom.

2. Being *"cast into hell fire,"* gehenna, is marked as the opposite of *"entering into life;"* "it is better for thee to enter into life, &c. rather than to be cast into hell fire." Now, if being *cast into hell fire* mean no more than being burnt in the valley of Hinnom as a penal sanction of the law of the land, then, *entering into life,* can mean no more than the enjoyment of existence in this world, in common with our race, in distinction from those who are put to death for their crimes. This conclusion cannot be avoided; for it would be absurd in the highest degree to suppose, on universalist principles, that entering into life refers to the future world, while being cast into hell fire relates exclusively to this

world. The text clearly implies that those who enter into life are not cast into hell fire; and that those who are cast into hell fire do not enter into life; whereas, if universalism be true, and if entering into life implies a state of happiness in the future world, then, being cast into hell fire can be no hindrance to entering into life, if by it nothing more be meant than being burnt to death in the valley of Hinnom. If there be no future hell, if all enter into life or enjoy a state of happiness immediately after death, as universalism asserts, it is easy to see that entering into life would be as short a passage from the valley of Hinnom as from any other place; indeed, in such case, hell fire would be the very door through which the soul would enter into life, and those who were cast into hell fire, would enter into life sooner than those who should behave so well as to escape the penalty of the law. It is clear then, that if by being cast into hell fire is meant, being burnt to death in the valley of Hinnom, then, by entering into life, we must understand that the individual, to whom the expression refers, has not rendered himself liable to be put to death for his crimes.

The argument then turns on this question: when Jesus Christ said, "It is better for thee to enter into life," did he mean no more than the preservation of the natural life, in opposition to being put to death for crime? If so, every honest man who is not burnt, hanged, or in some other way put to death for crime, may be said to enter into life, which is a manifest perversion of language. To say that a man enters into life, supposes that he enters into the enjoyment or possession of life in some sense or of some kind not before possessed, or enjoyed by him, which is not the case with the individual who merely escapes being burnt for his crimes. It is evident then that entering into life implies something more than not being burnt to death in the valley of Hinnom; and hence, it is equally clear that being cast into hell fire, *gehenna*, implies more than being thus literally burnt. Matt. xxiii. 33. "Ye serpents, ye generation of vipers, how can ye escape the damnation of (*gehenna,*) hell?" Suppose hell in this text to mean *the valley of Hinnom*, and its sense is, how can ye escape the damnation of the valley of Hinnom? That such is not its meaning is evident from the fact that they were not in danger of being condemned to the fire that is supposed to have been kept burning in that valley; and it is not probable that one of them was ever condemned to death by burning in that place. Should it be said, in reply to this, that the threatening of our Saviour, "how can ye escape the damnation of hell?" relates to the destruction of the Jews by the Romans, which actually took place, and that the *"damnation of hell,"* or being burnt in *gehenna,* is referred to as an alarming figure by which to represent the horrors, blood, and fire of that awful overthrow; we answer, such an exposition is an entire abandonment of the argument urged by Mr. Morse, and also by Mr. Balfour, in his entire work, which he has written on the word hell. The argument is, that the word *gehenna* did not originally refer to a place of punishment, but to the valley of Hinnom; it, therefore, does not in the New Testament refer to a place of future punishment. Mr. Balfour says: "The meaning of words in the New Testament must be determined by the original meaning in the Old;" from which he infers that as the words rendered hell did not originally signify a place of punishment in the future world, they, therefore, never have this meaning. Now it is as much a departure from this mode of reasoning, to say that Christ referred to the destruction of the Jews by the Romans when he threatened them with the "damnation of hell," as it is for us to say that he referred to future punishment in the same expression. If the "damnation of hell," being "cast into hell," &c. cannot mean future punishment because the original word, *gehenna*, did not primitively refer to the future world, for the same reason these expressions cannot refer to being slain and carried away captive by the Romans. We see then that the word *gehenna* in the above text, cannot refer directly and literally to the valley of Hinnom; that the Jews were not threatened with being cast into the literal fire that was there burning: it must therefore, refer to some other judgment or punishment. Now, as the Jews were directly threatened with some judgment or punishment, described by being "cast into hell fire," "the damnation of hell," &c. which did not relate to being cast literally into the fire that is supposed to have been burning in the valley of Hinnom, the circumstance that the original word *gehenna* which is used in these threatenings, primarily referred to this place, cannot prove that they do not describe a hell in the future world or even form an objection to such a conclusion. We beg leave to introduce one more text on this point and we will dismiss it. It is Matt. x. 28. "Fear not them which kill the body, but are not able to kill the soul; but rather fear him which is able to destroy both soul and body in hell." The parallel text, Luke xii. 4, 5, reads thus: "I say unto you, my friends. Be not afraid of them that kill the body, and after that have no more that they can do: But I will forewarn you whom ye shall fear; fear him, which, after he hath killed, hath power to cast into hell." That Jesus Christ does not here refer to being cast into the literal fire of the valley of Hinnom is clear, from the following circumstances:

1. The text clearly marks being cast into hell, *gehenna*, as a punishment to be inflicted after the death of the body. "Fear him which, *after he hath killed* hath power to *cast into hell*." Now if Christ refers to the valley of Hinnom, and not to a future hell, his instruction is this: fear not those who have power to put you to death, but fear those who after they have taken away your lives, have authority to burn the lifeless bodies in the valley of Hinnom;

and Christ is here made to say in effect, that the burning of the body after we are dead, is more to be feared than the loss of life. This is manifestly absurd. It is true that the thought of being burnt to ashes after we are dead might be revolting to us, but with the Saviour who,

> "ever from the skies,
> Looks down and watches all our dust,
> Till he shall bid it rise,"

it can make no difference where the ashes of his saints rest, whether in the valley of Hinnom, Nero's garden, or the rocky tomb.

2. The text particularly marks hell, *gehenna*, as the place where *souls* are punished, in distinction from their *bodies*. Fear not them that kill the body, *but are not able to kill the soul;* but rather fear him which *is able to destroy both soul and body in hell.* Here the soul and body are clearly distinguished from each other; the body may be killed and the soul still live—*them that kill the body*, but *are not able to kill the soul;*" or both soul and body may be destroyed in hell—"him which is able to destroy *both soul and body* in hell." Hell then is a place where souls are punished, here noted by being destroyed. Now, this cannot be true of the valley of Hinnom; it cannot be consistently maintained that souls were punished or destroyed in the valley of Hinnom any more than in Nero's garden, the Roman inquisition, or the retired chamber where the good man closes his eyes and gives up the ghost. Hell, therefore, in this text, does not mean the valley of Hinnom.

3. As the text speaks of the body as being killed, while the soul is not killed, and then of both soul and body as being liable to be cast into hell, or of being destroyed in hell, it marks distinctly the soul as being punished or destroyed in hell after the death of the body, and that hell, or *gehenna*, in which the soul is

cast *after the body is killed*, must be in a future state. If there was not another text in the Bible on the subject, this one would forever settle the question respecting the sense in which our Saviour used the term *gehenna*. But universalists attempt to screen themselves from the force of the arguments drawn from this text, by speculating upon the word *destruction*, "able to *destroy* both soul and body in hell." On this expression Mr. Morse in his reply to Mr. Parker, page 17, has made the following remarks: "But suppose God should *destroy* both soul and body in hell, or in any place—then neither soul nor body would remain either to suffer or to enjoy any thing. Soul and body would be *annihilated*. If his, (Mr. Parker's) decisive text proves anything unfavorable to universalism, it must be annihilation." To this we answer,

1. It is a mere evasion, and only serves to increase difficulties without removing any. Suppose we were to admit all that is here contended for, viz. that if this "text proves any thing unfavorable to universalism it must be annihilation," and still it will not relieve universalism from its decisive proof against it; for if men are annihilated they cannot be made holy and happy; hence, while it would throw difficulty in the way of the believer in endless misery, it would effectually and forever prove the doctrine of universal salvation to be false. From this retreat of universalists behind the doctrine of annihilation, it appears that they are not so anxious to prove the doctrine of universal salvation, as they are to disprove that of endless misery. It appears indeed, that they would be willing to give up the hope of eternal life, and die an eternal death of annihilation, if they can have the honor of dying like Samson, by embracing the pillars of their opponent's faith, and pulling down the Philistian [*sic*] fabric of endless misery over their heads.

2. We remark that destruction does not mean anni-

hilation when it signifies the punishment of the wicked, as a few examples will show. Matt. vii. 13 "Broad is the way that leadeth to destruction;" that is, *annihilation*. Romans iii. 16. "Destruction," that is, *annihilation*, "and misery are in their ways." 2 Thess. 1. 9. "Who shall be punished with everlasting destruction," that is, *annihilation* "from the presence of the Lord and from the glory of his power." Phil, iii. 19. "Whose end is destruction," that is, *annihilation* 2 Peter ii. 1. "And bring upon themselves swift destruction;" that is, *annihilation*. Chap. iii. 16, "Which they that are unlearned and unstable wrest as they do also the other scriptures unto their own destruction;" that is, their *annihilation*. These instances of the use of the word destruction clearly show that the wicked will be destroyed, while it is admitted by almost common consent, that they are not to be annihilated. Indeed, for a universalist to resort to the doctrine of annihilation, to defend himself against the arguments in favor of future or endless punishment, drawn from those scriptures which threaten the wicked with destruction, is not only an entire abandonment of their cause, but also betrays a want of honesty, by denouncing, when on the defense, the very premises they occupy themselves when they argue directly in support of their own theory. That the wicked are threatened with destruction cannot be denied; hence, when universalists urge that all will be saved, they argue on the ground that the wicked may be destroyed and saved too; and if this be true it is equally clear that they can be also destroyed and endlessly punished: hence, when they turn in defence and assert that if the wicked are destroyed, they must be annihilated, and, therefore cannot be punished endlessly, they contradict their own creed, and manifest a disregard for correct principles of argumentation.

We trust we have now removed every objection to the application of the word *gehenna*, drawn from its derivation and primitive use.

But, Mr. Morse says: "The word *gehenna* is found in the New Testament twelve times only." This circumstance can certainly form no objection to its application to future or endless punishment in the minds of those who have any confidence in the divine inspiration of the scriptures. If it were found in but one text, and that text was given by the inspiration of God, that is sufficient. But suppose the unfrequent use of this word to be an objection to its application to a future hell, and the argument may be employed with equal force against Mr. M's exposition of the term. If, because the word *gehenna* is used but twelve times in the New Testament, it cannot relate to a future hell, then, for the same reason it cannot have been the name in common use to designate a place near Jerusalem where a fire was kept burning to consume the filth of the city, and where criminals were executed, which must be the case to suppose that Christ referred to this place when he threatened the wicked with the damnation of hell. If, indeed, there is any force in this objection, it will annihilate some of the most prominent arguments in favour of universalism. The word *"restitution,"* which is the nucleus of universalism, is found but once in the New Testament. Acts iii. 21. There is but one text in all the Bible that says God "will have all men to be saved." 1 Tim. ii. 4. But once is it said that God "worketh all things after the counsel of his own will." Eph. i. 11. But once in all the scriptures does God say "his counsel shall stand." Isa. xlvi. 10. And yet universalists declaim over these expressions with as much confidence as though they occurred as often as the wicked are threatened with the damnation of hell, with being cast into hell, with hell fire, &c. But Mr. M. says that the word *gehenna* "was always addressed to the Jews. Nothing is said of *gehenna* to the gentiles." What bearing this can have on the question at issue, is not easy to conceive. It may prove this: that the authors of the scriptures used such words as were understood, and in common use among those whom they addressed. As this word was peculiar to the Jews, it is not a marvellous circumstance that its use should be restricted to them, by men who spoke and wrote as they were moved by the Holy Ghost, whether it mean the valley of Hinnom, or eternal torment in the future world.

We have now done with the four words in the original language, rendered hell in the English translation of the scriptures; and whether or not we have proved that there is a place of punishment in the future world, called *hell*, and answered and removed the objections founded on the primitive use and significations of the original words, we leave the candid reader to judge. We only have to remark in conclusion, on this subject, that if we have sustained our position and proved the existence of a place called hell, a place of punishment, where the wicked receive the reward of their doings, the question of future punishment is settled. If there is a hell, in the future world, and if the wicked are punished in hell, as we think we have proved, then it is clear that the wicked will be punished in the future world, or after death.

VIII. The punishment of the wicked is so connected with the happiness of the righteous, in point of time, as to prove its existence to be in a future state. If it can be shown that the threatenings of the gospel are fulfilled in the punishment of the wicked, at the same time that its promises are fulfilled in the salvation of the righteous, it must follow that such threatenings extend to the future state. Matt. Xiii. 41-43. "The Son of Man shall send forth his angels, and they shall gather out of his kingdom all things that offend, and them that do iniquity, and shall cast them into a furnace of fire; there shall be wailing and gnashing of teeth: *then* shall the righteous shine forth as the sun in the kingdom of their Father." The punishment of the wicked, and the glory of the righteous are both referred to in this text as existing at the same time. Then shall the righteous shine: then, at the same time in which those that do iniquity shall be cast into a furnace of fire and wail and gnash their teeth. If the punishment here spoken of is confined to this world, then the shining of the righteous in the kingdom of their Father must be confined to this world also. On the other hand if the righteous are to shine in the kingdom of their father in the future world; if, to them, "the glory remains when the light, (of this life) fades away," then the workers of iniquity will be punished and wail and gnash their teeth in a future world. That this whole subject refers to a future world is evident from Christ's own exposition of it. In relation to the same event he says, Matt. xiii. 38, 39, 40, "the field is the world." Again, "the harvest is the end of the world." And again, "So shall it be in the end of the world." It is, then, at the end of the world that the wicked are to be cast into a furnace of fire, and the righteous shine in the kingdom of their Father. It is true that universalists attempt to evade the force of all this by equivocating upon the Greek word *aion*, which is here rendered *world*; translating it *dispensation*, or *age*, and thereby referring the whole to the overthrow of the Jews and the destruction of their temple, and end of the Mosaic dispensation. As this word will hereafter be introduced on another question, we shall spare ourselves and the reader the trouble of original criticism in this place; we will attempt to show, however, in plain English that the common translation, "end of the world," best accords with the connection. The tares and wheat, by which we are to understand the children of the wicked one, and the children of the kingdom, are represented as growing together until the time of the harvest, verses 28, 29, 30. "Wilt thou then that we go and gather them up? But he said, Nay, lest while ye gather up the tares ye root up also the wheat with them. Let both grow together until the harvest, and in time of harvest I will say to the reapers, gather ye together first the tares, and bind them in bundles to burn them, but gather the wheat into my barn." Now all this is inapplicable to the destruction of Jerusalem for the following reasons:

1. At the time of harvest the angels are to be sent forth as reapers, to collect both the bad and the good, verse 41. "The Son of Man shall send forth his angels and they shall gather out of his kingdom," &c. Now, we ask, what angels were sent forth as reapers at the destruction of Jerusalem? It could not have been the Romans; for they scattered and dispersed instead of gathering together, especially, so far as the children of the kingdom, or the wheat, was concerned; for the disciples all fled at the approach of the Roman army. Nor could the Apostles have been intended by the gathering angels or reapers, for they were of the wheat; and hence, a part of that which was to be gathered.

2. The righteous, figured by the wheat, are represented as being gathered by the same angels or reapers by whom the tares are gathered, which is false if the gathering of the tares represent the punishment of the Jews by the Romans; for it would be too absurd to be maintained for a moment, to suppose that the Romans collected all the christians and secured them beyond the reach of the ruins of the siege.

3. The wicked are represented as being first gathered—"gather ye together first the tares;" which cannot be true if the harvest of the wheat refers to the preservation of the disciples from the ruin that came upon the Jews; for the disciples first fled and were all on the other side of Jordan before Jerusalem was closely encompassed.

4. Both the tares and the wheat are represented as being collected during the same harvest. "Gather ye together

first the tares," &c. "but gather the wheat into my barn." Now, if the gathering and burning of the tares represent the destruction of the Jews, there is no event connected in point of time, which answers to the gathering of the wheat into the barn. It will not answer to say that the preservation of the disciples constituted the harvest of the wheat; for such were the circumstances of this event as to render it altogether improperly represented by a harvest, in which the full ripe wheat is gathered into the barn, safe from the plundering herd and secure from the wasting storm. A harvest would better represent the gathering home of the saints into the garner of heaven, than the flight of the christians from the destruction of Jerusalem, in which they were turned out of their houses, exposed to the storm, and endured cold and hunger, and almost every evil but death itself; yea, much more than many suffered who lost their lives in the siege, such as were smitten dead at an early period, if, as their bodies fell, their souls leaped from the scene of action and mounted to the upper and better world. We think then that it is clear that this subject relates to a final retribution; and if so, it is equally evident, that when the righteous shall be gathered home to heaven, and shine in the kingdom of their father, the wicked will, at the same time be punished for their sins, and wail and gnash their teeth; they will therefore be punished in a future state.

Matt. viii. 11, 12. "I say unto you that many shall come from the east and west, and shall sit down with Abraham, and Isaac, and Jacob, in the kingdom of heaven, but the children of the kingdom shall be cast out into outer darkness; there shall be weeping and gnashing of teeth." By "the children of the kingdom," in this text, we understand the Jew, who rejected the Saviour, "to whom pertaineth the promises, and of whom, as concerning the flesh, Christ came." By those who are said to come from the east and west, we understand the Gentiles who believe the gospel and are saved. Now we ask, do they come from the east and west and sit down with Abraham, and Isaac, and Jacob in this life? This no one can pretend is the case, unless it be in some visionary or ideal sense. Will the righteous then come from the east and west, and sit down with Abraham and Isaac and Jacob in a future stale? This no one can doubt, who believes in the future happiness of any portion of the human family; and if so, it is in a future state that the unbelieving Jews will be cast out, and weep and gnash their teeth.

Luke xiii. 28. "There shall be weeping and gnashing of teeth when ye shall see Abraham, and Isaac, and Jacob, and all the prophets in the kingdom of God and you yourselves thrust out." Here their weeping and gnashing of teeth is fixed at a time *when* they shall see the patriarchs and prophets in the kingdom of God. Now, it cannot be consistently said that the Jews saw the patriarchs and prophets in the kingdom of God at the time of their destruction, or at any subsequent period. If then it is in the future world that they are to see the patriarchs and prophets in the kingdom of God, it follows that it is in a future state also, that they will see themselves thrust out, and weep and gnash their teeth — they will wail and gnash their teeth *when* they see Abraham, &c. in the kingdom of God, and this belongs to the vision of the future world.

This argument cannot be evaded by saying that these texts relate to the rejection of the Jews, and the call of the Gentiles here on earth; for in this sense they are not true.

1. Those, to whom these scriptures relate, are represented as being sensible of their exclusion from the kingdom of God, which is not true of the Jews in this world; for they contend that the Gospel dispensation, or the Christian Church, is not the kingdom of God, and maintain that they are his only true people.

2. They are represented as seeking admittance into the kingdom, saying, "Lord, Lord, open unto us," which is

not the case with the Jews here, for they have never sought admission into the christian church.

3. They are represented as being frowned away on making such application. "When once the master of the house hath risen up, and hath shut the door, and ye begin to stand without, and knock at the door, saying, Lord, Lord, open unto us; and he shall answer and say unto you, I know you not whence ye are; depart from me all ye workers of iniquity." This is not the present condition of the Jews. The door of the church is open to them; the gospel invitation is to all; the heralds of the cross invite them; Jesus bids them come, and God gives every returning Israelite a full welcome to the blessings of the Gospel kingdom. 2 Thess. i. 7-10. "The Lord Jesus shall be revealed from heaven, with his mighty angels in flaming fire, taking vengeance on them that know not God, and that obey not the gospel of our Lord Jesus Christ, who shall be punished with everlasting destruction from the presence of the Lord and from the glory of his power, *when* he shall come to be glorified in his saints, and to be admired in all them that believe." Here the wicked are threatened with a punishment awful in its description. Now, we ask when will this threatening be executed? The text itself answers, "*when* he shall come to be glorified in his saints." The wicked then are to be punished at the same time that Christ shall come to be glorified in his saints, and this, doubtless will be at the last day, when he shall come to judge the world, at the general resurrection. 1 Thess. iv. 16, 17. "The Lord himself shall descend from heaven with a shout, with the voice of the archangel, and with the trump of God, and the dead in Christ shall rise first; then we which are alive and remain shall be caught up together with them in the clouds to meet the Lord in the air, and so shall we be ever with the Lord."

We think we have shown, conclusively, in this argument that the promises and threatenings of the gospel are contemporary in their fulfilment, from which it must follow that the wicked will be punished after death, or else, that the promises of the gospel secure nothing to believers beyond the shades of the tomb; and to embrace the latter alternative universalists will have to abandon their present theory, and appear as infidels, without disguise.

IX. The scriptures teach that the punishment of the wicked is longer than man's entire earthly existence; and if so, it must follow that such punishment is in a future state.

1. When the scriptures speak of the life of man, they represent it to be very short, and employ the most expressive terms and figures to denote its brevity. 1 Peter i. 24. "All flesh is as grass, and all the glory of man as the flower of grass; the grass withereth, and the flower thereof falleth away." James iv. 14. "What is your life? it is even a vapour that appeareth for a moment and then vanisheth away." Psalm ciii. 15, 16. "As for man, his days are as grass, for the wind passeth over it and it is gone." Job. vii. 6. "My days are swifter than a weaver's shuttle;" viii. 9. "Our days upon earth are a shadow." xiv. 1.2. "Man is of few days; he cometh forth like a flower, and is cut down; he fleeth also as a shadow."

2. When the scriptures speak of the punishment of the wicked, they represent it to be very long, and employ the strongest terms to express its duration. Matt. xxv. 41. "Depart from me, ye cursed, into *everlasting fire;*" 46. "These shall go away into *everlasting* punishment." 2 Thess. i. 9. "Who shall be punished with *everlasting* destruction" Rev. XX. 10. "Shall be tormented day and night *forever and ever.*" Let it be understood that these texts are not introduced in this place to prove endless punishment. This will be attended to in its proper place. The present object is to show that the scriptures represent the punishment of

the wicked to be very long, longer than man's entire earthly existence. Men often commit the most atrocious crimes, after which they do not live a year, a month, a week, a day, an hour, and sometimes not a moment. Now do they endure a very *long* punishment in a very *short* time? Will *"everlasting* fire" burn out in a *year?* Can "everlasting punishment" be all endured in a month?—Will the sinner recover from *everlasting* destruction in a week? Is it possible to "be tormented *for ever and ever"* in a day or an hour? But suppose the sinner to live a life of common length, still it follows that he cannot receive in this life, all the punishment which the Bible threatens; for the punishment is longer than the whole of his earthly existence. It cannot be consistently denied that the terms *everlasting, for ever and ever,* &c. express longer duration than the terms and figures which are used to express the brevity of life. "Everlasting punishment" must be longer than a life that "is a vapor that appeareth for a moment and vanisheth away." "Everlasting destruction" must last longer than the life of a man, whose "days upon earth are a shadow." He who is "tormented forever and ever" must suffer longer than the earthly existence of a man who "is of few days." We say then that the scriptures teach that the punishment of sinners, is longer than the entire earthly existence of man and that punishment which is longer than the life of man must exist in a future state.

X. The scriptures teach that men will possess the same moral character in a future state, with which they leave this, and if so, those who die sinners will be sinners after death; and if sinners, subjects of punishment. Prov. xiv. 32. "The wicked is driven away in his wickedness, but the righteous hath hope in his death." In this text, being driven away in wickedness, stands opposed to hope in death. It follows then that the righteous have hope in their death, and that the wicked are without hope in death. Now, hope always relates to the future; hence, in death, amid the pangs of dissolving nature, as the world recedes from our vision, hope must take hold of the realities of a future state; and as the wicked are driven away in their wickedness, in distinction from the righteous who have hope in their death, their states must be different in the future world. If sin only affects the sinner in this life, he must have as much hope in his death as the expiring saint; and certainly he has more reason to appreciate that hope, if his punishment is all this side of death, and all is happiness beyond. The peculiar phraseology of the text shows that the sinner's guilt will cleave to him in a future state. The wicked is driven away *in* his wickedness, not driven away *from* it; hence, his wickedness goes with him into the future world. John v. 28, 29. "The hour is coming in the which all that are in their graves shall hear his voice, and shall come forth; they that have done good unto the resurrection of life, and they that have done evil unto the resurrection of damnation." Let it be remarked, that a man's character is not reckoned in view of what he may have been, but in view of what he is; hence a man may have done evil, and yet, if he ceases to do evil, and learns to do well, he is not reckoned an evil doer, but a well doer, (see Ezek. xxxiii. 13-16.) Those therefore who die in a state of well doing, will be among those who have done well, when the dead shall be raised; and those who die in a state of evil doing, will be among those who have done evil: the former will be raised to the resurrection of life, and the latter to the resurrection of damnation; and both will possess the same moral character with which they left this world. Ezek. xviii. 26. "When the righteous man turneth away from his righteousness, and committeth iniquity, and dieth in them, for his iniquity that he hath done shall he die." This text not only teaches that men will possess the same moral character in a future state with which they leave this; but it proves directly, that moral death will exist after the death of the body. Mark the peculiar language: the apostate is here said, first, to die in his iniquity, and then to die for it. This clearly proves that he who dies a sinner; will be a sinner in the future state, and will there experience that death which is the wages of sin, (see Rom. vi. 23.) That men will possess the same moral character in a future state, with which they leave this, farther appears from the fact that sin attaches itself to the soul. If sin attached itself to the body only, it might be contended that it dies with the body; but having its seat in the soul, it will live with it when the body dies. Death cannot destroy sin, for death itself is an effect of sin, as has been shown in Chap. I. and an effect can never destroy the cause that produced it; hence, if the soul is polluted with sin when it leaves the body, it will be polluted still after it has left the body; and if sin begets misery, those who die in sin will be miserable in a future state; and if sin deserves punishment while it exists, the sinner will deserve punishment in a future state.

XI. The punishment of the wicked is so connected with the existence and punishment of the devils, as to prove it to be in a future state. But universalists, or that class of them who deny future punishment, also deny the existence of a devil or devils: we will therefore attempt to prove that there are real personal devils. The scriptures abundantly speak of a devil, and of devils; and something must be meant, and what is it? Those who reject the common opinion of the church, that there are real demons who are our invisible foes, are not uniform in their faith on the point. Some suppose that by the devil is meant the wicked disposition of men, the carnal mind, or evil propensities of human nature; some suppose that a personified principle of evil is intended by the devil; some say that any enemy is a devil in a scriptural sense, and that men or any opposer may be intended; and others say that by devils, bodily diseases are intended, especially in those cases where devils are said to have been cast out. To show that the scriptures speak of other devils, not included in this list, real personal devils, shall now be the object of a few remarks.

1. The temptation of such as were not possessed of evil propensities, must go to prove that an evil disposition, or a personified principle of evil cannot be meant, when the devil is spoken of as a tempter. Our first parents as they came from the hand of their creator, could not have been possessed of evil propensities, or propensities to evil, as has been proved in Chap. I. Man in his first state of existence could not have possessed any thing which he did not receive from his creator; and as God is holy, he could not be the author of evil propensities, unholy affections, or sinful lusts: and yet the mother of our race was beguiled and led into sin. Gen. iii. 13. "The serpent beguiled me and I did eat." 2 Cor. xi. 3. "But I fear lest by any means, as the serpent beguiled Eve through his subtlety, so your minds should be corrupted from the simplicity of Christ." 1 Tim. ii. 14. "But the woman being deceived was in the transgression." The temptation of Christ is another instance to me point, see Matt. iv. 1-11, inclusive. Jesus Christ was tempted by some being or thing, which could not have been any evil propensity or propensity to evil. This appears from two considerations. *First*, the tempter came to Christ and departed from him; *secondly*, Jesus Christ could not have possessed, in his own nature, any propensity or incentive to evil. If the human nature of Jesus Christ was prone to evil, or contained in itself incentives to evil, it must have

been an evil nature, and could not have been an acceptable sacrifice to God.

2. Some persons have been possessed of many devils at the same time. Luke viii. 30. "And he said legion, because many devils were entered into him." Luke viii. 2. "Mary called Magdalene, out of whom went seven devils."

3. The devil has an existence separately from, and independently of, man. Luke viii. 33. "Then went the devils out of the man and entered into the swine." The devils, then, must have existed after they went out of the man, which could not have been the case, if the devils in question had been evil propensities or diseases. Man's evil propensities cannot exist separately from himself, and disease has no existence separately from the constitution upon which it preys.

4. The devil has attributes and passions ascribed to him which imply personal and intellectual being. Matt. viii. 31. "So the devils besought him, saying, If thou cast us out, suffer us to go into the herd of swine." This shows that the devils possessed reason, volition and desire. 1 Peter v. 8. "Your adversary the devil walketh about seeking whom he may devour." This represents the devil as acting from design. James ii. 19. "The devils believe and tremble." This proves that the devils have intelligence, which is implied in believing; and fear, which causes them to tremble.

5. The devil, (the prince or chief of the devils) has angels. If by the devil is meant the evil propensities of our nature, a personified principle of evil, or some malignant disease, who or what are his angels? Matt. xxv. 31. "The devil and *his angels.*"

6. The devil has names and titles ascribed to him, which imply personal being. Eph. ii. 2. "The prince of the power of the air." Eph. vi. 12. "We wrestle not against flesh and blood, but against *principalities* and against *powers*, the rulers of the darkness of this world." John viii. 44. "Ye

are of your *father* the *devil,* he was a *murderer* from the beginning, and abode not in the truth, because there is no truth in him. When he speaketh a lie he speaketh of his own, for he is a *liar* and the father of it." Such names, titles and epithets must imply a personal being.

7. The devil is an active agent, and has personal actions ascribed to him. Matt. xiii. 39. "The enemy that sowed them is the devil." 1. Cor. vii. 5. "That satan tempt you not." 2. Cor. ii. 11. "Lest satan should get an advantage of us, for we are not ignorant of his devices." The devil is represented as a murderer, a liar, a deceiver, &c. Such performances can be ascribed only to personal and active agents.

8. The devil is an accountable agent, and punishable for his misconduct. Matt. viii. 29. "They cried out, saying, what have we to do with thee, Jesus thou Son of God? art thou come to torment us before the time? Matt. xxv. 41. "Punishment prepared for the devil and his angels." Rev. xx. 10. "And the devil that deceived them was cast into the lake of fire and brimstone, where the beast and false prophets are, and shall be *tormented* day and night, for ever and ever." Nothing but personal and responsive beings can be subjects of punishment.

9. It appears to have been the opinion of the orthodox Jews, that there were real personal devils. Matt. xii. 34. "But when the Pharisees heard it, they said, this fellow doth not cast out devils but by Beelzebub the prince of the devils;" see also Matt. ix. 24. If the Pharisees believed in no devils, any more than universalists of the present day, what did they mean by Beelzebub the prince of devils? And what did they mean when they affirmed that Christ cast out devils by this prince of the satanic host? Did they mean that Christ employed the worst of man's evil propensities to cast out those of less turpitude? Or did they mean that he employed the worst of diseases to cure those of a more mild character?

10. The writers of the New Testament express themselves as though they believed in real devils, and demoniac possessions. Mark i. 34. "And he healed many that were sick of divers diseases, and cast out many devils, and suffered not the devils to speak because they knew him." Here the writer distinguishes diseases from devils, and says that Christ suffered not the devils to speak, as though he really believed that the devils thus cast out were beings capable of speaking, and understanding the character and mission of the Son of God. What cried out if there are no devils that are personal beings? and who did St. Luke suppose cried out if he did not believe in real demoniac possessions?

11. Jesus Christ pursued a course directly calculated to confirm his disciples in the opinion that they were real and personal beings that he cast out. Luke x. 17, 18. "And the seventy returned, saying, Lord, even the devils are subject unto us through thy name; and he said unto them, I beheld satan as lightning fall from heaven." If they believed in devils, this reply was calculated to confirm them in that belief; and if they did not believe in devils, what would Christ have the disciples believe it was that he saw fall from heaven? Luke iv. 35. "And Jesus rebuked him saying, hold thy peace and come out of him." Here Christ, in casting out what is called a devil, speaks with authority, not to the man, but to the devil he was casting out of the man. "And Jesus rebuked him, (the devil) and said, come out of him," (the man.) Did they believe in the existence of real demoniac possessions, the solemn and direct address of our Lord, to their imaginary demons was certainly calculated to confirm them in the error, if it be an error; and if they did not believe in the existence of devils, to whom would Jesus have had the by-stander suppose he was addressing himself, with such commanding authority?

12. The disciples had "authority over all devils," to cast

them out. See Luke ix. 1. By devils here cannot be meant bad men of any class or degree, nor any evil propensities in our nature, nor any personified principle of evil; for the disciples never had authority over these, nor could they have such authority consistently with moral agency on the part of the controlled. Had the disciples of our Lord possessed such power over evil, or even over the evil dispositions of men, they could have reformed every sinner at pleasure.

But before we close this subject, we may do well to devote a few moments to the consideration of some of the principal objections which have been urged against the commonly received opinion on the subject of devils.

I. It has sometimes been urged that the existence of devils cannot be accounted for on any principle consistent with enlightened reason, or honorable to God. It has often been asked with an air of triumph, who made the devil, or from whence came he.

This objection supposes that God created all beings, and that it would be absurd to suppose that he would or could create a devil or a host of devils. To this objection we reply:

1. Universalists, who are so very tenacious for the divine honour and holiness on the subject of the existence of devils, deny the doctrine of the fall of man; supposing it to be perfectly consistent with wisdom, justice, goodness and holiness, for God to create man with all his present propensities to evil, many of whom appear inferior to the orthodox devil only in point of ability to do evil. Now, if God could create such a wicked race of beings as men have proved themselves to be, as universalists profess to believe, it can require but a very small degree of credulity more, to enable them to believe that he might create a race of devils. But if, as we believe, God created man "very good" and he has become depraved through the abuse of his moral powers, we think it easy

to conceive that devils may have been originated in the same way. Taking this view of the subject, we see that universalists must abandon their opposition to the doctrine of the fall, or else admit that God can create wicked beings; and hence, this objection to the existence of devils falls.

2. Leaving universalists to contend with the above difficulties of their own creating, we would remark that we believe the devils to be fallen spirits. In this position we think ourselves borne out by the scriptures of divine truth. It is true that this subject is wrapped in much obscurity, but this is no objection to the doctrine of fallen angels, since the fact itself is revealed. No clearly revealed truth is to be rejected because all the circumstances that pertain to it are not revealed. As the scriptures were given for man's special benefit, it could not be expected that they should record circumstantially the events of other worlds, but only advert to them as they in some way shed light upon our present allotment, future destiny; and such references the scriptures make to the fall of angels. 2 Peter ii. 4. "God spared not the angels that sinned, but cast them down to hell, and delivered them into chains of darkness to be reserved unto judgment." Jude 6. "And the angels which kept not their first estate, but left their own habitation, he hath reserved in everlasting chains under darkness unto the judgment of the great day." Here are two direct references to the fall of angels, for the purpose of illustrating the dealings of God with men. The argument is that of induction, in which it is shown that certain false teachers cannot escape punishment, from the fact of the punishment which God inflicted upon transgressors in past time. To show this, that God has heretofore punished the rebellious, three cases are adduced, viz. the angels that sinned were cast down to hell; the inhabitants of the old world were destroyed by a flood brought in upon the ungodly; and the cities of Sodom

and Gomorrah were condemned with an overthrow, turned into ashes, and made an example; unto those who should after live ungodly. The fall of angels is not only referred to, but is classed with those awful events, the drowning of the old world by a flood, and the consuming of Sodom and Gomorrah by a storm of fire; and it is worthy of remark that St. Peter notices these events in the order of time in which they occurred. Here then is an event, the sin and punishment of angels, awful from the very association in which inspiration has placed it, as well as from the description given of it. Now we ask what this event was, if the commonly received notion of the fall of angels is not true? That some rational accountable beings are intended by *"the angels that sinned,"* no one can doubt, for none but rational accountable beings can sin and become subjects of punishment; and as we have no account of any order or race of beings, save angels and men, there can be no doubt but one or the other of these is intended. If then it is clear that by "the angels that sinned," we are to understand apostate angels, according to the commonly received doctrine, or men of some particular class, character or office, here called angels, it only remains to show that the latter cannot be true, and the former will appear to be the true sense of the text. We will then show from the text itself, that to suppose men are intended by *"the angels that sinned,"* is utterly inconsistent with universalism, and must prove it to be false. The Apostle says, Jude 6. "The angels which kept not their first estate but left their own habitation, he hath reserved in everlasting chains under darkness unto the judgment of the great day." On this we remark:

1. The expression, "the angels which kept not their first estate but left their own habitation," clearly describes an action in past time, and shows that the sin of the angels, or beings here spoken of, was committed at some period prior to the time of the Apostle's writing.

2. The expression, "he hath reserved in everlasting chains under darkness," clearly marks an event past, yet extending to the present time; showing that the angels or beings referred to were then, at the time the Apostle wrote, in confinement held in reserve.

3. The expression, "unto the judgment of the great day," connected with the last, thus: "he hath reserved in everlasting chains under darkness *unto the judgment of the great day*," clearly points out a future event as the object of their confinement; their judgment and punishment at some future day of retribution, here called "the judgment of the great day." Note then, that if men are intended by the angels that sinned, the apostle here speaks of men who had sinned in past time, who were then in chains under darkness for their crimes, and who were to be reserved in these chains to be judged and punished at some future day; which must for ever refute the notion that men receive their full punishment as they pass through life, and establish the doctrine of future punishment as clearly as it can be made out in form of words. We say then, as angels or men must be intended by the apostle, and as universalists cannot, consistently with their theory, admit the latter, they must subscribe to the former; and that this is really the doctrine of the text, is clear from the fact that the term *angel* is the one which the scriptures uniformly employ to designate the inhabitants of the invisible world. The united testimony of these two apostles, speaking on the same subject, we think sufficient to settle the question concerning the fall of angels; but still we will add a few more quotations from the scriptures, which we think refer to the same event 1 John iii. 8. "He that committeth sin is of the devil, for the devil sinneth *from the beginning*." Here the devil is represented as being the first sinner, with whom moral evil originated. John viii. 44. "Ye

are of your father the devil, he was a murderer from the beginning, and abode not in the truth." This text clearly proves that the devil is a fallen being, for it says "he abode not in the truth;" now, he must have once been in the truth to justify such an expression. Luke x. 18. "And he said unto them I beheld satan as lightning fall from heaven." If this does not teach the doctrine of satan's fall it must be hard to conceive in what language it could be taught. Job iv. 18, 19. "Behold he put no trust in his servant? and his angels he charged with folly, how much less in them that dwell in houses of clay, whose foundation is in the dust." Here is an allusion to the fall of angels too plain to be overlooked. The text says expressly that "he charged his angels with folly;" and what clearly proves that the inhabitants of the world of spirits is meant by angels is, the comparison which is instituted between these angels and men, whom the writer distinguishes by the expression, *"them that dwell in houses of clay."* The meaning appears to be this. If he put no trust in his servants, the angels, who are disembodied, but charged them with folly, how much less shall he put confidence in men who are embodied or dwell in houses of clay.

II. It has been objected to the common doctrine of satanic influence or temptation, that if the devil is chained in hell as represented in the preceding quotations and remarks, then he cannot be about in this world as the tempter of the human family. This objection we recollect to have seen very gravely stated in a universalist periodical. Now, to reply to this, it is only necessary to enquire what is meant by the fallen angels' being chained. It is presumed that no one supposes that the devil is chained literally, with a material chain, as we hand-cuff a criminal, and chain him down to the floor of his prison; such a notion, when applied to spirits, is too absurd to be indulged by the most superstitious and vulgar. What then is meant by the fallen angels' being chained? Their chains may signify their hopeless despair, there being with them no hope or prospect of ever escaping from their wretched condition. Or their being chained may denote that they are so held in on all sides, by the divine power as not to be able to go beyond certain limits in their work of malevolence, temptation and ruin. Had not satan his chain in this respect, beyond the length of which he cannot go, we should no doubt see other marks of his goings than those that now appear. Now, what is there in all this contrary to the common belief in satanic influence in this world. Should it be thought absurd to suppose that God can lay any restraint upon satan, and yet not confine him entirely, so as altogether to prevent his evil influence in this world, a sufficient answer will be found in the reply to the following objection.

III. It has sometimes been objected that it is inconsistent with the divine power and goodness that such a satanic majesty, as the devil is supposed to be, should exist and be permitted to roam with such destroying influence through the world and church of God. This argument is sometimes stated thus: God has power to destroy or control the devil, or he has not; if he has not the power, he cannot be omnipotent, and the devil becomes a kind of omnipotent being, at least equal with God; and if God has power to destroy or control the devil, and will not do it, he becomes accessary [sic] to his deeds, and can be but little better than the devil himself. That this argument is fallacious is evident from the circumstance that it may be applied to disprove what is plain matter of fact. It proved just as much against the existence of wicked men, as it does against the existence of devils. It is said, Prov. ix. 18. "One sinner destroyeth much good." Now, God has power to destroy or control this sinner, so as to prevent his destroying much good, or he has not. If God cannot destroy or control the sinner he cannot be omnipotent, and the sinner becomes a kind of omnipotent being, at least equal with God; and if God can destroy or control the sinner, so as to prevent his destroying much good, and will not, he becomes accessary [sic] to his deeds and can be but little better than the sinner himself. We see then that this argument proves just as much against the existence of wicked men as it does against the existence of devils; and the existence and evil influence of wicked men it can never disprove, since these are plain matters of fact; therefore it can never disprove the existence of devils. What God has power to do, and what he may see it proper to do, are two things quite distinct from each other. We know not but God may have power to annihilate the devil by one look from off his throne; but if it be so it cannot prove that it is consistent for him so to do. That God's peculiar people are sometimes tempted and led astray by wicked men, is a fact too plain to be denied, and it can detract, no more from the power or goodness of God to suppose that a similar evil influence is exerted by the devil.

IV. It has been objected to the doctrine of satanic influence, that if the devil tempts men as generally, and in all parts of the world as is believed, he must be capable of being in many places at the same time, or he must be omnipresent, which can never be ceded to any created being. The fallacy of this objection consists in supposing that absolute ubiquity is essential to satanic influence as generally believed. On this subject we beg leave to remark,

1. That every created being has his own sphere of being, which he is capable of filling; more than which he cannot fill, beyond which he cannot go, and out of which he cannot act: as no being can act where he is not. Some beings however may fill a larger sphere than others.

2. Spiritual or disembodied beings may, no doubt, con-

vey themselves from one place to another with great facility, which unquestionably is the case with the devil. We know not but he can pass around the globe quick as the motion of light. The movements of disembodied spirits, for aught we can know, are as easy as our thoughts which pass to the most distant orb in the smallest imaginable period of time.

3. To the above we would add, that there may be more devils than there are men in the world. The apostle informs us that angels sinned; but how many sinned and fell we are not told. We also read of the devil and his angels; while we are informed that seven devils were cast out of one individual and a legion out of another. These circumstances render it more than probable that devils are more numerous than human beings, and that where we read of *the* devil, reference is had to the chief, prince, or leader of the infernal host; hence, to him so much wickedness is attributed, though he has myriads under his command in its accomplishment.

We trust we have now proved the existence of devils, who are subjects of punishment in the invisible world, and have also removed the principal objections urged against our theory on this head. Now we say that the punishment of wicked men is connected, both in point of time and place, with the punishment of the devils, who inhabit the invisible world. Matt. xxv. 41. "Depart from me ye cursed into everlasting fire, prepared for the devil and his angels." Now, as there are devils that inhabit the world of spirits, and as wicked men are to be punished with them, it clearly follows that wicked men will be punished in the future world.

XII. The scriptures teach that the good works of the righteous performed in this life, will be rewarded in a future state, and if so, it not only follows that the non-performance of these works on the part of the wicked, will affect them in the same proportion, they losing what the righteous gain; but in addition to their loss, they will receive at the same time, in positive punishment, the reward which is due for the non- performance of duty as well as for sins they may have committed. Those who deny future punishment, we believe, always limit the effect of human actions to this state of existence; denying that virtue or vice affect their votaries after the close of this transient life. If then it can be shown that a virtuous life, will receive a reward in a future state, it will follow that the sinner will also receive his reward, after having finished the work of life and passed the limits of his present career. But before we enter upon the proof of the position, it should be remarked, that when we speak of the reward of obedience, we mean a reward of *grace*, and not of *debt*. Though we can merit nothing at the hand of God, by our obedience, yet God of his free grace in Christ Jesus, has promised a future reward to all such as obey the gospel in this life. We will now attempt to show that our conduct in this life will have a bearing upon our condition in a future state. Luke xiv. 13, 14, "When thou makest a feast call the poor, the maimed, the lame, the blind, and thou shalt be blessed, for they cannot recompense thee; for thou shalt be recompensed at the resurrection of the just." Here benevolence has the promise of a reward *at the resurrection of the just*; which proves such reward to be in a future state. The man then, who from true christian love, bestows his goods to feed the poor, will enjoy a reward in the future world, in which the sordid miser will have no part; and yet, which he might secure if he would pursue the same course. Therefore the case of the benevolent and the miserly, will both be affected in a future state, by their conduct in the present life. Heb. xi. 35. "And others were tortured, not accepting deliverance, that they might obtain a better resurrection."

This clearly shows that holy martyrs died in the belief, that their fidelity and sufferings would be rewarded with a better resurrection in the future world; which clearly implies, that such as accept deliverance, or procure exemption from suffering in this life, by a renunciation of the truth, or by betraying in any way the cause of God, will be raised from the dead, less to their advantage in the world to come. Rev. ii. 10. "Be thou faithful unto death and I will give thee a crown of life." This text is too plain to need comment. The faithful here have the promise of a reward *after death*. And will not the unfaithfulness of the sinner affect him after death, by depriving him of that reward? We might multiply quotations on this subject, but it is unnecessary; the above plain scriptural evidence must convince every candid reader, that we are all acting in this life for the retributions of a future world.

XIII. The scriptures teach that there is to be a day of general judgment, when the whole human family will be judged and rewarded according to their moral characters, or conduct in this life. If men receive all the punishment due to their sins, in this life, then every man must be judged as he passes along in life's career; hence, if we can show that there will be a day of general judgment, the doctrine of future punishment will follow as a necessary consequence. There are several classes of scripture texts which might be urged in proof of a future and general judgment.

1. It is worthy of notice, that the scriptures speak of the judgment as an event yet future, and not as though it had taken place, or as though it were now transpiring every day. Eccl. xii. 14. "For God shall bring every work into judgment with every secret thing, whether it be good or whether it be evil." Mark the expression, God *shall bring*, not has brought, nor does bring, every work into judgment. Rom. xiv. 10. "For

we must," not do, "all stand before the judgment seat of Christ." 2 Cor. v. 10. "For we must," not do, "all appear before the judgment seat of Christ."

2. Another class of scriptures fix the judgment at a set time or on an appointed day. Acts xvii. 31. "He hath *appointed a day* in the which he will judge the world in righteousness." Rom. ii. 16. "In *the day* when God shall judge the secrets of men by Jesus Christ." Jude 6. "The judgment of the *great day*." 2 Pet. ii. 9. "The day of judgment." John xii. 48. "He that rejecteth me and receiveth not my words hath one that judgeth him. The word that I speak, the same shall judge him at the *last day*." These expressions, "the day of judgment," "the day when God shall judge the secrets of men," "the judgment of the great day," "that day," "the last day," &c. were common among the Jews; and how they understood them, and consequently how they are to be understood when they occur in the scriptures, may be seen by the following extract from Josephus. "For all men, the just as well as the unjust, shall be brought before *God the word*, for to him hath the *Father committed all judgment*. This person, exercising a righteous judgment of the Father towards all men, hath prepared a just sentence for every one according to his works; at whose judgment seat when all men and angels, and demons shall stand, they will send forth one voice, and say, JUST IS THE JUDGMENT." See discourse on Hades.

3. The scriptures speak of the judgment of former generations as yet to come. Matt. x. 15. "It shall be more tolerable for the land of Sodom and Gomorrah in the day of judgment than for that city." xi. 23, 24. "And thou Capernaum, it shall be more tolerable for the land of Sodom, in the day of judgment than for thee." Luke xi. 31, 32. "The queen of the south shall rise up in the judgment with this generation, and condemn it. The men of

Nineveh shall rise up in judgment with this generation, and shall condemn it." It is here declared that it shall be more tolerable, in the day of judgment, for the land of Sodom and Gomorrah, than for those cities where Jesus preached and wrought miracles without effecting their moral reform. Mark the peculiar language; Christ does not say *it was more tolerable* for the land of Sodom than it *shall be* for thee, in the day of judgment, but *it shall be more tolerable*, &c. referring the whole to the future, clearly implying that those ancient cities, which in ages past had withered from existence under the divine displeasure, had not yet received their final judgment, and that they were yet to be judged together with the unbelieving Jews of our Lord's time. This clearly shows that the final judgment and punishment of sinners are matters which belong to the future world. Again, it is said in the above quotations, that the queen of the south, and the men of Nineveh, shall rise in judgment with those to whom Christ preached, and condemn them. Now, the Ninevites, here referred to, lived eight hundred and six-two years before Christ, and the queen of the south made her visit to see the wisdom of Solomon about one thousand years before Christ; and yet these are said to rise up in the judgment with the Jews of our Lord's days. And now can this be unless a general judgment is referred to? Surely, generations so remote from each other in point of time, between whose earthly allotments, nations rose and fell, and millions came and went on the waves of intervening ages; we say, two such generations declared to rise up in the same judgment, and at some future time, must prove beyond all doubt a future and general judgment.

XIV. The scriptures teach that the judgment, and consequently the punishment of the wicked, are to take place after death, and at the general resurrection; which must determine the punishment to be in a future state. 2 Tim. iv. 1. "I charge thee therefore, before God and the Lord

Jesus Christ, who shall judge the quick and the dead at his appearing." 1 Peter iv. 5. "Who shall give account to him that is ready to judge the quick and the dead." Acts x. 42. "And he commanded us to preach unto the people, and to testify that it is he which was ordained of God to be judge of quick and dead." In these texts, by the quick, we are to understand those who shall be alive upon the earth when the judgment shall sit; and by the dead, we are to understand such as die previously to the judgment who will be raised from the dead.

What most clearly confirms the point, that these scriptures relate to a judgment after death, and at the general resurrection, is the circumstance that Christ is declared to be the judge. There can be no doubt but it is in the Redeemer's glorified character that he will judge the world; and if so, it follows that the judgment must be after death, and at the general resurrection; otherwise all those generations and nations of men, who had their being, and passed into the future world before the death and resurrection of Jesus Christ, have no part in the judgment; whereas, Christ, in his glorified character, is constituted judge of the world, of the quick and dead." If Christ is the judge of all men in his glorified character, the judgment must be subsequent to his resurrection and exaltation, which proves beyond the possibility of doubt that, men are judged after death; for the inhabitants of four thousand years had lived and were dead before this event. This view is sustained by the Apostle, Acts xvii. 31. "He hath appointed a day in the which he will judge the world in righteousness, by that man whom he hath ordained whereof he hath given assurance unto all men, in that he hath raised him from the dead." This text contains so many reasons in support of the above view that it deserves particular attention.

1. It speaks of the appointment of a day of judgment "in the which he will judge the WORLD.["] The

world then is to be judged by Jesus Christ, and by the world, in this text, nothing less than all men can be understood. Nor can this be set aside by universalists, by saying that it is the Jewish world which is here spoken of, and that it was fulfilled in the destruction of Jerusalem; for this discourse was not directed to the Jews, nor was it spoken concerning them. The text in question is a part of that celebrated discourse delivered by St. Paul in Athens, to the idolatrous and philosophical Greeks. The connexion shows that the judgment is universal. The Apostle says, "the times of this ignorance God winked at," which shows that the heathen world is the subject of discourse. He farther says, God "now commanded *all men every where* to repent; because he hath appointed a day in the which he will judge the world." The expression *"all men every where,"* pointing out the subjects of the divine command, enjoining repentance, corresponds with the expression *"world,"* pointing out the subjects of judgment; hence, if all men every where are commanded to repent, then, all men every where are to be judged. Here then is a day of judgment predicted which does not relate to the Jews, nor to the destruction of their city, nor subversion of their polity. It would have been a very singular mode of reasoning to urge the necessity of repentance upon the Greeks, because God had appointed a day in the which he would judge the Jews in righteousness, and burn up their city and disperse them among the surrounding nations.

2. The resurrection of Jesus Christ is set forth in the text, as an evidence or an assurance of this universal judgment. There are two points of light in which the resurrection of Christ is an assurance of a general judgment. First, it confirmed the doctrines of the gospel, one of which is that of a general judgment; and secondly, it furnished clear evidence of a general resurrection; for "if Christ be

preached that he rose from the dead, how say some among you that there is no resurrection of the dead? but if there be no resurrection of the dead then is Christ not risen. But now is Christ risen from the dead and become the first fruits of them that slept." See 1 Cor. xv. 12, 13, 20. It must be difficult to see on what other ground the resurrection of Jesus Christ can be an assurance that all men will be judged; and if this is the correct view of the subject, it follows that the judgment is subsequent to death, and at the general resurrection. As Christ's resurrection is an assurance of a general judgment by being a proof of a general resurrection, it follows that a general resurrection is essential to the judgment of the world, of which the apostle speaks; and must precede it. As we have proved beyond all doubt that this text speaks of a general judgment which did not relate peculiarly to the Jews, and consequently has not been fulfilled in them, it may be well to compare it with the preceding texts, which have been introduced in this argument, that it may appear that they all relate to the same event. Three texts have been introduced. 2 Tim. iv. 1. 1 Peter iv. 5, &c. Acts x. 42. which declare Christ to be judge of quick and *dead,* and this text declares that his resurrection is an assurance of such judgment. This argues strongly that the literally dead are intended—Christ is proved to be judge of the *dead* by his own *resurrection from the dead.* Again, one of the texts, Acts x. 42, which declares Christ to be judge of quick and dead, says, "he was *ordained* of God to be Judge," while the text, Acts xvii. 31. which we have shown to relate to a general judgment, says, God will "judge the world by the man Christ Jesus whom he hath *ordained.*" Both texts, in effect, declare that Christ is ordained "judge;" one says, judge of quick and dead, and the other, judge of the world. These parallels, drawn between these different texts, show that they all relate to the same event, and that the dead, who are in their graves, are intended. But there are other scriptures which speak of judgment after death, and at a general resurrection. Rev. xx. 12, 13. "And I saw the dead, small and great, stand before God, and the books were opened, and the dead were judged out of the things which were written in the books, according to their works; and the sea gave up the dead that were in it;" &c. This text speaks of all the dead, of their standing before God and of their being judged; and to render it more certain if possible, the judgment of the dead is connected with the resurrection of the body; "and the sea gave up the dead that were in it," &c. This shows, that by the dead, those who have died the death of the body are intended. Heb. ix. 27. "It is appointed unto men once to die and after this the judgment." This text is so plain as not to need comment, had not universalists belaboured it, in a manner very much to distort its features. According to their exposition, the apostle is here made to say that it was appointed unto the high priest to die figuratively in the sacrifices, which he offered annually as an atonement for sin; and that after this the judgment came, whereby the congregation was judged and pronounced righteous in view of the atonement that had been made. Or, as some will have it, the apostle speaks of the natural death of the high priest, and the judgment which follows relates to the events which were connected in law with his demise. Now, it appears to us that nothing was more foreign to the apostle's mind than either of these expositions. The points essentially connected with the text in question, in the apostle's reasoning, are, the two-fold appearing of Christ; once as a sin offering "to put away sin," and once "without sin, (without a sin offering,) unto salvation." The apostle declares that it is not necessary that Christ "should offer himself often as the high priest entereth into the holy place every year with the blood of others, but now once in the end of the world, (the Jewish dispensation,) hath he appeared to put away sin by the sacrifice of himself." But this is not all, for as men not only die but are to be judged after death, so Christ has not only appeared once, to die, but "shall appear the second time" to judge the world; and this second appearing shall be without a sin offering: "and unto those that look for him," that is, those who believe and trust in him, his second appearing shall be "unto salvation." Such appears to us to be the chain of the Apostle's reasoning, the substance of which may be thus stated: As men are subject to one temporal death, and one only, so it was necessary for Christ to die once and once only, as their substitute to redeem them; and as men are accountable for the improvement they make upon his grace, and hence must be judged after death, after the opportunity for such improvement is past, so Christ must appear a second time to judge them. As men die once, so Christ died once to redeem them, and as men are to be judged after death, so Christ is to come as judge subsequently to his death; and as he came at the end of the Mosaic dispensation as redeemer, so will he come at the end of the Gospel dispensation, that is, the end of the world, as judge. We think we have now established the point that the judgment is after death, and at a general resurrection, and if so, it as clearly follows that sinners will be punished after death.

XV. The judgment, and of course the punishment of the wicked, are connected with a second coming of Christ, in a manner which proves the judgment to be future and general, and the punishment to be in a future state. Matt. xxv. 31, 32. "When the Son of Man shall come in his glory and all the holy angels with him, then shall he sit upon the throne of his glory, and before him shall be gathered all nations.

So far as we have been able to learn the opinions of others, it is generally agreed that this text relates to one of two events: universalists maintain that it was fulfilled in the destruction of Jerusalem, while anti-universalists consider it descriptive of a future and general judgment. To refute the former of these opinions and to establish the latter, is the intended work of this argument; to effect which we shall, first, examine the text itself, and then compare it with other texts which are supposed to relate to the same event. But before we attempt to rear an argument, we will endeavor to remove some of the rubbish which universalists have thrown in our way, on this subject, by considering what they urge in support of their own exposition of this text. Universalists explain this paragraph by the preceding chapter which treats of the destruction of Jerusalem, and where Christ says, verse 34, "This generation shall not pass, till all these things be fulfilled." Now, because Christ speaks of the sun's being darkened, and of the moon's not giving her light, and of the falling of the stars of heaven; of the coming of the Son of Man, &c. it is argued that the second coming of Christ took place at the destruction of Jerusalem, and hence, that the xxivth and xxvth chapters relate to the same event. To this we object on the following ground:

1. Though it is clear that Christ does speak of the destruction of Jerusalem in the xxivth chapter, yet it is not clear that his discourse is exclusively on that subject. He first said to his disciples, of the temple "there shall not be left here one stone upon another that shall not be thrown down." This led the disciples to enquire, verse 3, "When shall these things be? and what shall be the sign of thy coming and of the end of the world? On this Dr. A. Clarke has the following remarks: "There appear to be *three* questions asked here by the disciples. 1st. *When shall these things be?* viz. the *destruction* of the *city, temple* and *Jewish state*: 2dly, *What shall be the sign of thy coming?* viz. to *execute* these judgments upon them, and to *establish* thy own church: and 3dly, *When shall this world end?* When wilt thou come to *judge* the *quick* and *dead?*" Now, as there are three questions blended together, it is rea-

sonable to suppose that the answers should be found in like manner, in the same discourse; and hence, it may be supposed that some things are said here which relate to the destruction of the temple, and others to the final destruction of the world. Should it be insisted that the expression, "this generation shall not pass till *all these things* be fulfilled," forbids such an idea, we answer that it is very far from being clear that by *"this generation"* we are to understand the natural life of the then existing inhabitants. The expression may be intended to designate the Jews as a distinct race or nation of men. We do not mean to say that the word is never used to signify the people who live in the same age; but we deny that it is always used in this sense, and maintain that it is sometimes employed to denote a peculiar class or race of people, extending through many ages. A few instances, in which it is used in this sense will satisfy the reader of this fact. Ps. xiv. 5. "God is in the generation of the righteous." Here the righteous are called a generation, as a class or race of persons running through all ages of time. Ps. xxiv. 6. "This is the generation of them that seek him, that seek thy face, O God of Jacob." By adverting to the fourth verse, it will be seen that in this text such as have clean hands and pure hearts, &c. are declared to be a generation, which does not denote people living at the same time, but people of a certain character, in whatever age or place they live. Prov. xxx. 12. "There is a generation that are pure in their own eyes, and yet is not washed from their filthiness." Here wicked persons of a certain description are called a generation, not because all of this particular stamp are contemporary with each other, but because they are the same in character in every age; presenting the features of a distinct and peculiar race of the wicked. In Isa. liii. 8. it is said of the Messiah, "who shall declare his generation? for he was cut off out of the land of the living." Here generation must mean either pedigree or progeny, either of which implies a race, and not a period of time. 1 Pet. ii. 9. "Ye are a chosen generation, a royal priesthood, a holy nation, a peculiar people." Here christians are termed a generation, and this is spoken of christians in general as a peculiar race or class of men, and not as having their being at the same time. It is clear then that the scriptures do sometimes employ the term generation to signify a peculiar people or distinct race; and if so, this may be the sense in which Christ uses it when he says "This generation shall not pass away till all these things be fulfilled:" that is, this people, the Jews shall be preserved as a distinct race as a standing proof of the predictions I now utter. One prediction appears very much to favour this construction. In Luke xxi. 24, 32. where Christ is speaking on the same subject we read, "Jerusalem shall be trodden down of the gentiles until the times of the gentiles be fulfilled." Here then, it is plainly declared that Jerusalem shall be trodden down until the times of the gentiles be fulfilled, which implies that the times of the gentiles should be fulfilled, and that Jerusalem should cease to be trodden down; and all this before that generation should pass away. Now if we understand by the expression, *"this generation,"* the class of inhabitants then living, this prediction cannot be true, for that generation has passed away, and the times of the gentiles appear not to be fulfilled, and Jerusalem is still trodden down by them. But if we understand by this generation, the Jews as a distinct and peculiar race, the prediction appears to be literally true, and consistent with other prophecies which relate to the same event. Rom. xi. 25. "For I would not brethren, that ye should be ignorant of this mystery, that blindness in part is happened to Israel *until the fullness of the gentiles be come in.*" If this view be correct, then the supposed difficulty in this subject vanishes at once; for the generation or race of the Jews have not passed away to this day, they are still a distinct people, and there is nothing absurd in supposing that they will be preserved so until the end of time, "to the judgment of the great day."

2. Were it admitted that the xxivth of Matt. the xxist of Luke 9 &c. relate exclusively to the destruction of Jerusalem, and that by "this generation" we are to understand the set of inhabitants then living, confining the whole within the lifetime of some of those to whom this solemn discourse was delivered, still it will not follow that the last paragraph of the xxvth of Matt, relates to the same event; or that there is no future coming of Christ predicted in the scriptures, as universalists must infer, to render it in the least subservient to their cause. Suppose Christ, in giving an account of the ruin which was soon to come upon the people, city and temple of the Jews, represented that special providence as his coming, that he represented the rapid march of the Roman army, his ministers of justice, who entered Judea on the east, by "the lightning that cometh out of the east and shineth even unto the west;" suppose he represented the entire abolition of the Jewish religion, by the sun's being darkened, and the overthrow of the Jewish state, by the moon's refusing to give her light, and the subversion of the judges and doctors, by the falling of the stars from heaven; we say admit all this, and what does it prove more than that these are figurative expressions borrowed from literal correspondent events? Is there a second figurative coming of Christ, a figurative judgment, a figurative passing away of the heavens, and no such literal events from which these figures are borrowed? If so we have yet to learn the origin, the nature, and import of figurative language. These expressions then, applied to the destruction of Jerusalem, are so far from disproving the second coming of Christ at the end of the world, that they beyond dispute establish the very point.

Admitting then that all this is figurative, it does not

follow from thence that the xxvth of Matt, is also figurative. The one may be a representation of the destruction of Jerusalem in the use of figures borrowed from the events of the last day, and the other may be a literal narration of those events. This is now what we shall attempt to prove, viz. that the last paragraph of the xxvth of Matt, contains an account of a second coming of Christ, yet to take place.

1. Christ is here said to come in his glory: which cannot relate to the destruction of Jerusalem. We often read of the appearances of the divine glory, as when the angel of God appeared to the shepherds on Judah's hills, Luke ii. 9. Christ also speaks of the glory he had with the Father "before the world was," John xvii. 5. But in no sense did Christ come in his glory when Jerusalem fell under the pressure of Roman arms. Let the Christian look upon the record of that event, and fancy that he hears the clangour of swords and shields, the shouts of the victors and the groans of the wounded and dying, and that he sees the flames and rising columns of smoke from the dissolving city—we say let that christian look upon these things, and then ask himself if this is the glory of the son of man. Is this the glory he hopes to enjoy with his divine Lord? Christ prayed, "Father glorify thou me with the glory I had with thee before the world was;" and St. Paul, in speaking of the high calling of the christian, says, Rom, viii. 17. "If children, then heirs, heirs of God and joint heirs with Jesus Christ, if so be we suffer with him that we may be *glorified together*." But if Christ came in his glory at the destruction of Jerusalem, we should pray, Lord, save us from thy glory.

2. In the text Christ is said to come with all the holy angels; which was not the case at the destruction of Jerusalem. In a controversy, which the writer once held with a universalist, this objection was raised to his application of this subject, to which he replied, that by the holy an-

gels the Roman army was intended. It was then stated that the Roman army was composed of heathen, which were never in scripture termed holy; and the words of Daniel were quoted as applied by Christ, Matt. xiiv. 15, 16. "When ye shall see the abomination of desolation, spoken of by Daniel the prophet, stand in the holy place, then let them that be in Judea flee into the mountains." On this text, we remarked that the Roman army are so far from being termed *holy angels*, that they are called the *abomination of desolation*. The abetter of universalism then changing his ground, as its advocates are apt to do, said that by the holy angels was meant the apostles and christians. To this it was replied that no apostles or christians were at Jerusalem at that time; that instead of *coming* at that time they *fled away*, according to the word of their master above quoted, "Then flee ye to the mountains." No farther reply was offered, and we consider the argument as good now as it was then.

3. It is declared in the text that Christ shall sit upon the throne of his glory at his coming here referred to, which was not the case at the destruction of Jerusalem. Wherein did Christ sit upon the throne of his glory at the destruction of Jerusalem, any more than at the fall of Babylon, or at the dissolution of the Roman empire?

4. In the text it is said that all nations shall be gathered before Christ at his coming here referred to. Now there was no gathering of nations at the destruction of Jerusalem, but rather a scattering: the christians and all strangers fled on the approach of the Roman army. In the controversy above alluded to, it was replied by the opposite party, that by all nations, nothing more was meant than a collection of some of all nations, and that this was fulfilled in the approach of the Roman army, which, it was said, was composed of some of every nation on earth. In answer to this it was maintained that there is no evidence, or even probability, that there were some of every nation

in the Roman army, though it was composed of a collection from different provinces. The author of this handy method of making out a collection of all nations, was also reminded of what he had just said concerning the promise of God to Abraham, that in his seed all nations should be blessed, in which he contended that, by all nations, every individual of all nations, must be understood. On this it was remarked that if all nations could be gathered together, where there were only a few individuals selected out of all nations, it must be perfectly plain that all nations could be blessed in the seed of Abraham, though but some of all nations actually enjoyed the blessing.

5. It is said in the text, that Christ shall separate them, (nations,) one from another. Now we ask, what nations were separated at the destruction of Jerusalem, by being parted from each other, or by each being severed in its own members? The Roman army, which is made to comprise all nations, were not separated one from another. The Jews were not separated from all other nations at this time, but were taken and sold as slaves among other nations. If it be said that the Jews were separated from each other, we answer this was but the separation of one nation, whereas the text speaks of all nations.

6. When Christ shall come, as predicted in this text, the obedient are to be rewarded or blessed, upon consideration of their former good character. "Come, ye blessed of my Father, inherit the kingdom prepared for you from the foundation of the world, for I was a hungered and ye gave me meat," &c. What is this kingdom prepared from the foundation of the world, which the righteous now inherit? It cannot mean the gospel kingdom on earth, to which the gentiles were then called; for the call of the gentiles took place long before this period: it being an acknowledged fact that the gospel had been preached throughout the Roman empire before the fall of Jerusalem. Again, the righteous, in this text, are rewarded for

what they had done, or on the ground of their former good conduct, which was not the case in the call of the gentiles; for they were received into the gospel church on condition of their present repentance and faith, and not on account of what they had been or had done. It will be equally futile to say that by the reward here promised to the faithful, we are to understand their preservation amid the ruins of that bloody siege. A temporal deliverance, or a deliverance from temporal death is not well described by "a kingdom prepared from the foundation of the world." As well might it be said that the same reward was extended to the three worthies on their coming forth from the fiery furnace, or to Daniel, on his deliverance from the den of lions. As well might every christian be said to inherit a kingdom prepared from the foundation of the world when he is in any way delivered from impending danger.

7. At the coming of Christ, described in the text, the wicked will be punished with a punishment prepared for the devil and his angels. Now, we trust it has been shown in a preceeding [sic] argument, (see Argument vii.) that there are real and personal devils, inhabitants of the invisible world, from which it must follow that the calamities which befell the Jews cannot be intended, by a punishment prepared for the devil and his angels.

Having examined the text itself, and drawn out such arguments, as it appears to contain in support of a second coming of Christ to judge the world, we will endeavor farther to support the position, by comparing it with other texts which are supposed to relate to the same event. 1 Thess. iv. 15. "The Lord himself shall descend from heaven, with a shout, with the voice of the arch-angel and with the trump of God, and the dead in Christ shall rise first." This text speaks of Christ's coming at the resurrection of the dead, which proves that he will come at the end of the world, when all the dead will be raised. That the resurrection here referred to, is the resurrection of the body, is certain, from the reference which the text contains, to the manner of the general resurrection, by the sounding of the last trump. It must be admitted that the same writer is to be understood to mean the same thing, when he uses similar expressions in different places, unless the nature of the subject absolutely requires a different construction. All admit that 1 Cor. xv. contains an account of the resurrection of the dead; and in this chapter, verse 52, the apostle describes the manner in which the resurrection will be effected, viz. by sounding the trumpet—"for the trumpet shall sound, and the dead shall be raised." If this then refers to the general resurrection, how clear must it be that the same writer refers to the same event when he says, "The Lord shall descend from heaven with the trump of God, and the dead shall rise." Having shown that 1 Thess. iv. 16. speaks of Christ's coming at the general resurrection we will proceed to compare it with Matt. xxv. 31-46, in farther proof that it relates to the same event. Please mark the points of resemblance between the language of Christ in Matt, and St. Paul in Thessalonians.

1. Christ says, "The Son of Man shall come in his glory;" Paul says, "The Lord himself shall descend from heaven with a shout, with the voice of the arch-angel and the trump of God."

2. Christ says, "The Son of Man shall come, and *all the holy angels with him;*" Paul says, as above, that he "shall descend *with a shout, with the voice of the arch-angel,* &c. His coming with a shout, answers to his coming with all the holy angels, for a shout supposes that he will have attendants who will give the shout.

3. Christ says, "All nations shall be gathered before him;" Paul says, "The dead shall rise."

4. Christ speaks to the faithful, "Come ye blessed of

my father inherit the kingdom prepared for you from the foundation of the world." These shall go "into life eternal." Paul says, of the righteous, "they shall be caught up to meet the Lord in the air, so shall they ever be with the Lord."

It appears to us that nothing but a determination to support an opinion, at all hazards, could lead the mind to apply these texts to different events. They seem to refer to the same event, with this difference only—Christ treats of both the righteous and the wicked, while St. Paul speaks of the righteous only. But the apostle, in his second letter to the same people, treats of both the righteous and the wicked. 2. Thess. i. 7-10. "When the Lord Jesus shall be revealed from heaven in flaming fire, taking vengeance on them that know not God, and obey not the gospel of our Lord Jesus Christ, who shall be punished with everlasting destruction from the presence of the Lord, and from the glory of his power, *when* he shall come to be glorified in his saints." That this text relates to the same event described in the former one, must appear, when we consider,

1. That they were both penned by the same hand.
2. They were both directed to the same people.
3. They resemble each other so nearly as not to admit of an application to different events without an express warrant from the author. Note, the first of these texts says, "The Lord himself shall descend from heaven." The second says, "The Lord Jesus shall be revealed from heaven." One says, "He shall descend with the voice of the archangel." The other says, "He shall be revealed with his mighty angels." Now, that 2 Thess. i. 7- 10, does not relate to the destruction of Jerusalem must appear from a consideration of the subjects to whom it was addressed.

1. The church at Thessalonica was not composed of Jews but principally of devout Greeks and converted heathen. "Hence," says Dr. Clarke, "we find in the epistle but few

allusions to the Jews, and but few references to the peculiarities of their religious or civil institutions."
2. The Thessalonians were too remote from Jerusalem to be materially affected by the judgments which befel [sic] this devoted city. Thessalonica was a city in Europe distant nearly one thousand miles from the noise and blood of the siege that proved the overthrow of the Jews. In view of these circumstances to suppose that St. Paul appealed to their hopes and fears on the ground of the fall of Jerusalem, describing the event by a revelation of the Lord Jesus from heaven with his mighty angels in flaming fire, is too absurd to be believed. We will introduce one text more which refers to the second coming of Christ and leave the subject. It is 1 Cor. xi. 26. "As oft as ye eat this bread and drink this cup, ye do show the Lord's death till he come." This text clearly implies that the death of Christ is to be celebrated in the holy sacrament until the Lord comes, and no longer; from which it follows that the sacrament has been invalid since the destruction of Jerusalem, or else that Christ did not come then, has not yet come, but is to come hereafter, at a time when gospel ordinances will no longer be perpetuated. This argument we do not expect will weigh much with the unceremonious quaker, but with universalists, who *sometimes* pretend to administer the sacrament, and with all others, who believe in its validity it must prove conclusive.

We trust we have now shown that the judgment and punishment of the wicked are connected with a second coming of Christ, yet future, from which it most clearly follows that the wicked are to be punished in a future state.

XVI. The scriptures connect the judgment and punishment of the wicked with the end of the world, or the dissolution of this whole mundane system, which must determine the punishment to be in a future state. If it can be proved that the wicked will be judged and punished at a time when this world will cease to be, the argument will be irresistible in proof that they will be punished in a future state. We are not prepared to say whether universalists, generally, will admit that this world will have an end and cease to be, having never fallen in with any decisive expression on this subject; but whether they will admit it or not, we think it may be easily proved. Heb. i. 10-12. "Thou Lord in the beginning hast laid the foundation of the earth, and the heavens are the work of thine hands; they shall perish, but thou remainest; and they all shall wax old as doth a garment and a vesture shalt thou fold them up, and they shall be changed; but thou art the same, and thy years shall not fail." That the literal heavens and earth are intended in this text, is evident from the plain reference to the Mosaic account of the creation which it contains. Gen. i. 1. "In the beginning God created the heavens and the earth." Now, it is clear that the same beginning is referred to in the text above quoted. "Thou, Lord *in the beginning* hast laid the foundations of the earth and the heavens are the work of thy hands;" and if the same beginning is referred to in both texts, it must follow that the same heavens and earth are also intended. It is then clear that the literal heavens and earth, which God created in the beginning are to perish, wax old, as doth a garment, and as a vesture be folded up. Having shown that this world will have an end, we will produce some of those texts which connect the judgment and punishment of ungodly men with this solemn event. 2 Pet. iii. 7, 10, 12. "But the heavens and the earth that are now, are kept in store, reserved unto fire, against the day of judgment and perdition of ungodly men. But the day of the Lord will come as a thief in the night, in the which the heavens shall pass away with a great noise and the elements shall melt with fervent heat; the earth also, and the works that are therein shall be burned up. Looking for, and hastening unto the coming of the day of God, wherein the heavens being on fire shall be dissolved, and the elements shall melt with fervent heat." Rev. xx. 11, 12. "And I saw a great white throne, and him that sat upon it, from whose face the earth and the heavens fled away and there was found no place for them. And I saw the dead, small and great stand before God, and the dead were judged," &c. These texts clearly connect the judgment of the world, and the punishment of the wicked, with the end of time, or the dissolution of this whole mundane system; and *that* punishment which is to be inflicted when time shall be gone, and when the world shall be no more, must be in a future state.

XVII. Men generally have a consciousness of future retribution, insomuch, that it is a common sentiment in the world that sin will be punished after death.

That it is the prevailing opinion among Christians, Jews and Mahometans, cannot be denied. But let us inquire if it be a common sentiment in the heathen world also.

The Chinese are said to believe in punishment after death. Confucius who is said to have been born 550 years before Christ, taught that it was the indipensable [sic] duty of every man to perform sacred rights to the memory of his ancestors, and that whosoever neglected this duty, would be punished after death, by the exclusion of his soul from the hall of his ancestors, &c. Another sect among this people are said to teach that there is a great distinction between good and evil, and that the good are rewarded and the wicked punished after death, in places suited to the spirits of each.

The Japanese also believe in punishment after death. The most prevalent religious sects in Japan, are those of *Sinto* and *Budsdo*. Of that of Sinto, which is the most ancient, it is said: "They have some conception of the soul's immortality and believe that a happy abode immediately under heaven is assigned to the spirits that are virtuous; while those of the wicked shall be doomed to wander to and fro under the firmament." Budsdo taught that "the souls of the wicked are condemned to undergo punishment and purification after death, by passing into the bodies of the lower animals."

Of the Thibetians and Tartars it is said: "They believe in one God and a trinity, but full of errors, and a paradise, hell and purgatory, but full of errors also."

It is said, "all the Hindoo sects believe in the immortality of the soul, transmigration, and a future state of rewards and punishment."

Of the Aborigines of New-England it is said: "The immortality of the soul was in some way universally believed among them. When good men die, they say their spirits go to *Kitchtan*, where they meet their friends and enjoy all manner of pleasures. When wicked men die they go to Kitchtan also, but are commanded to walk away and wander about in restless discontent and darkness forever." *See Religious Ceremonies and Customs, by Charles A. Goodrich.*

The following is from the last speech of Socrates, the Grecian Philosopher, who was put to death about four hundred years before the christian era. The condemned orator after labouring to prove the immortality of the soul, improves upon this doctrine as follows: "My friends there is still one thing which is very just to believe; and this is, that if the soul be immortal, it requires to be cultivated with attention, not only for what we call the time of life, but for that which is to follow, I mean eternity; and the least neglect in this point may be attended with endless consequences. If death were the final dissolution of being, the wicked would be great gainers by it, as being delivered at once from their bodies, their souls, and their vices; but as the soul is immortal, it has no other means of being freed from its evils, nor any safety for itself but in becoming very good and very prudent; for it carries nothing away with it but its good or bad deeds, its virtues or vices, which are commonly the consequence of the education it has received, and the cause of, eternal happiness or misery.

"When the dead are arrived at the fatal rendezvous of departed souls, whither demons conduct them, they are all judged. Those who are judged to be incurable on account of the greatness of their crimes, the fatal destiny that passes judgment upon them, hurls them into Tartarus, from whence they shall never depart.

"But for those who have passed through life with peculiar sanctity of manners, delivered from their base earthly abodes as fi om a prison, they are received on high, in a pure region which they inhabit, and live without their bodies through all eternity in a series of joys and delights which it is not easy to describe." Rollin's History, Vol. iv. pages, 38, 39.

It appears then, that the doctrine of future retribution is a common sentiment in the world, common among all nations and tribes of men, and common to all religions.

The doctrine of future punishment is proclaimed in the language of heathen oracles; it is taught at the temple of Juggernaut, and believed on the banks of the Ganges; it is read in the Koran, and believed by all true Mahomedans. Go to the Jews and they will teach you the same sentiment; and inquire at the shrine of Christianity and you will see future retribution inscribed upon her sacred altars, with the exception of a few, erected by universalists. Now, we ask from whence is this general conviction of future punishment derived? If it be said, as universalists have often said, that it is a heathen tradition, we ask from whence the heathen received it at first, and how does it happen that this is a general sentiment in the world, when, in other respects, each heathen nation, generally, has sentiments and rites peculiar to itself? If the doctrine of future punishment be an error, it is the most general one that ever entered the world, and must have been introduced in the most insidious manner. Other errors may generally be traced to their sources, and their authors, and the time of their introduction be pointed out; but no account of the origin of the doctrine of future punishment can be given, on the supposition that it is false. If some errors cannot be traced back to their origin, they are not general in the world, but are peculiar to particular nations, tribes, or sects; while the sentiment in question is a general one, and prevails most where the scriptures are most known and read. The doctrine of future punishment must have had its origin; and as it prevails generally in the world, and as no account can be given of its introduction, it follows that it must have sprung from some one of the following sources: — It must be instinct, the result of natural reason, the light of nature, the impression of God's spirit on the mind, or the principle of revelation contained in the Bible. Now, if it be instinct, it must be from the Creator; if it be the result of natural reason, it cannot be unreasonable; if it be the light of nature, it is a revelation from God; if it be the impression of God's Spirit on the mind, it is no less a divine revelation; and if it be the sentiment of the Bible, none but infidels will deny it. If universalists can prove that the doctrine in question had some other origin, or if some other sentiment can be named, manifestly false, and equally common in the world, of the origin of which no account can be given, we acknowledge that they will evade the force of this argument; but until this be done the argument must prove ruinous to their theory.

VI
The Duration of Future Punishment

IN THE PRECEDING chapter, we have confined our remarks to the simple fact of punishment in a future state, without any reference to its limited or endless duration, and having, as we believe, established the fact of punishment after death, we shall devote the present chapter to a consideration of its duration, in which we shall attempt to prove that it will be endless. And after what has been said in proof of future punishment, we think the reader will justify us in proceeding in the proof of endless punishment, on the supposition that punishment will exist in the future world; hence, this chapter and the preceding one will reciprocally support each other. So far as the fact of punishment in the future world appears unfavorable to the final reformation and salvation of all lost spirits, the preceding chapter comes in with its whole weight of argument to the support of this, while the present, so far as it contains arguments in favour of endless punishment, which are not dependent on the circumstance that the punishment is in the future world, must support the preceding; for just as far as arguments go towards proving endless punishment, they, at the same time, prove that such punishment must be in a future state. The question upon which we now enter, is one of awful moment, and in our theological war with universalists is the main post against which they of every class and opinion, equally direct their assaults with an unsparing effort. The Universalists, the Restorationers, and Destructionists, all direct their battering rams against this castle of endless punishment; and well they may, for it is a commanding position, which, if they do not succeed in silencing, its batteries will drive them from every position they may see fit to occupy, and beat down every bulwark of defence they can rear. Opposed to this stands the main sentiment of universalism, which asserts the final holiness and happiness of all men, in defence of which all universalists unite. And having as we believe demolished their outposts, we propose assaulting the citadel itself, in the present chapter, by proving the fact of endless punishment.

1. We urge, in support of the doctrine of endless punishment, those terms which the scriptures employ to express the duration of punishment. Such as, everlasting, forever, forever and ever, eternal, dieth not, unquenchable, &c. Matt. xxv. 46. "These shall go away into everlasting punishment" Matt, xviii. 8. "It is better for thee to enter into life halt or maimed rather than having two hands or two feet to be cast into everlasting fire." 2 Thess. i. 9. "Who shall be punished with everlasting destruction."

These texts clearly prove that the punishment of the wicked will be everlasting. Everlasting punishment, everlasting fire, and everlasting destruction, are expressions too plain to need any comment. It will not be denied that everlasting literally signifies endless, and that when the word is used to signify any thing short of endless, it is not used in its proper sense. Dr. Johnson defines the word thus: everlasting; perpetual, without end." Dr. Webster: 1. "Lasting or enduring forever, eternal, continuing without end, immortal. 2. Perpetual, continuing indefinitely, or during the present state of things. 3. In *popular language* endless, continued, unintermitted." But while there is no room for dispute about the English word everlasting, it is often contended by universalists that the original is not properly rendered by it, at least in those cases in which it is applied to the punishment of the wicked. The following ground is taken, on this point, by Mr. Morse in his reply to Mr. Parker. On page 14 the author says: "If he" (Mr. Parker) "had looked into his Greek Testament, he would have seen that the phrase rendered 'eternal damnation' is *aionion kriseos* which does not *necessarily* signify endless suffering. The word, *kriseos*, damnation, is equivalent to condemnation or punishment. The word *aionion* is equivalent to long, lasting, or according to scriptural usage, everlasting." And what the meaning of everlasting is, he tells us on page 13, where he says: "The scriptural meaning of the word everlasting may be easily understood by observing that the land of Canaan was promised to the seed of Abraham for an everlasting possession. Gen. 17. 8. and they have long since ceased to possess it." This, we believe, is the ground generally taken by universalists, the substance of which is, the words rendered everlasting, eternal, &c. are applied to some things which have an end, therefore the punishment of the wicked to which they are applied, to describe its duration, must have an end also. Before we enter upon the main argument, drawn from these words, a few remarks shall be devoted to the above quotation from Mr. Morse, which will apply equally well to what others have said and written on the same subject.

1. Mr. M. says, "The word *aionios* is equivalent to long, lasting, or everlasting." Here the truth is told in the end; we suppose the word *aionios* to be properly translated by the word everlasting. But why does Mr. M. cause his readers to blunder over two errors to come to this truth, by saying first, that the word in question is equivalent to long, or lasting? The object, no doubt, is to give his readers to understand that the word is as properly rendered by *long* as by everlasting, which is not true. The word *aionios* is never rendered long, nor can it be so rendered without destroying the sense of the sacred text, as a few examples will show. If the word in question can be properly rendered long, as Mr. M. more than intimates, then where the word occurs in the original, and is rendered everlasting, and eternal, it will make good sense to read, long, in the place of these words. By this then we will test Mr. M's criticism. We read, John iii. 15. "Whosoever believeth in him shall not perish, but have eternal life; according to Mr. M. *long life*. This rendering makes the gospel promise long life to the believer, which is contradicted by matter of fact, for St. Stephen believed, and his faith, instead of procuring long life, was the occasion of his premature death. Chap. v. 39. "Search the scriptures, for in them ye think ye have eternal life;" that is, according to Mr. M. the Jews thought they had *long life* in the scriptures. But to sustain this rendering it must be shown that the Jews lived to a greater age than the surrounding nations, who were destitute of the scriptures. How otherwise could they think they had long life in the scriptures? Chap. vi. 29. "Labour not for the meat that perisheth but for that meat which endureth unto everlasting life;" that is, long life. Verse 68. "Then Simon Peter said unto him. Lord, to whom shall we go, thou hast the words of eternal life;" that is, thou hast the words of long life. Chap. xvii. 3. "This

is life eternal that they might know thee;" that is, life long. Acts xiii. 48. "As many as were ordained to eternal life believed." According to Mr. M's criticism, this must mean that as many as were destined or determined (as some render the word *tetagmenoi*, ordain,) to live long believed the gospel. Rom. xvi. 36. "The everlasting God;" that is, according to Mr. M. the lasting or long lived God. Verse 27. "to God only wise be glory through Jesus Christ forever;" that is, for a long time. These illustrations must show how utterly unfounded Mr. M's statement is that the word *aionios* is equivalent to long or lasting, unless lasting be understood in an unlimited sense. If universalism rests upon such garbling criticism as he has given us in this instance, it has but a poor foundation.

2. Mr. Morse says, "The scriptural meaning of the word *everlasting*, may be easily understood by observing that the land of Canaan was promised to the seed of Abraham for an everlasting possession, and that they have long since ceased to possess it. To this we reply, "The scriptural meaning of the word everlasting may be easily understood by observing" that God is said to be an everlasting God; that the kingdom of God is an everlasting kingdom, and that the gift of God through Jesus Christ is everlasting life. Rom. xvi. 26. Matt. vi. 13. Rom. v. 21. vi. 23. Now if Mr. M. has done any thing towards proving that the word everlasting does not express endless duration, we have done just as much towards proving that it does express endless duration. If the word *everlasting* cannot mean endless, because it is sometimes applied to things which are not endless, then, it cannot mean any thing less than endless because it is applied to the existence of God, the duration of his kingdom, and the happiness of the saints, which are absolutely endless.

3. The circumstance that the land of Canaan was promised to the seed of Abraham for an everlasting posses-

sion, and that they have ceased to possess it, does not prove that the word is used in a restricted sense even in this instance. It is perfectly plain that the seed of Abraham were not dispossessed of the land of Canaan by a dissolution of the covenant by limitation, which secured it to them, but by forfeiture of its privileges, by a non-compliance with its conditions on their part. To argue as Mr. M. does, that the word everlasting means a limited period because the land of Canaan was promised to the Jews forever, and because they notwithstanding, have ceased to possess it, implies that it was promised to them for a limited period; and that such period has expired, in consequence of which, they are dispossessed of the promised land, like a man who is dispossessed of his farm by the expiration of his lease by which he holds it, it being given for a term of years, which is not the case. The Jews were dispossessed of the land of Canaan more like a man who holds what we call an everlasting lease of his farm, and is dispossessed of it by a forfeiture of its conditions. The covenant was conditional, as appears from Deut. xxxviii. 15, 63, 64. "But it shall came to pass that if thou wilt not hearken unto the voice of the Lord thy God to observe to do all his commandments that all these curses shall come upon thee, and ye shall be plucked from off the land whither thou goest to possess it, and the Lord shall scatter thee among all people." The Jews then were plucked from the promised land in consequence of their sins, and not because the word everlasting, in the use of which it was promised to them, did not secure it to them for a longer period. Had they obeyed the voice of the Lord their God, they would, no doubt, now have been in possession of the land of their fathers; and it is now the general opinion of the church that the outcasts of the children of Israel shall yet be gathered under the gospel banner, and be put again into the possession of the land of their former inheritance. But it may be said that even in such case everlasting can mean no longer than natural life, or the whole period of time, at most, as the land of Canaan cannot be possessed in a future world. This is true, so far as the land of Canaan is literally concerned; but it should be remembered that the promise, which secured the land of Canaan, included other blessings of a spiritual and heavenly character, and that the promised land is to be regarded as an earnest and type of heaven, which is everlasting in the highest sense. But it is often said, that we read that the priesthood of Aaron was everlasting, and of the everlasting hills, &c. as well as the land of Canaan as an everlasting possession. These facts are uttered by universalists, with as much of an air of triumph as though they were utterly irreconcilable with the belief that the same word, when applied to the punishment of the wicked, expresses endless duration. But we have already shown that the same word is applied to the existence of God, which is absolutely endless; we have therefore just as good a right to conclude from thence that it must mean endless duration when it is applied to the punishment of the wicked. But all this proves no more than that the word is applied, sometimes to things which have an end, and sometimes to things which are absolutely endless, leaving us to determine from other considerations in which sense it is used in each case. Now it is generally agreed that the word must be construed according to the nature of the subject to which it is applied. Not however that the nature of the subject fixes the meaning of the word, but on the principle that the word is used in a proper, and in an accommodated sense, and that the nature of the subject determines in which of these senses it is used in that particular instance; the word being applied to some things which are everlasting only in an accommodated sense, and to others which are properly endless. Guided then by this rule, for which universalists themselves contend, let us test the strength of their defence against the argument drawn from this and kindred words, in favour of the doctrine of endless punishment.

The hills are said to be everlasting hills, and the punishment of the wicked is said to be everlasting punishment. In what sense then are the hills everlasting? They are everlasting in an accommodated sense, in two respects. They will endure as long as the earth, of which they form a part, and as long as time, in which they have their existence. The hills will never come to an end as hills abstractly considered, but will end only when the earth itself shall be burned up at the end of time, in which they exist. Now, let us apply the same principle of interpretation to the punishment of the wicked. The hill is everlasting because it is as lasting as the earth to which it is attached, and if so, to render punishment everlasting, must it not be as lasting as the soul on which it is inflicted; which will render it absolutely endless in the opinion of all who believe in the immortality of the soul? Again the bill is everlasting, because it will endure as long as time, in which it exists, and if so, to render punishment everlasting, must it not be as lasting as the age in which it takes place? and this we have shown in the preceding chapter to be the future world. This must render the punishment of the wicked absolutely endless, in the opinion of all who believe in an endless hereafter.

The same mode of reasoning may be employed in relation to the priesthood of Aaron, which was everlasting in an accommodated sense, because it was as lasting as the dispensation under which it was established. The priesthood had no end, as a distinct feature or branch of the Mosaic economy, but was ended by the abrogation of the whole dispensation, of which it formed a part; and if so, punishment, which will form a part of the divine dispensation in the future world, will be as endless as all the other realities of eternity.

Having as we believe removed the bulwarks, which

universalists have reared to shelter themselves from the argument founded on the strength of the terms applied to punishment to describe its duration, we will assault their citadel, by proceeding to the statement of the main argument itself.

1. We maintain that the proper meaning of the original word *aionios*, which is rendered everlasting, and eternal, is endless. This word Mr. Groves defines thus: *Eternal, immortal, perpetual, former, past, ancient.*" He says it is derived from *aei*, which signifies *ever*, and *on* which signifies *being*. These two terms put together, make *ever being*. Dr. A. Clark, has the following remark, in his notes on Gen. xxi. 33. "Abraham called upon the name of the Lord the EVERLASTING GOD." "The Septuagint renders the words *Theos aionios*, the ever existing God. From this application of both words we learn *olam* and *aion* originally signified ETERNAL, or *duration without end*. *Aion*, according to Aristotle, and a higher authority need not be sought, is compounded of *aei, always* and *on, being*. Hence we see that no words can more forcibly express the grand characteristics of eternity than these. It is that duration which is *always existing*, still *running* ON, but never *runs* OUT." The Dr. continues, in fine, on this chapter, "In all languages, words have, in process of time, deviated from their original acceptations, and have become accommodated to particular purposes and limited to particular meanings. This has happened, both to the Hebrew *olam*, and the Greek *aion*; they have been both used to express a *limited* time, but in general a time the limits of which are unknown; and thus a pointed reference to the *original ideal meaning* is still kept up. Those who bring any of these terms, in an accommodated sense to favour a particular doctrine must depend upon the good graces of their opponents for permission to use them in this way. For as the real grammatical meaning of both words is *eternal* and all other meaning only accommodated ones,

sound criticism in all matters of dispute, concerning the import of a word or term, must have recourse to the grammatical meaning, and to the earliest and best writers of the language, and will determine all accommodated meanings by this alone. Now the first and best writers in both these languages apply *olam* and *aion* to express eternal, in the proper meaning of that word; and this is their proper meaning in the Old and New Testaments, when applied to God, his attributes, his operations, taken in connection with the *ends* for which he performs them, for *whatsoever he doeth it shall be forever*. The word is with the same strict propriety applied to the duration of the rewards and punishments in a future state, and the argument that pretends to prove, and it is only pretence, that in the future punishment of the wicked the worm *shall die*, and the fire *shall be quenched*, will apply as forcibly to the state of happy spirits, and as fully prove that a point in eternity shall arrive, when the repose of the righteous shall be interrupted and the glorification of the children of God have an eternal end. On Matt. xxv. 46. "These shall go away into everlasting punishment but the righteous into life eternal," the Dr. remarks thus: "But some are of opinion that this punishment shall have *an end*: this is as likely as that the glory of the righteous shall have *an end*: for the same word is used to express the duration of the punishment, *kolasin aionion*, as is used to express the duration of the state of glory: *zoen aionion*. I have seen the best things that have been written in favour of the final redemption of damned spirits, but I never saw an answer to the argument against that doctrine drawn from this verse, but what sound learning and criticism should be ashamed to own." We might add authority to authority on this point were we disposed to cover some few pages with the names of critics, but that this is the voice of critics generally, from the earliest period to the present day, the critical reader already knows, and we will not detain the plain reader with criticisms on the original Greek, but address ourselves to his understanding, and attempt to settle the point in his mind in plain English. The point at which we aim here, is to show that the proper and grammatical sense of the Greek noun *aion*, and its corresponding adjective *aionios*, is endless. Whether or not these words, when applied to the punishment of the wicked, are used in their proper sense is a question hereafter to be settled. That such is their meaning appears from the fact that if these terms do not express endless duration, there are no terms in the Greek language which do properly express endless duration; and it would be preposterous in the highest degree to suppose that a language in which God has revealed his will to man, in which he has declared his own eternity and set forth the endless destiny of the human family and the undying realities of the future world, in which universalists contend he has clearly and unequivocally revealed the final and endless happiness of all men, should have no words in it which properly express endless duration. Has God declared to us his own eternity in the use of words which do not properly express absolute eternity! Has he revealed to us the endless happiness of the saints, or as universalists contend, that of all men, in the use of words which do not properly denote endless duration? Such a declaration would be an insult to common sense. The terms in question are those which the scriptures employ to express the eternity of God, the perpetuity of his kingdom and the endless happiness of the saints. Rom. i. 25. "The Creator who is blessed, *aionios*, forever." ix. 5. God blessed, *aionios*, forever." xvi. 27. "To God only wise be glory, aionios, forever." Matt, vi. 13. "Thine is the kingdom and the power and the glory *aionios*, forever." John vi. 51. "I am the living bread which came down from heaven; if any man eat of this bread he shall live, *aiona*, forever." These quotations show that the word in question is used to express absolute eternity or endless duration; the proper meaning therefore must be, endless, or else the eternity of God and the perpetual happiness of the saints are expressed only by words used in an accommodated sense, in which they are made to express as much more than their proper meaning as eternity extends beyond a period in time. This is absurd in two respects. First, it is highly absurd to suppose that the eternity of God and the endless felicity of the saints are not expressed in the proper use of words, but only by words used in a figurative or an accommodated sense. If this be the case, it follows that these points are not absolutely expressed, or else that they are absolutely expressed in the use of words which do not express them in their proper signification; and if words which do not properly signify endless duration can, nevertheless, be so accommodated to the subject as to express absolutely the eternity of God and the endless felicity of the saints, the same words can most clearly, by the same accommodation, express the eternity of punishment, and the controversy about the meaning of words is at an end.

Again, words are never used, in an accommodated sense, to express more than their proper signification, but always less, if not used in their proper sense. As swift as the wind, as large as a mountain, as cold as ice, as lasting as the hills, are hyperbolical expressions, in which words are used to express less than what they properly signify; but, with us, it would be a difficult task to use words in an accommodated sense, so as to express more by them than what they properly express. If words are not used in their proper sense, they must be used figuratively, and hence, must belong to some one of the figures of speech, which may be pointed out as such according to the rules of rhetoric. But rhetoric treats of no figures which consist in the use of words to signify more than what they properly express. To illustrate the point, we remark that God is said to be the everlasting God, and a hill is said to be an *everlasting* hill. Now in one or the other of these instances the word everlasting is used figuratively. Suppose, then, that the proper meaning of the word is endless or ever existing, and it is used in its proper sense when it is applied to God, and figuratively when it is applied to the hill. Here we have a plain figure called in rhetoric, hyperbole. Dr. Blair, who is good authority on all questions of rhetoric, says: "Hyperbole consists in magnifying an object beyond its proper bounds;" and here we have it, a hill which is not, strictly speaking, everlasting, is asserted to be everlasting, by which it is "magnified beyond its proper bounds." But reverse the case by supposing that the word everlasting properly means only a limited period, and it must be used in its proper sense, if it have any, when it is applied to the hill, and if so, it must be used figuratively when it is applied to God. But this is a nameless figure, or rather it is no figure at all according to any known laws of language. We say the word *aionios*, which is translated by *forever, everlasting* and *eternal* is applied to limited and unlimited objects, to those which end, and to those which are endless; and as words are used to signify less than their proper meaning when they are employed figuratively, *aionios*, rendered everlasting, must be used figuratively when it is applied to things which have an end, and in its proper sense when applied to things which are endless; its proper meaning therefore is, endless. We think we have now fully shown that the proper meaning of eternal, everlasting, and forever, is endless.

2. We maintain that words are always to be understood in their proper sense, unless the connection be such as to require a different construction. The common sense of every reader must sanction this position, were no author-

ity produced: we will however adduce testimony on the point. The following is extracted from the rules of interpretation contained in Hedge's Logic. Rule 8. "Words which admit of different senses should be taken in their most common and obvious meaning, unless such a construction lead to absurd consequences, or be inconsistent with the known intention of the writer." Rule 12. "When there are no special reasons to the contrary, words should be construed in their literal rather than in their figurative sense." The Rev. Mr. Sawyer, A. M. in his "Elements of Biblical Interpretation," says, on page 12. "The most common meaning is always to be chosen where the nature of the subject or context does not clearly indicate another." And on page 15, the author says again: "The literal meaning of words is never to be departed from without evident reason and necessity." Other authorities might be added, but we forbear, as we presume universalists will not dispute this proposition.

3. We maintain that when the term *aionios*, in English, *forever, everlasting*, and *eternal*, is applied to the punishment of the wicked, there is nothing in the connection or nature of the subject which requires it to be understood in a restricted sense, and that therefore it is to be understood in its proper sense, which is, endless. To this universalists object, but before their objections can be heard, they must prove that the connection or the nature of the subject requires that the terms in question be understood in a restricted sense, when applied to the punishment of the wicked. The burden of proof must fall upon them, for as we have shown the proper meaning of these words to be, endless, they are, as a matter of course, to be understood in this sense, until it be shown that the nature of the subject or the connection requires a different construction. They often attempt this, by affirming that the doctrine of endless punishment is false; that other portions of the scriptures teach the final happiness of all men: but

this is a mere begging of the question, by taking for granted the main point in dispute. Though we are not required to prove a negative in this place, by showing that the subject or connection does not require a restricted sense, yet we will offer some remarks to this effect.

1. This is the most common sense in which it occurs in the scriptures. "*Aion,*" says Dr. Edwards, "reckoning the repuplications of it, as *oi aiones ton aionon,* to be but single instances of its use, occurs in the New Testament in one hundred and four instances; in thirty two of which it means a temporary duration. In seven, it may be taken in either the temporary or endless sense. In sixty-five, including six instances in which it is applied to future punishment, it plainly signifies an endless duration."

"The adjective *aionios* is found in seventy-one places in the whole New Testament; sixty-six, besides the five in which Dr. C*. allows it is applied to future punishment. In every one of the sixty-six instances except two it may, to say the least, be understood in the endless sense." If then, the word is applied to punishment five times, and to God, to his kingdom, to the Holy Ghost, to the happiness of the saints, and to other subjects sixty-six times, in sixty-four of which it may be understood in the endless sense, it is rational to understand it in this sense in the five instances in which it is applied to punishment, unless very strong reasons can be urged to the contrary.

2. The terms in question are used to express the duration of punishment, and the duration of the happiness of the saints, in the same connection, and sometimes in the same verse. Matt. xxv. 46. "These shall go away into *kolasin aionion,* everlasting punishment, but the righteous into *zoen aionion,* life eternal. The word *aionion* is here rendered everlasting in the first clause of the text, and *eternal* in the last clause, from which it must be seen that

---

* Dr. Chauncy, a universalist author.

the same word describes the duration both of the punishment and the life spoken of in the text. The question is, does this text speak of endless life? This cannot be doubted if the text refer at all to a future state, and that it does, we think, has been abundantly shown already. See Chap. V. Argument xv. If then *aionion* in this text, is to be understood in the endless sense in one case, it should undoubtedly be so understood in both cases. It would be absurd to suppose that the Saviour, in the same discourse, the same sentence, and with the same breath, used a word in two different senses, as far from each other, as finite is from infinite, without giving any intimation of the same. This in connection with the fact that the word *aionios* is frequently applied to the happiness of the saints, which ever stands opposed to the punishment of the wicked, furnishes, in our opinion, strong ground for understanding it in its proper and endless sense, when it describes the duration of punishment.

3. The peculiar connection in which *aionios* is used, when applied to punishment, requires that it be understood in its proper meaning in order to maintain the sense of the sacred text. Matt. xxv. 34, 41. "Then shall the king say to them on his right hand, inherit the kingdom prepared for you from the foundation of the world. Then shall he say unto them on his left hand, depart from me into *pur aionion*, everlasting fire." The wicked are here represented as being cast into *aionion*, fire, at the same time that the righteous are welcomed to the kingdom prepared from the foundation of the world; and being cast into the fire, and being received into the kingdom, stand opposed to each other. Now, as the one must be considered final and unalterable, so should the other; and if the righteous are always to possess the kingdom, then will the *aionion*, fire, be endless with the wicked. Mark iii. 29. "But he that shall blaspheme against the Holy Ghost hath never forgiveness but is in danger of *aionion*

kriseos, eternal damnation." Here the word *aionion*, rendered eternal, is shown to be used in its most unlimited and endless sense, by the connection in which it stands. In the text, forgiveness and damnation are opposed to each other; hence, as he who blasphemes against the Holy Ghost is not forgiven, he must be damned, and as he *"hath never forgiveness,"* he must be damned forever; he is therefore in danger of eternal damnation, *aionion kriseos*. We will now close this argument, which stands thus:

1. The proper and grammatical meaning of the original words rendered forever, everlasting and eternal, is endless, or always being or existing.

2. Words are always to be understood in their proper and grammatical sense unless the connection or nature of the subject require a different construction.

3. In the application of the terms in question to the punishment of the wicked, as they are thus applied in the scriptures, there is nothing in the nature of the subject or connection which requires that they should be understood in an accommodated sense, they must therefore be understood in their proper sense, which is endless; and hence, it follows that the scriptures teach the doctrine of endless punishment.

II. The scriptures describe the punishment of the wicked, and the salvation of the righteous in contrast, in a manner which shows that they are opposed to each other, so that those who are punished all their sins deserve cannot be saved. This point has been proved in Chapter IV. the whole of which goes to show that salvation implies a deliverance from the punishment which sin deserves. Now, if we have sustained the argument in the fourth chapter to which the reader is referred, which we think we have beyond all doubt, it must appear that there is an impassable gulf lying between the salvation of the righteous and the punishment of the wicked, and the point is settled, that such as are punished to the extent of the divine penalty, can never be saved; we shall not therefore repeat the arguments in this place, but simply introduce a few plain scriptural proofs to show that salvation and punishment are described in contrast. Matt. xxv. 46. "These shall go away into everlasting punishment, but the righteous into life eternal." That this text relates to a future state of being the reader will find ample proof in Argument xv. of the preceding chapter, and that the punishment of the wicked is here opposed to the salvation of the righteous, needs no proof, more than is apparent on the very face of the text. Do those who are said to go into everlasting punishment, go also into life eternal? Just as consistently might it be argued that those who go into life eternal will also go into everlasting punishment. If then those who go away into everlasting punishment, do not go into everlasting life, the contrast between the respective dooms of the righteous and wicked is marked as wide as the space between heaven and hell, and the punishment of the one will be as lasting as the eternal life of the other.

John iii. 16. "God so loved the world that he gave his only begotten Son, that whosoever believeth in him should not perish but have everlasting life." Here, perishing stands opposed to everlasting life, in a manner which clearly proves that those who perish do not have everlasting life, and that those who have everlasting life do not perish. Now, as perishing can mean nothing more nor less than the just punishment of sin, it follows that salvation and punishment are opposed to each other, so that if a man is punished for his sins all he deserves he cannot be saved. Rom. ii. 6, 7, 8. "Who will render to every man according to his deeds; to them who by patient continuance in well doing seek for glory and honor and immortality, eternal life. But unto them that are contentious and do not obey the truth, but obey unrighteousness, indignation and wrath." This text is decisive, as a few remarks must show to every unprejudiced mind.

1. A contrast is clearly drawn between the respective rewards of the saint and sinner: God "will render to every man according to his deeds;" and this reward will be to the righteous, *"eternal life,"* and to the wicked, *"indignation and wrath."* Now it cannot with any degree of propriety be maintained that those who are rewarded with *indignation and wrath* will also be rewarded with *eternal life*—this would be a contradiction of the Apostle's declaration; for he asserts that God will render to every man according to his deeds. He then states what reward will be in accordance with the deeds of both saint and sinner; that *eternal life* is in accordance with the deeds of the righteous, and that *indignation and wrath* are in accordance with the deeds of them that obey not the truth. To suppose that those who are worthy of indignation, will also receive eternal life, assigns to them a portion which is denied them by the apostle, and must be just as absurd as to suppose that those, who are worthy of eternal life, will also receive indignation and wrath. When the Apostle asserts that eternal life is according to the deeds of the righteous, and that indignation and wrath are according to the deeds of the wicked, he, in effect says, that indignation and wrath are not according to the deeds of the righteous, and that eternal life is not according to the deeds of the wicked. Now, God will render to every man according to his deeds, he will therefore never render eternal life to them that obey not the truth.

2. That this whole subject relates to the future destinies of men appears, not only from the fact that we have already proved that sin will be punished in the future world, but also from the phraseology of the text itself. To whom will God render eternal life? "To them who by patient continuance in well doing seek for *glory* and HONOUR and IMMORTALITY." Now, it cannot be supposed that

any enlightened christian seeks for immortality as a portion attainable in this world, and as they seek for glory and honor and immortality in the world to come, and as God will render to them according to their deeds, it follows that God will render to them eternal life in the future world, and that this eternal life involves the entire object of their pursuit, glory, and honour, and immortality. As the righteous will have rendered to them glory and honour, in a state of immortality in the future world, and as we have shown above that the wicked, who will receive indignation and wrath, in distinction from this reward, cannot also be made to partake thereof, it follows that such as are punished for their sins, the disobedient who receive according to their deeds, cannot be made holy and happy. Should it be supposed that the above implies that the wicked will not be rendered immortal, and hence that they will be annihilated, we deny the inference. The most that can be made of the above reasoning is, that the scriptural expression, *eternal life* implies glory and honour and immortality, and that the wicked will not enjoy this eternal life. All this we believe. The glory of the saint may consist in the fashion of his person, when his soul shall be cleansed from all sin, and his body be made like unto Christ's glorious body; and his honor may consist in the distinguished rank he shall have assigned him by his judge, while his immortality will confirm him in this state and rank, world without end. To deny this eternal life to the wicked does not deny their immortality, nor imply their annihilation; for they may be rendered immortal though they do not seek for immortality; and they may possess immortality though they do not possess with it glory and honour, which must be added to it to constitute eternal life in a scriptural sense. But their immortality, with deformity instead of glory, and disgrace instead of honour, will be their heavy curse. Many more scriptures of a similar character might be produced, in proof that the punishment of the wicked and the salvation of the righteous are directly opposed to each other: but we will close the argument by stating it in form.

1. Some men will be punished for their sins according to their deserts. This is a proposition too plain to be denied and has been already established.

2. Those who are punished for their sins according to their deserts, can never be saved. This is the contested proposition in the argument, and has been established not only by the above reasoning, but also by Chapter IV. the whole of which goes to confirm it.

Therefore there are some men who will never be saved, and the doctrine of universal salvation is proved to be false.

III. The scriptures teach that salvation is conditional, and therefore may be lost, by a non-compliance with the terms on which it is proffered. It cannot be denied that whatever is conditional may be lost; the proposition, therefore, which asserts the conditionality of salvation, is the only one in this argument about which there can be any dispute, and this we will attempt to prove.

1. We urge the doctrine of conditional salvation from man's moral agency. If man is a moral agent, and hence, capable of performing moral actions, it will follow from thence that something must be required of him in order to happiness, and salvation will appear conditional. But here also we have to confront the objections of universalists, for they, or many of them, deny the doctrine of moral agency, and assert the doctrine of fate. Now, as we wish to take nothing for granted which our opponents deny, we will here insert a few arguments in favor of moral agency, and against the opposite doctrine of fate.

1st. If a man is not a moral agent, that is, free in his volitions, he cannot be the subject of a moral government. To constitute a proper subject of a moral government, man must be capable of moral actions, and in order to render an action moral, it must be performed voluntarily or from choice, under circumstances which would admit of its being otherwise. The circumstance that a man acts freely or from choice, does not, in our view, constitute moral liberty, or give moral quality to action, unless the actor be capable, at the same time, of making a different choice, and of acting differently. Now, as none but moral actions can be recognized by a righteous moral law, none but moral beings, as above defined, can be made the subjects of moral discipline. Taking this view, we see that if man is not a moral agent, he cannot be the subject of a moral government, and, so far as relates to man, God cannot be a moral ruler—cannot maintain a moral government over this world.

2d. If man is not a moral agent, is not free in his volitions, he cannot be accountable for what he does, cannot be either punishable or rewardable for his conduct. To deny the doctrine of man's moral agency, not only annihilates the orthodox hell, but also the restorationist's hell of limited duration, and the universalist's hell of a horrible conscience. If men were not free in their actions there could be no hell of conscience, for nothing is more clear, than that a man can never feel condemnation for having done what he could not have refrained from doing, or for having left undone, what he could not have done; hence, if man is not free in his volitions, whatever the ignorant may feel, who do not know they are mere machines, universalists, who know the truth on this subject, can feel no condemnation let their conduct be what it may, if so be that they are not free to do differently from what they do.

3d. If man is not a moral agent he is not a sinner, and there can be no such thing as sin [in] the world, or, if there is, God must be its author. There can be no sin without a violation of the moral law, and in order to convict a man of violating a law, it must first appear that he had power to have obeyed it, which supposes that the sinner might have done differently, and if so, this is the very point for which we contend. This view shows that man is a moral agent, or else, that he is not a sinner. The will of God is the highest authority in the universe, therefore there can be no sin without a violation of this supreme law, the will of the Creator; but if man is not a moral agent—is not free in his volitions, his actions must be just as his Creator designed they should be, his will therefore is not violated in any thing which man performs; hence, the very notion of sin vanishes.

4th. If man is not free in his volitions, if he has not power to do differently from what he does, all the precepts, promises and threatenings, which the scriptures so pointedly address to his conscience, his understanding and his interests, are a mere hoax. If man cannot do differently from what he does, why do the scriptures point him to a path different from the one in which he treads, saying, this is the way, walk in it? Why do they hold over his head the darkening thunderbolts of divine wrath, to check his vanity and damp his worldly joys; or open upon his vision through the promises of the gospel, the glories of the throne, to allure him to the skies? Why do the scriptures enjoin the duty of repentance, promise pardon, and talk so much of renewing grace, if man has done in all things just as God intended he should do? These things can never be accounted for, only on the principle that man is a moral agent.

5th. To deny man's moral agency, and suppose God to be the efficient cause of all his actions, is to set the Author of the Bible at variance with his own word, and make him appear insincere in most of the declarations of his will concerning us.

It cannot be denied that God has declared it to be his

will that we should do many things which we do not, and that it is his will that we should not do many things which we do. Now, these things are his will, or they are not. If they are not his will, then God is insincere in the declarations of his will concerning us; he has not in such case given us his real will in the Bible: hence his will appears to be one thing and his word another, and they are opposed to each other. On the other hand if these things, which God has commanded, and which we do not, are his will, then man's actions are opposed to the will of God, and if so, he does not govern us absolutely, and cannot be the cause of those actions, which are opposed to his will, unless it be said that God is opposed to his own will!

6th. Every man's conscience tells him that he acts freely, and that he is capable of acting differently from what he does. It may be possible for men to consult their own heads or their imaginations, and think that they are governed by some unseen hand of fate, but if they will consult their consciences, they will receive an answer that will cause them to feel that they are moral agents, and that they are the authors of their own actions. Did the reader ever hear the soul cheering whisper of an approving conscience, for having done his duty; for having performed an act of virtue or benevolence? Why this placid smile of the soul? Why this internal pleasure? Why does the soul smile on herself when acts are performed which the judgment approves, if she does not consider herself the author of her own conduct? Did the reader ever feel the sting of a guilty conscience for having done wrong? Why this sense of guilt? Why does the soul turn and goad herself, and obscure her light by the darkness of her own frown, when something has been done which the judgment pronounces wrong, if she does not consider herself the author of her own deeds?

7th. All men confirm the doctrine of man's moral agency by the plaudits and censures which they so bountifully bestow upon their fellows around them. All men have their notions of right and wrong; the one they applaud, and the other they censure; and this is common to all ranks, from the throne to the humble seat of the beggar. Why do kings complain of each other, and from off their thrones hurl the thunderbolts of war, if they do not consider each other free in their actions? Why does neighbour complain of neighbour for his conduct? Why does the beggar by the way side complain of the penuriousness of the passers-by, if he supposes God or fate controls their wills as absolutely as their wills control their own purse strings? There is no way to dispose of these things, only to say that they are all under the government of the same fate, that the man who complains is no more free than the one of whom he complains, and that he cannot therefore help complaining of his fellow, though he knows at the same time that the conduct of which he complains could not have been prevented. This ground was once taken by a universalist in publick controversy with the writer of these pages. This view makes the same predestination operate equally upon both sides of the warring elements of this world of mind and passion; and all the mind and muscle, that have been engaged, when truth and error have struggled; when individuals have wrestled in single combat, and nation strove with nation, have been mere instruments in the hand of God with which he has been contending with himself. How far such notions come short of the old heathen doctrine that there exist in Deity a good and evil principle, which are the respective sources of all the good and evil in the world, we leave the candid reader to judge.

We think we have now shown, though very briefly in comparison with what might be said on the subject, that man is a moral agent; we will therefore proceed to bring the doctrine to bear on the conditionality of salvation. God having created man a moral agent, it is reasonable to suppose that he will not, that he cannot, consistently, govern or save him only through a due exercise of his moral liberty. When God created man a moral agent, he must have designed that he should exercise his moral liberty, and that he should exercise it in a right way, and that all this should lead to a proper end; hence, if there is any connection between the means which God institutes, and the end which he proposes, it must appear essential for man to exercise his moral liberty, or to improve on his moral powers in a proper way, in order to secure his own happiness. Now, if man, as a moral agent, is obliged to put forth his moral powers in a particular direction in order to secure his own happiness, his salvation must be a matter of conditionality. The following series of propositions will lead us to the same conclusions:

1st. Man being a moral agent, or, as some express themselves, a free agent, which with us means the same thing, he cannot be saved only through his own consent or choice of his own free will.

2d. As man can be saved only through his own consent or choice of his own free will, salvation, so far as choosing or refusing, accepting or rejecting is concerned, depends upon man's own choice or act.

3d. As salvation depends, in the above sense, upon man's own choice or act, it is conditional bey6nd all dispute.

If we have succeeded in establishing the doctrine of man's moral agency, we see that the conditionality of his salvation follows as a matter of course. But we will not rest the proposition on this one argument, founded on man's moral agency, but proceed by remarking,

2. If salvation is not conditional, then it cannot be the sinner's own fault that he is not saved now, nor can any reason be given why he is not now saved, unless it be said that God is not able or willing to save him. If salvation is not conditional it follows that the sinner can do nothing to induce salvation, on one hand, or to prevent it

on the other; it cannot therefore be his fault that he does not now enjoy the salvation of God. And on this principle, the cause why man is not saved now is not to be found in the sinner, nor can he by any thing he can do, ever render himself any more the subject of salvation than he now is. Why then are not sinners now saved? If it be said, because God cannot now save them, we ask when will he be more able to save than at the present time? And if it be said that God is able but is not now willing to save, we reply, if he is immutable he will never be more willing than he now is, since, if salvation is not conditional, no change nor work on the part of the sinner can take place which can be urged hereafter as a reason for a different procedure on the part of the divine administration. Such are the fatal conclusions to which a denial of the conditionality of salvation must lead, while our theory of moral agency, and a conditional salvation is unincumbered [sic] by such consequences. Man being a moral agent and salvation being conditional, the sinner may always find the reason in himself why he is not saved.

3. If salvation it not conditional, and yet certain, it follows, that to be the greatest sinner, is to secure the greatest salvation! This conclusion cannot be denied; and we do not know that universalists wish to deny it— perhaps they will glory in so grand a consequence of their doctrine; but we will submit it to the candid reader whether or not it is consistent with reason and the word of God, and tends to the moral restraint and improvement of mankind. But the scriptures shall settle the question of the conditionality of salvation.

4. The scriptures speak on this subject too plain to be misunderstood or misapplied. A few quotations however must suffice. Matt. xix. 16, 17. "And behold one came and said unto him, good master, what good thing shall I do that I may have eternal life? And he said unto him, if thou wilt enter into life keep the commandments." Mark

xvi. 16. "He that believeth and is baptised shall be saved, and he that believeth not shall be damned." John iii. 36. "He that believeth on the Son hath everlasting life, and he that believeth not the Son shall not see life." Rev. ii. "Be thou faithful unto death and I will give thee a crown of life." John vi. 40. "This is the will of him that sent me, that every one, which seeth the Son and believeth on him may have everlasting life," Verse 47. "Verily, verily I say unto you he that believeth on me hath everlasting life." John v. 40. "Ye will not come unto me that ye might have life." John iii. 14, 15. "So must the son of man be lifted up, that whosoever believeth in him should not perish but have everlasting life." Rev. iii. 5. "He that overcometh shall be clothed in white raiment, and I will not blot out his name out of the book of life, but I will confess his name before my Father and before his angels." Verse 21. "To him that overcometh will I grant to sit with me on my throne, even as I also overcame and am set down with my Father on his throne." The above quotations abundantly show that salvation, eternal and everlasting life, crown of life, the robe of white, an acknowledgment of our discipleship before the Father and his angels, interest in the book of life, and a seat with Christ in his throne are conditionally promised in the scriptures, and if these do not express the final salvation of men, we know not in the use of what expressions and figures the ultimate salvation, even of any, is taught in the Bible. We think we have now proved that salvation is conditional. This argument may be thus stated.

1. Whatever is conditional may be lost, or forfeited by a non-compliance with the conditions on which it is suspended.

2. Salvation is conditional, and therefore it may be forfeited and lost; and if the sinner can forfeit the salvation of his soul, and come short of the interest he has in the gospel by a non-compliance with its condi-

tions, the doctrine of the certain salvation of all men cannot be true, and the endless punishment of a portion of the human family, such as do not comply with the conditions of the Gospel, is certain, unless a shelter is sought from it in the absurd doctrine of annihilation, which has neither reason nor scripture for its support; and even in such an alternative the doctrine of universal salvation must be given up.

IV. The scriptures teach that there is a possibility and even danger of coming short of salvation. Heb. iv. 1. "Let us therefore fear, lest a promise being left us of entering into his rest, any of you should seem to come short of it." On this text Dr. A. Clark remarks thus: "Seeing the Israelites lost the rest of Canaan through obstinacy and unbelief, let us be afraid, lest we come short of the heavenly rest through the same cause." Heb xii. 15. "Looking diligently lest any man fail of the grace of God." On this text Mr. Morse in his reply to Mr. Parker, page 15, has given the following comment. "The apostle left out one word which should have been inserted, if he meant to state any thing to Mr. P's. purpose—that word is *endlessly*. If the Apostle had said 'lest any man endlessly fail of the grace of God,' we should be obliged in candor to admit it as evidence of never ending wo. As it is, it affords no such evidence." In reply to this very extraordinary comment we say.

1. Mr. M. has laid down a rule of evidence here which, if applied to his own theory will ruin it forever. According to his remark, "*endless wo*" cannot be proved without the use of the word *endless*, and if so, endless salvation is not taught in the scriptures: there is not a blessing promised in all the Bible in the use of the word endless. To place this matter in a clear point of light, we will apply Mr. M's own words to the promise of God, which he quotes, and on which he much relies. On page 10, he quotes the promise of God made to Abraham, as repeated,

Acts iii. 25. "In thy seed shall all the kindreds of the earth be blessed." Now, hear Mr. M. "The apostle," (God in this instance,) "left out one word which should have been inserted if he meant to state any thing to" Mr. M's "purpose—that word is *endlessly*. If the Apostle," (God in this case,) "had said, in thy seed shall all the kindreds of the earth be endlessly blessed, we should be obliged in candor to admit it as evidence of never ending" happiness. "As it is, it affords no such evidence." Mr. M's remarks will apply equally well to every other promise which can be adduced in proof of universal salvation.

2. Mr. M's pert remark may be retorted upon himself in view of the same text which gave rise to it, thus: "Had the Apostle said, lest any man fail of the grace of God" for a season, for life, or for a limited period in eternity, "we should be obliged in candor to admit" that it furnishes no "evidence of endless wo." As it is, it furnishes clear evidence. In the text, nothing is said of times or seasons, but the expression is unqualified, "lest any man fail of the grace of God." Now, no man, who is saved by grace forever, can be said unqualifiedly to fail of that grace by which he is saved. Mr. M. farther remarks on this text thus: "Every rational being must perceive that there is a great difference between failing of the grace of God at any particular time, and failing of that grace, finally." This is no doubt correct, and we presume also that they will perceive that as nothing is said in the text of *"any particular time"* the apostle warns them against failing of the grace of God *"finally and eternally."* The expression, "lest any man fail of the grace of God, unconnected as it is, with any reference to a particular time or period, clearly implies that the failure is a final one; and for Mr. M. to take it for granted that the Apostle had reference to some temporary or limited period only, is no better than to beg the whole question at issue.

2. Cor. vi. 1. "We then as workers together with him,

beseech you also that ye receive not the grace of God in vain."

By referring to the closing words of the preceding chapter, we shall see what is meant by the grace of God in this text. "Now then we are ambassadors for Christ as though God did beseech you by us, we pray you in Christ's stead be ye reconciled to God; for he hath made him to be sin," (a sin offering,) "for us, who knew no sin, that we might be made the righteousness of God in him. We then beseech you also that ye receive not the grace of God in vain." From this connection we see that by the grace of God is meant, the grace of reconciliation whereby we are *"reconciled to* God," which is the proper benefit of the atonement or of Christ's being made an offering for our sin. The benefits of the atonement then, may be received in vain, that is, those for whom it was made, to whom the word of reconciliation is preached, who for a time receive this grace, may, after all, fail to be ultimately benefitted by it. Now we have shown in Chapter III. that the death of Jesus Christ was an offering for sinners, by virtue of which, and by which only, they can be saved; hence, as it is here shown that they may come short of the benefits of his offering for them, it follows that in such case they must be lost for ever. The text under consideration clearly teaches that we may receive the grace of God in vain; and can any one, who receives the grace of God in vain, nevertheless be saved by that grace? Or can any one, who is saved forever by grace, still receive such grace in vain? It is impossible. Should it be said by universalists that the sinner may receive certain gift of grace in vain, and then be saved by after and more abundant gifts, or that he may receive the grace of God in vain for a season, and then be saved by grace afterwards, we reply that such a position would be fatal to the doctrine of the certain salvation of all men. If any portion of the grace of God can be received in vain, another portion may, and all on the same principle. Or if the sinner may receive the grace of God in vain for a season, on the same principle he may receive it in vain longer, and forever. As sinners can be saved only by grace. if such grace can be received in vain, they may come short of salvation forever; we see therefore that this text is fatal to universalism, for it clearly teaches that the grace of God may be received in vain. The apostle would not have besought the Corinthians not to receive the grace of God in vain if there can be no such thing—if the thing is in itself impossible.

Matt. vii. 13, 14. "Enter ye in at the strait gate, for wide is the gate and broad is the way that leadeth to destruction and many there be that go in thereat; because strait is the gate and narrow is the way that leadeth unto life, and few there be that find it." On this text Dr. Clarke among other remarks has the following: "Our Saviour seems to allude here to the distinction between the publick and private ways mentioned by the Jewish lawyers. The publick roads were allowed to be sixteen cubits broad, the private ways only four. Enter in (to the kingdom of heaven) through THIS strait gate of *doing to every one as you would he should do unto you,* for this alone appears to be the *strait gate* which our Lord alludes to. With those who say, it means repentance and forsaking of sin, I can have no controversy. That is certainly a *gate,* and a *strait* one too, through which every sinner must turn to God in order to find salvation. Gate among the Jews signifies metaphorically the entrance, introduction, or means of acquiring any thing. So they talk of the gate of repentance, the gate of prayers, and the gate of tears. When God, say they, shut the gate of paradise against Adam, he opened to him the gate of repentance." On the expression, "broad is the gate," the Doctor says, "a spacious roomy place, that leadeth forward into that destruction, meaning eternal misery." There is no necessity or room for controversy about the meaning of the term gate, as used in this text, for it must be obvious to all that it here has reference to our moral characters and conduct; nor is it on the meaning of the word gate that the strength of the argument depends, but on the meaning of the terms *life* and *destruction* as used in this text. The text informs us that there are two gates or ways, that is, two courses of moral conduct pursued by man, that one of these, the strait gate, leads to *life*, and the other, the broad gate, to *destruction*. What then is to be understood by life and destruction? If these refer to the rewards and punishments of a future state, the question is settled that the text teaches that there is danger of coming short of salvation, for as these two gates are opposed to each other, if one leads to endless life, the other, of course leads to endless destruction. Now, that the text really speaks of that eternal life which will be conferred on the righteous in a future state, appears as follows. The text cannot be true in relation to any temporal blessing. It most clearly teaches that the strait gate, by which we must understand a course of duty and virtue, leads to life. Now, suppose we understand natural life, and by the opposite destruction, natural death, and the text is false, for there is no gate, strait or broad, that leads to life in this sense. This would make the text say that sin leads to the death of the body, and that duty and virtue, the strait gate, lead to exemption from the death of the body, to an earthly immortality, which every one knows to be false. Nor will it relieve the difficulty to suppose that the text refers to the destruction of the Jews; for, keeping temporal life and death in view, the text is still untrue in this sense. The Jews were not all slain—did not experience temporal death, though it must be admitted that those who were captured by the Romans passed the wide gate and pursued the broad road. On the other hand many of the christians perished before the overthrow of the Jews. Stephen was stoned, and James was slain with the sword, and many others perished, if by perishing temporal death be meant in the text; though it cannot be denied that every true christian entered in at the strait gate, and pursued the narrow way which leadeth unto life. We see then, that by life, to which the strait gate leads, we cannot understand natural life, or the life of the body; and by destruction to which the wide gate leads, we cannot understand natural death, or the death of the body. Nor will it afford any relief to understand these terms in a very highly figurative sense, as expressing prosperity on one hand, and a state of calamity and affliction on the other, for the text is no more true in this sense than in the preceding one. To sustain this view, it must be made to appear that the strait gate, that is, the path of duty and piety, always leads to prosperity; and that the wide gate, that is, the way of sin and unbelief, always leads to calamity and distress in this life, neither of which is true. It cannot be denied that many of the pious in all ages of the world, who have entered in at the strait gate, (if this is a work common to the righteous, which cannot be contradicted,) have, notwithstanding, endured the deepest afflictions, and most distressing calamities to which flesh can be heir in this world; hence, if by life any temporal prosperity is meant, in opposition to affliction and distress, the strait gate does not lead to life, and therefore the text cannot be true. On the other hand, many, who pursue the broad way of sin, are, notwithstanding, so prosperous as to have it said of them that they receive their "good things," that they "have their portion in this life." If then misfortunes and suffering in this life, are meant by destruction, the broad way does not certainly lead to destruction, whereas Christ declares that it does. What life is meant then in the text? We answer, it must be that "eternal life" which God will "render to those who through patient continuance in well doing seek for glory and honour and immortality." In other words, this life is that blessing to which duty and virtue will conduct us. Nor can this be disposed of by saying, as universalists often assert, that this is the blessing which the obedient enjoy in this world, as the fruit of their piety, for their piety is the way which leads to the life—"strait is the gate and narrow is the way which leadeth unto life:" the strait gate must be passed, and the narrow way must be kept as the means of coming at this life, which is represented as lying at the end of the way; hence, whatever is meant by entering in at the strait gate and passing the narrow way, it is a work which must be performed before we can arrive at life, and as by this work nothing less can be meant than the proper duties of the present state, the blessing must be at the end of life's career, and the strait gate and the narrow way that *lead to life*, will conduct us to that life which shall be enjoyed when the pilgrim's footsteps shall take hold upon the realities of the future world. Now, as the strait gate leads to *endless life*, in the future world, then, the wide gate and the broad way, which are opposed thereto, and which do not lead to the same place, must conduct those who enter, to endless destruction and misery, and Christ says, "many go in thereat." The text, then, clearly teaches that there is danger of coming short of salvation. This view is further sustained by Luke, xiii. 24. "Strive to enter in at the strait gate, for many, I say unto you, shall seek to enter in and shall not be able." On this text Mr. Morse, in his vindication of universalism in reply to Mr. Parker's Lectures, page 5, has given the following paraphrase as expressing its true meaning.

"Strive to enter into the gospel dispensation, for at a particular time many Jews will seek to enter in and shall not be able, because they strive to enter through the Mosaic Law." This certainly is making the text speak what it does not speak of itself. This paraphrase we consider defective in the following particulars.

1. The application which it makes of the text to an entry, into the gospel dispensation is wholly assumed: the text says nothing of entering into the gospel dispensation. If by the strait gate, the christian religion, with its high and holy privileges and duties, be understood, we will not contend, for this we believe to be the way to eternal life, for which we should strive; but that Christ here exhorts to strive to enter into the gospel dispensation, in distinction from the Jews and heathen who are without the pale of the gospel church, with exclusive reference to the present life, is wholly unfounded.

2. Mr. M's expression, "enter into the gospel dispensation," is unmeaning, or at least unintelligible. What is the gospel dispensation? Dispensation is the act of dealing out any thing; hence, the gospel dispensation is that method of dealing with us, which God has revealed in the gospel, and that distribution of the divine favors which God makes through the gospel. Now we ask how can a man enter into the gospel dispensation, that is, enter into the method of dealing with us revealed in, or the blessing dispensed through, the gospel? We may be under this dispensation, we may receive the revelation which the gospel makes of God's gracious dispensation, or we may enjoy the blessings which are dispensed through the gospel; but to tell of entering into the gospel dispensation is to talk without saying any thing. What does Mr. M. mean by striving to enter into. the gospel dispensation? Does he mean that an effort should be made to receive the gospel, believe the gospel, or to obey the gospel? Why did he not say so? We should have then understood him.

3. Mr. M's exposition of this subject makes the gospel dispensation comprise no more than temporal blessings. The expression, "strive to enter in at the strait gate," &c. was spoken as an answer to a question which was asked, "are there few that be saved." On this question Mr. M. says, "it is plain that he who asked the question 'are there few that be saved,' had his mind upon temporal salvation—and our Saviour's answer was adapted to the condition of the enquirer's mind." This makes the conversation stand thus: Are there few that be saved with a temporal salvation? And he said strive to enter into the gospel dispensation. Now if, as Mr. M. says, "our Saviour's answer was adapted to the condition of the enquirer's mind" it follows that the gospel is a dispensation of temporal blessings.

4. Mr. M's paraphrase makes the text speak an untruth, by saying that "at a particular time many Jews shall seek to enter into the gospel dispensation and shall not be able, because they strive to enter through the Mosaic law." The truth is, the Jews have never sought "to enter into the gospel dispensation" in any way, nor is it now probable that they ever will make an ineffectual effort to become christians. The door of the gospel church has always been open to the Jews, and will be until they shall be brought in with the fullness of the gentiles.

5. The reason which Mr. M. assigns why they shall not be able to enter, is assumed, absurd in itself, and contrary to the plain sense and spirit of the text. He says "many Jews will seek to enter in," (to the gospel dispensation,) "and shall not be able *because they strive to enter through the Mosaic law.*" This is assumed because there is nothing said or intimated in the text about the Mosaic law. It is absurd in itself, because it supposes the Jews to seek to become christians with their peculiar adherence to the law of Moses. No Jew can be supposed to strive to enter into the gospel dispensation, until he is convinced

that the gospel is true; and no Jew, when convinced that the gospel is true, can maintain his peculiar attachment to the law of Moses, and therefore cannot seek to enter into the gospel dispensation through the Mosaic law. The Jews may seek to enter into heaven, or into the enjoyment of salvation and not be able, because they seek it through the Mosaic law; but it is not possible to conceive that they can seek to enter into the gospel dispensation through this medium. We can just as easily suppose that they wish to be christians while they are Jews, ana wish to be Jews while they are christians; or that they are, in point of belief, Jews while they are christians at the same time This reason is contrary to the plain sense and spirit of the text in two respects, and as this is an essential point we will note it distinctly.

1st. The exhortation, "strive to enter in," is founded on the fact that "many will seek to enter in and shall not be able," which would be no good reason for such an exhortation if they were unable only in consequence of striving in a wrong way. This makes our Saviour say, *strive*, because many of you Jews will *strive wrong*. Because others *misdirect their efforts* is no reason why I should *make an effort*, but only a reason why I should be sure *to give mine a proper direction*, provided I make one; but if others fail of an important object, *because they are not sufficiently engaged*, it is a good reason why I should be more engaged and *strive*.

2d. The text clearly implies another reason, why we should, strive to enter in, than that assigned by Mr. M.; Christ says "strive to enter in, because many shall seek to enter in and shall not be able." Here is a clear distinction marked between *striving* and *seeking*: striving implying the greater effort. Now, if many who seek, fail because they are not sufficiently engaged, for want of a sufficient effort, it is a good reason why we should strive. We think we have now shown that Mr. M's exposition of this text is entirely unfounded, that it involves as many absurdities as it contains distinct expressions; and it must appear that a system that requires such an absurd exposition, to dispose of as plain a text as the one under consideration, must be a system of absurdities. But we have yet our own reasons to give for believing that this text has a bearing on the future destinies of men.

As the text was spoken in answer to the question, "are there few that be saved?" (a strange question for a universalist to ask,) the sense of the text must be determined by the nature of the salvation, concerning which the enquiry was made. "Are there few that be saved?" This Mr. M. says relates to temporal salvation, which we deny. Now, on the ground that it is a temporal salvation, to what does it allude? Are there few that be saved? How, or from what? There is but one event to which this question can be referred if a temporal salvation be intended, and that is the escape of the christians at the destruction of Jerusalem. This is the rallying point of universalism in the explanation of every text that speaks of judgment or punishment, or that implies them. If it does not relate to this, there is no temporal salvation, of which we have any knowledge, to which it can relate. Now, that it does not relate to this event, we think, will appear as follows: The question, "are there few that be saved?" was asked by one who believed the gospel as preached by Jesus Christ, or by one who did not believe it. If it was asked by one who believed the gospel, then he had already entered into the gospel dispensation, to use Mr. M's language, and to such an one, "Christ would not have said strive to enter into the gospel dispensation," as he supposes. It would be highly absurd to suppose Christ bade one who had already entered into the gospel dispensation to strive to enter in because some who had not entered in, should at a particular time be unable to enter in. It is clear then that if the question was asked by one who had already embraced the gospel, Mr. M's exposition cannot be true. And if the question was asked by one who did not believe the gospel, it cannot refer to the destruction of Jerusalem or the salvation of christians from that destruction; for no unbelieving Jew would ask such a question, in relation to this event, for in their view no such event was to take place. We see, then, that Christ would not have answered a disciple thus, in relation to this event, the destruction of Jerusalem; and none but a disciple would have asked such a question in relation to this event, therefore, the question cannot relate to this subject. We hence conclude that the salvation, concerning which the inquiry was made, is that with which Christ came to save the lost, and that the answer, "strive to enter in at the strait gate" implies that personal effort which we have to make for ourselves in order to secure eternal salvation, as saith the Apostle. 1 Tim. vi. 12. "Fight the good fight of faith, lay hold on eternal life;" and if this be the meaning of the text, it clearly teaches that there is danger of coming short of salvation.

1 Cor. ix. 27. "But I keep under my body and bring it into subjection, lest after I have preached to others, I myself should be a castaway." The only question on which there need be any controversy, in relation to this text, is, What does the Apostle mean by being a *castaway?* That he contemplates some evil or punishment in this expression, cannot be doubted, but the question is, what is this evil? That it could not be the loss of character or fortune that he feared is evident, for these he had already sacrificed at the altar of Christianity. Nor could it have been the temporal judgments which befel his nation that he feared, for he so perfectly understood this coming event that there could have been no necessity of his suffering himself to be surrounded in Jerusalem by the Roman army. We say then that St. Paul feared being a castaway by coming short of a crown of glory in the future world,

which is evident from the connection. Take the last three verses in the connection and this is the only consistent construction that it will bear. The Apostle refers to the publick games, in which men contended for a prize, from which he takes occasion to advert to the effort which the christian should make for an immortal prize. He says "every man that striveth for the mastery is temperate in all things. Now they do it to obtain a corruptible crown, but we an incorruptible. I therefore run, not as uncertainly, so fight I, not as one that beateth the air, but I keep under my body lest after I have preached to others, I myself should be a castaway." From this it is clear that the apostle was contending for an INCORRUPTIBLE CROWN, and that by being a castaway he meant being rejected as not having won this immortal prize; hence, it is clear that St. Paul really supposed that there was danger of his coming short of salvation, and that he acted in view of this danger, really contending in his christian and ministerial career for an incorruptible crown. Universalism confines every motive, and the consequences of every act, to a period which lies this side of our final destiny, but from this subject we see that the Apostle's motives were more lofty, lifting his aspiring soul to the unfading glories of the heavenly world. This class of proof texts might be multiplied to almost any extent, but as we have extended our remarks on those already adduced to such a length, we shall add no more on this point. We think we have now clearly shown that the scriptures teach that there is a possibility and even danger of coming short of salvation, and if so, the doctrine of the certain salvation of all men cannot be true, and the doctrine of endless punishment follows of course.

V. The scriptures teach that sinners can and do actually resist the means which God employs to bring them to repentance and salvation, and if the means of salvation are resisted, their object is defeated and the unyielding soul cannot be saved. No reliance can be placed upon any means or mode of salvation, only such as are revealed in the scriptures, and if it can be shown that these means are all resisted by some sinners, it will be clear that the salvation of all men cannot be proved as a matter of certainty, and that the endless punishment of such as do resist is, to say the least, a possible issue. The only debatable question, in this argument, is, whether or not the means which God employs to bring sinners to salvation may be resisted, and rendered ineffectual by the sinner, and this point we propose, to prove from the declarations of God's own word. So far as God has revealed his own modes of operation, (and no argument can be founded on what he has not revealed,) the following are the principal means which he employs to reclaim and save sinners, viz. the force of truth, the striving of the Holy Spirit, the influence of mercies, and the restraining force of judgments or punishment, all of which are sometimes resisted.

1. The sinner resists the force of truth, and thereby renders the word preached ineffectual, so far as any saving benefit accruing to himself, is concerned. The prophet exclaims, Isa. liii. 1. "Who hath believed our report, and to whom is the arm of the Lord revealed?" The Apostle declares, Heb. iv. 2. "The word preached did not profit them, not being mixed with faith in them that heard it." iii. 16. "For some when they had heard did provoke." Acts xiii. 46. "Then Paul and Barnabas said, it was necessary that the word of God should first have been spoken to you, but seeing you put it from you and judge yourselves unworthy of everlasting life, lo, we turn to the Gentiles." Here the unbelieving Jews are said to put the word of God from them, which clearly proves that they resisted its influence. 2. Tim. iii. 8. "Now, as Jannes and Jambres withstood Moses so do these resist the truth." Matt. xiii. 58. "And he did not many mighty works there because of their unbelief." Matt. xxiii. 37. "How often would I

have gathered thy children together but ye would not." These quotations clearly show that sinners do resist the force of divine truth as brought to view in the gospel of the Son of God. This truth indeed is matter of every day's experience, with universalists as well as others; for notwithstanding the boasted reasonableness and attractive charms of their theory, which they pretend to be commissioned from God to preach, to the overthrow of superstition and priestcraft, they after all find as much difficulty as others in bringing community under the influence of their doctrines. This could not be the case, if they are right, did not men resist the force of divine truth.

2. Men resist the strivings of the Holy Spirit. Isa. lxiii. 10. "But they rebelled and vexed his Holy Spirit." 1 Thess. v. 19. "Quench not the spirit." Eph. iv. 30. "Grieve not the Holy Spirit of God." Acts vii. 51. "Ye do always resist the Holy Ghost." These quotations show that men vex, quench, grieve, and resist the Holy Spirit.

3. Men resist the influence of divine mercy. This is implied in the preceding remarks, for as men resist the force of truth and the influence of the spirit, in so doing, they, resist the influence of divine mercy; for the gospel, and the influence of the spirit are mercy's own gifts. But a few other instances shall be adduced. Isa. v. 4. "What could have been done more to my vineyard that I have not done in it? Wherefore when I looked that it should bring forth grapes, brought it forth wild grapes." This text teaches, beyond all dispute, that the mercies bestowed upon the Jewish nation, did not effect their intended object. The dying prayer of our crucified Redeemer for his wicked murderers, Luke xxiii. 34. was a most striking display of divine mercy and compassion, and yet it failed to melt down their hard hearts. Nothing can be more plain than that goodness and mercy have followed sinners all their days; sinners who have lived in sin and blasphemy, and died unreformed. That sinners do resist the influence of

divine mercy, and rebel against the filial regard of the hand that formed them, God himself bears testimony while he calls heaven and earth to witness the astonishing fact. Isa. i. 2. "Hear, O heavens! and give ear, O earth! for the Lord hath spoken; I have nourished and brought up children and they have rebelled against me."

4. Sinners sometimes resist and harden themselves under the dispensation of divine punishment. Rev. xvi. 9. "And men were scorched with great heat, and blasphemed the name of God which hath power over these plagues, and they repented not to give him glory." Verse 11. "And men blasphemed the God of heaven because of their pains, and repented not of their deeds." Verse 21. "And men blasphemed God because of the plague of the hail, for the plague thereof was exceeding great" We have now shown that sinners do sometimes resist all the principal means which God employs to bring them to repentance and salvation, and hence, the salvation of all men cannot be certain, on one hand, while, on the other hand, the endless punishment of those who resist the means of their salvation, is the roost probable issue.

VI. The scriptures teach that there will come a time when it will be too late to seek and obtain salvation. Gen. vi. 3. "And the Lord said, my spirit shall not always strive with man." That the influence of the divine spirit is essential to salvation cannot be doubted by any who believe the Bible, and yet sinners are threatened with a withdrawal of this spirit, in which case it must be forever too late to seek salvation. On this text Dr. Clark remarks as follows: "It was only by the influence of the spirit of God that the carnal mind could be subdued and destroyed: but those who wilfully resisted and grieved this spirit, must be ultimately left to the hardness and blindness of their own hearts." Psa. xxxii. 6. "For this shall every one that is godly pray unto thee in a time when thou mayest be found" This text clearly implies that there will come a time when God will not be found; hence, we read, Isa. lv. 6. "Seek ye the Lord while he may be found, call ye upon him while he is near." An exhortation to seek God, "*while he may be found,*" most clearly supposes that a time is coming when he will not be found; and to "*call while he is near,*" supposes that a time is coming when he will not be near. In accordance with this we read, Prov. i. 24, 26, 28. "Because I have called and ye refused, I have stretched out my hand and no man regarded; I also will laugh at your calamity, I will mock when your fear cometh; then shall they call upon me but I will not answer, they shall seek me early but shall not find me." Chap. v. 11. "And thou mourn at the last, when thy flesh and thy body is consumed." Isa. xxxviii. 18. "For the grave cannot praise thee, death cannot celebrate thee: they that go down into the pit cannot hope for thy truth." Whether the word, here rendered pit, signifies the grave or hell itself, will not alter the nature of the evidence, which the text furnishes, in proof that there will come a time when it will be too late to seek salvation. If they that go down into the grave cannot hope for the truth of God, it follows that the only time and place in which we have the proffers of divine truth, and consequently of salvation, are in this world, and that those who reject the truth of God in this life, and descend to the grave in unbelief cannot hope for the renewal of its proffers in the world to come. 2. Cor. vi. 2. "For he saith, I have heard thee in a time acceptable, and in the day of salvation have I succored thee; behold, now is the accepted time, behold, now is the day of salvation." This most clearly implies that the accepted time and day of salvation are limited, and that a time is coming which will not be accepted, and which will not be a day of salvation. What then is the accepted time, and day of salvation? We answer the time of preaching the gospel, as the apostle says, at the close of the preceding chapter, of himself and all other true gospel ministers, "we are embassadors [sic] for Christ, as though God did beseech you by us, we pray you in Christ's stead, be ye reconciled to God." Now, while this ministry of reconciliation is holding forth in the name of God, offering terms of peace to rebel man, is the accepted time and day of salvation; and this closes with each individual sinner at death, and will close with all sinners at the end of time, when all the watchmen shall be gathered in from Zion's walls, and all sinners be called to an account. Heb. iii. 13. "But exhort one another while it is called to-day, lest any of you be hardened through the deceitfulness of sin." Verse 15. "While it is said, to-day, if you will hear his voice harden not your hearts as in the provocation." By the expression, *"to-day,"* in these passages are understood the present state of gospel privileges and gracious overtures, in opposition to the state which is to succeed. In literal phraseology, *to-day*, distinguishes the present period of time from the future, which is called *to-morrow*; hence, when applied to the time of preaching the gospel, or to the time of God's gracious call to sinners through the gospel, it distinguishes the present time, that is, this life, during which "it is said *to-day*," as a time of gracious probation, within the limits of which sinners may hear the voice of God, in opposition to a time or state to come, when it will be too late to hear effectually unto salvation. Luke xiii. 25. "When once the master of the house is risen up and hath shut to the door, and ye begin to stand without and to knock at the door, saying. Lord, Lord, open unto us, and he shall say unto you, I know you not whence ye are." Matt. xxv. 11, 12. "Afterward came also the other virgins, saying. Lord, Lord, open to us. But he answered and said, verily I say unto you, I know you not." Here the case of sinners is brought to view by representing them in the condition of persons excluded from a marriage feast, in consequence of being too late in their application for admittance. The door is represented as being open only for a given period during which admission may be obtained, at the expiration of this period the door will be closed when it will be too late to enter. Now, if this serves at all to illustrate the impending destiny of sinners, and the principles of the divine administration as revealed in the gospel, of which there can be no doubt, it follows, that there is a limited period, during which the door of gospel salvation is open to all who will enter in and be saved, and that a time is coming when this door will be shut, that is, when the offers of salvation will no longer be held out to the sinner, and, consequently, when it will be too late to seek and obtain salvation. If the texts above quoted do not mean this, they can have no bearing at all on the sinner's condition, and consequently, can have no meaning. It would be worse than trifling to pretend to deny, that the closing of the door and the shutting out of certain characters represents an exclusion from gospel blessings, and to suppose that it relates merely to a temporary exclusion here in this world. This would be false, for sinners are not shut out, in this sense, in this life: no sinner knocks at the door of the gospel church, or at the door of mercy and salvation, and receives for an answer, "I know you not whence ye are." Even the Jews, of forlorn condition, are not excluded in this sense; to them the door of gospel salvation is open; hence, this exclusion from the benefits of religion, must be a future and a final one, when it will be too late to seek and obtain salvation. Rev. xxii. 11, 12. "He that is unjust let him be unjust still, and he which is filthy let him be filthy still. And behold I come quickly, and my reward is with me, to give unto every man according as his work shall be." This text clearly teaches that there is a time coming when our moral characters will be forever settled; when it shall be said, "he that is filthy, *let him be filthy still,*" it must be too late to seek and obtain salvation; and when it shall be pronounced, "he that is holy, let him be holy still," there will be no more apostacy. Should it be said that this text has no reference to the final judgment, or to the fixing of our final condition, it is replied that were this granted it would not destroy the argument. The text clearly speaks of the coming of Christ, with his reward with him, to give unto every man according as his works shall be. Now, to make the least of this, it relates to some temporal calamity which threatened the destruction of the wicked; and if it be said of the wicked in view of a temporal destruction, that is, temporal death, "he that is unjust, let him be unjust still, and he that is filthy, let him be filthy still," it follows that it will be too late to reform after death—that those who die morally filthy, will be filthy forever. If the text relates to the destruction of the Jews, as universalists suppose almost every threatening relates to this event, then, it follows that those Jews which were destroyed, arc filthy still. At least, the text proves that some sinners, at some time, either in this world or the world to come, have been, or are to be, unalterably confirmed in their injustice and pollution, and with these it must be, at such time, forever too late to seek salvation. We think we have now shown from scripture, that here will come a time when it will be too late to secure salvation; from which it must follow, that all who do not repent and obtain salvation, within the limits of this probationary state, must be forever lost.

VII. The scriptures speak of rewards and punishments in a manner which clearly implies the doctrine of endless punishment. These scriptures are various, some restricting salvation to certain characters, and others speaking of the punishment of the wicked. Matt. v. 8. "Blessed are the pure in heart, for they shall see God." This text most clearly speaks of the future blessedness of the saints. Note, the condition, purity of heart, is in the *present tense*, and the blessing is in the *future tense*. "Blessed are the pure in heart," *those who are now pure in heart*, "for they shall see God" *hereafter*, not do now see God. If seeing God then relates to the admission of the saints into the divine presence hereafter, to "ever be with the Lord," it follows, that the impure in heart will be forever excluded from the society of the blessed. The text marks the blessedness of seeing God as peculiar to the pure in heart, which cannot be true if all are to see God, which must be the case if universalism be true; it would be equally true to say, blessed are the impure in heart, and wicked in life, for they shall see God. Herein universalism differs from the doctrine of Christ. Christ says, "Blessed are the pure in heart, for they shall see God;" but universalism says, in effect, the *impure*, as well as the *pure*, shall see God. But it may be said, in reply to this, that all will become pure, and then all will see God. True, if all become pure all will see God; but this is what the text does not assert; indeed, it implies directly the reverse. To promise the pure in heart that they shall see God, implies that some may remain impure, and not see God. Not only so, but to take it for granted that all will become pure, is to beg the main question at issue. 2 Tim. iv. 7, 8. "I have fought a good fight, I have finished my course, I have kept the faith; henceforth there is laid up for me a crown of righteousness, which the Lord the righteous Judge shall give me at that day; and not to me only, but to all them that love his appearing." There can be no doubt that this text refers to eternal life in the future world, or to the final salvation of St Paul. The expressions in the text, *"that day,"* and *"his appearing,"* cannot be applied to the destruction of Jerusalem; for St. Paul did not participate in the scenes of that event, but closed his career in Rome, from whence he wrote his epistle just before his death. Indeed it is clear that sentence of death had been pronounced upon him before he wrote this epistle, and that it was in view of this sentence, which was soon to be executed, he penned the text under consideration, exclaiming, "I am now ready to be offered, and the time of my departure is at hand, I have fought a good fight," &c. This clearly shows that the apostle had reference to a reward in the future world. Now, nothing can be more plain than that the apostle looked upon his fidelity in this world as a condition of the reward in the world to come. He says "I have fought a good fight," &c. "henceforth there is laid up for me a crown of righteousness." This clearly implies that there would have been no crown laid up for him, if he had not fought a good fight, kept the faith, and finished his course. Now, if St. Paul's crown was secured by his fidelity, it follows that all those who do not, like him, fight the good fight, such as make shipwreck of faith, and run off the course of the christian race, must come short of a crown of righteousness in the future world; that is, they will come short of heaven. In perfect agreement with this, is Rev. ii. 10. "Be thou faithful unto death and I will give thee a crown of life." That this text promises a reward in the future state there can be no doubt, for faithfulness *unto death* is stated as a condition. Now, as the condition extends up to death, and as the crown must be received after the time of complying with the condition, it follows that this crown of life must be received after death, and in the future state. Here, then, is a plain promise of a crown of life, in the future world, to all such as are faithful unto death, in this world, which implies, beyond all doubt, that such as are not faithful unto death, shall not have a crown of life in the future world. To suppose that all are to have a crown of life, would make the scriptures speak the following absurd language; "Be thou faithful unto death and I will give thee a crown of life;" and I will give a crown of life also to all such as are not faithful unto death. Matt. x. 39. "He that findeth his life shall lose it, and he that loseth his life for my sake shall find it." Mark viii. 35. "For whosoever will save his life shall lose it; but whosoever shall lose his life, for my sake and the gospel's, the same shall save it." Luke ix. 24. "For whosoever will save his life shall lose it; but whosoever will lose his life for my sake, the same shall save it." John xii. 25. "He that loveth his life shall lose it; and he that hateth his life in this world shall keep it unto life eternal." Here are two kinds of life and death referred to; the first is the life and death of the body, or natural life and death; the second is the life and death of the soul, or moral or spiritual life and death. On no other plan can these texts be true; "he that loseth his life shall save it," cannot both be true of the same life, but it may be true that whosoever will save his natural life, by betraying the cause of truth, shall lose his moral life or life of his soul; and that he who shall lose his natural life, as a martyr, shall save the life of his soul, or "preserve it unto life eternal." Here then are two cases; one person thinks more of this life than he does of the life to come, and the other thinks more of the life to come than he does of the present life. Now, it is said that he who seeks to preserve the present life shall lose the future life, and he who is willing to sacrifice the present, shall preserve the future; which clearly implies that some will not enjoy spiritual life in the world to come. One man is said to preserve his life unto life eternal, and another, in distinction from this, is said to lose his life, the same which the other preserves unto life eternal, by endeavoring to save his present life. Nothing can be more plain than that both kinds of life here spoken of, cannot be enjoyed, in the sense of the text, by the same person, and yet one is represented as saving the one, this life, and another as preserving the other, eternal life; hence, it is clear that the person, who would have eternal life, cannot preserve or enjoy this life, in the sense of the text; and that he who does preserve this life in the sense of the text, cannot have eternal life in the future world. 1 Tim. vi. 12. "Fight the good fight of faith, lay hold on eternal life." Here eternal life is represented as taken by the good fight of faith; and yet it cannot be contended that all fight this good fight, for "all men have not faith." This class of texts, which limits salvation to certain characters, is so numerous as to require a volume in order to give room to comment on them all; what has been said, therefore, must suffice. We will now examine some of the threatenings of God's word, which imply the doctrine in question. Matt. xxvi. 24. "Wo unto the man by whom the Son of Man is betrayed; it had been good for that man if he had not been born." We shall not bewilder the plain reader with an appeal to the original Greek on this very plain text. The expression, "it had been good for that man if he had not been born," can mean nothing more nor less, than that it would have been better to have had no existence, than to exist under the circumstances of him by whom the Son of man was betrayed; which cannot be true of any one who shall be finally and eternally saved. Here then is an individual of whom it is said, "it had been good for that man if he had not been born;" but this could not be said of any who shall be finally and eternally saved; therefore, here is an individual who cannot be finally and eternally saved; hence, the doctrine of universal salvation is false, and the doctrine of endless punishment is true. It will be no fair reply to this to say, as universalists often have said, that the argument if admitted, would prove the endless punishment of only one individual out of all the human family; for if the endless punishment of one individual be proved, the principles which endless punishment involve are established, and as the ways of God are equal, or the moral principles of his government the same in every case, the endless punishment of one involves the endless punishment of all of similar moral character.

James ii. 13. "He shall have judgment without mercy, that hath showed no mercy." If judgment *without mercy* implies the doctrine of endless punishment, then it is implied in this text. If men cannot be saved without mercy, then this text proves that some will never be saved. If men can be saved without mercy; be made forever happy and not have one drop of mercy mingled in the full cup of their blessing, then we admit that the unmerciful can be saved; but until this strange hypothesis be proved, the gates of heaven must appear barred against them, so long as it is written "he that hath showed no mercy shall have judgment without mercy." Prov. xxix. 1. "He that being often reproved, hardeneth his neck, shall suddenly be destroyed, and that without remedy." If irremediable destruction implies endless punishment, then it is implied in this text. If men can be destroyed, with a destruction for which there can be no remedy, and be saved too, then all may be saved; but not without. Universalism says, in effect, there is no evil, no destruction to the wicked which shall not find a remedy in the final and eternal salvation of God; but the Bible says certain characters shall be destroyed without remedy, and the reader is left to judge which he is to believe, universalism or the Bible.

Matt. xiii. 47,48,49. "Again the kingdom of heaven is like unto a net that was cast into the sea, and gathered of every kind, which, when it was full, they drew to shore, and sat down and gathered the good into vessels, but cast the bad away; so shall it be at the end of the world." This certainly implies the doctrine in question. Note, some are good and others are bad, the good are saved and the bad cast away; and all this is to take place at the end of the world. Now, unless being cast away, and being saved, mean the same thing, all cannot be saved. Mark, universalism says all shall be saved, bad as well as good, or that the bad shall all become good; but Christ says, the good shall be saved and the bad be cast away.

But universalists attempt to evade the force of this, by criticising upon the phrase, *"end of the world,"* rendering it *end of the age* or *dispensation*; but it will not bear this construction here, unless it be the end of the gospel dispensation. The end of the world in this case, is shown to be the end of time, by its being the time when the gospel net is to be drawn to land, by which must be meant the close of the gospel dispensation. While the commission, "Go ye into all the world and preach the gospel to every creature," is in force, and while ministers are, in accordance with this commission, extending the field of their operations, and pushing the triumphs of the cross wider and wider through the world, the gospel net cannot be said to be drawn to land; but when time shall end, the gospel be preached no more, and all be called to give an account for the improvement they have made on the gospel and its privileges, then will the kingdom of heaven, or the gospel dispensation be like a net drawn to land full of fish, both good and bad, and then will the good be saved, and the bad be castaway. Rev. xxii. 19. "And if any man shall take away from the words of the book of this prophecy, God shall take away his part out of the Book of life, and out of the holy city, and from the things which are written in this book." It must have been a possible case to "take away from the words of the book of this prophecy," or the individual who should do it would not have been threatened. It would be absurd to suppose that God would threaten men with the heaviest penalty, if they shall do what it is not possible for them to do. It is clear then that there must have been a possibility of taking from the words of the book, whether it be now possible to do it in the sense of the text or not. Now, the person who should do this, is threatened with three evils, either of which implies endless punishment.

1. "God shall take away his part out of the book of life." An allusion is had here to the custom of keeping publick records; books in which the names of all the citizens were written, and from which the names of public offenders were blotted. So God is represented as having a book of life, in which the names of all his children are written, by which circumstance of having the name written or not written in this book, the future destinies of all will be determined. In chap. xx. 15, it is said, "whosoever was not found written in the book of life was cast into the lake of fire." Now we ask, on what the hope of heaven can be based, of those whose names God blots from the Lamb's book of life?

2. "God shall take his part out of the holy city." The holy city here is the same as that mentioned, chap. xxi. 1, 2. "And I saw a new heaven and a new earth. And I, John saw the holy city New Jerusalem coming down from God out of heaven." We will not here agitate the question whether or not, this subject relates to the present or future world; for, to make the least of it possible, it describes the christian church, either in this world or in its triumphant state; and he whose part God shall take away out of the church, involving as it does, all the interests of our holy religion, must be effectually lost.

3. "God shall take away his part out of the things which are written in this book." As this is a threatening, it relates to all the promissory portions of the book. Now, if salvation, heaven and eternal life, are written in this book, from all these the individual has his part taken, and must be forever lost. If there were not another text in the Bible implying the endless punishment of sinners, this would seal their endless and hopeless ruin.

VIII. The scriptures absolutely deny salvation to certain persons and characters. Matt. v. 20. "For I say unto you, that except your righteousness exceed the righteousness of the Scribes and Pharisees, ye shall in no case enter into the kingdom of heaven." It is clear that some may not exceed the Scribes and Pharisees in righteousness, or this text never would have been uttered, and to such the text absolutely denies salvation. They shall "in *no case* enter into the kingdom of heaven;" and if they cannot enter into the kingdom of heaven, they cannot be saved. Universalism says, that all shall enter into the kingdom of heaven, but Christ says of certain characters, that they shall in no case enter into the kingdom of heaven. John iii. 3. "Except a man be born again he cannot see the kingdom of God." This text absolutely denies salvation to all such as are not born again. The text clearly implies that men may, or may not be born again; and that if they are not, they cannot see the kingdom of God, in which case they cannot be saved. To suppose that men can be saved, without ever seeing the kingdom of God, is in the highest degree absurd. Universalism says all shall see the kingdom of God and enjoy it forever; but Jesus Christ says, such as are not born again *"cannot see the kingdom of God."* Gal. v. 21. "Envyings, murders, drunkenness, revellings, and such like, of the which I tell you before, as I have also told you in time past, that they which do such things shall not inherit the kingdom of God." It is worthy of remark, that, in this text, the verb which expresses the forbidden conduct, is in the present tense, "they which *do* such things," while the verb which expresses the punishment, is in the future tense, *"shall not inherit*; not, do not inherit. This clearly marks the sense thus: those who do such things *here* shall not inherit the kingdom of God *hereafter*. Eph. v. 5. "For this ye know that no whoremonger, nor unclean person, nor covetous man, who is an idolator, hath any inheritance in the kingdom of God." Universalism says that every man has an inheritance in the kingdom of God, and in this it is opposed to the word of God.

But universalists attempt to evade the force of these passages, by denying that they have any reference to a future state, and by maintaining that the phrases, "kingdom of God," and "kingdom of heaven," mean no more than the gospel dispensation. To this we reply,

1. That these phrases do not always and exclusively signify the gospel dispensation, here on earth, but sometimes signify a future state of happiness. That the terms kingdom of God, and kingdom of heaven, sometimes mean the gospel dispensation, is admitted; but that they never mean a place of happiness in the future world is denied. Matt. viii. 11. "Many shall come from the east and west, and shall sit down with Abraham and Isaac and Jacob in the kingdom of heaven." This text was spoken hundreds of years after Abraham, Isaac and Jacob were dead, after they had dwelt for ages in the future world, while the collection from the east and west to sit down with the Patriarchs in the kingdom of heaven, is described as an event yet to take place; therefore, the kingdom of heaven in this text must refer to the future world. 1 Cor. xv. 50. "Now, this I say brethren, that flesh and blood cannot inherit the kingdom of God; neither doth corruption inherit incorruption." The Apostle is here speaking of the resurrection of the body, in which he declares "it is sown in corruption, it is raised in incorruption, it is sown a natural body it is raised a spiritual body;" and in view of this change he says, "flesh and blood cannot inherit the kingdom of God." From this it is clear, beyond all doubt, that by the kingdom of God, in this text, is meant an inheritance which cannot be possessed in this world, while we tabernacle in flesh and blood, but which awaits us in the future world to be possessed after the resurrection of the body.

2. If it were admitted that by the kingdom of God, in

the above texts, we are to understand the gospel dispensation, still it would not in the least lessen their evidence in proof of endless punishment. The texts affirm that certain characters "shall in no case enter into the kingdom of heaven," that they "cannot see the kingdom of God," that they "have no inheritance in the kingdom of God," and that they "shall not inherit the kingdom of God." Now, suppose that the gospel dispensation is to be understood, and what then can be meant by these expressions? The texts will then read thus: Except your righteousness exceed the righteousness of the Scribes and Pharisees, ye shall in no case enter into the gospel dispensation. Except a man be born again he cannot see the gospel dispensation. Shall not inherit the gospel dispensation. Now, on the supposition that these texts refer exclusively to the gospel dispensation, it is clear that the persons to whom they relate are denied all interest in the gospel dispensation, as absolutely as they are denied all interest in heaven, on the supposition that they relate to a future state of happiness; and as there can be no introduction into heaven only through the gospel dispensation, that is, through the provisions of the Gospel, it is clear that those who are denied all interest in the kingdom of God cannot be saved, whether by the phrase we understand the gospel dispensation or a future state of happiness. If, as restorationers contend, sinners are to have the offers of the gospel held out to them in the future world, and be made the subjects of grace and moral reform in hell, it will be as necessary to enter into the gospel dispensation, to pass from hell to heaven, as it is to pass from earth to heaven; hence, those who "shall in no case enter into the kingdom of heaven," "cannot see the kingdom of God," and who "have no inheritance in the kingdom of God," can never find their way into heaven itself. Matt. vii. 21. "Not every one that saith unto me, Lord, Lord, shall enter into the kingdom of heaven, but he that doeth the will of my Father which is in heaven." This text clearly denies admission into the kingdom of heaven, to all such as say Lord, Lord, and do not the will of God. And in this case it cannot be pretended with any degree of plausibility, that the gospel dispensation is intended, by the kingdom of heaven; for the meaning of this phrase must be determined, in this instance, by the term *heaven*, which occurs a second time in the text. In the two expressions "kingdom of heaven," and "my Father which is in heaven," the term heaven is, unquestionably to be understood in the same sense. Now, understand by the first of these expressions, the gospel dispensation, and Christ is made to say in the latter, my Father which is in the gospel dispensation! Such a construction outrages common sense. It is clear, then, that the kingdom of heaven, in this text means the place of the divine presence, where those who do the will of God are to dwell forever with him, and as it is said, "Not every one that saith unto me, Lord, Lord, shall enter into the kingdom of heaven," it is clear, that there are some who will never be saved.

Luke xiv. 24. "For I say unto you, that none of those men which were bidden, shall taste of my supper." This relates to the gospel supper, or provision which the gospel contains for the salvation of sinners. This supper is a feast consisting of the blessings which the gospel proffers to all. Now, of certain persons it is said, none of these men which were bidden shall taste of my supper." John viii. 21. "Then said Jesus again unto them, I go my way and ye shall seek me, and shall die in your sins; whither I go ye cannot come." Where did Jesus Christ go? He went to heaven, there can be no doubt in the mind of any; hence unbelievers who die in their sins, can never go to heaven, for to such Christ says, "whither I go ye cannot come." John iii. 36. "He that believeth on the Son hath everlasting life, and he that believeth not the Son shall not see life." We know not how to express what we conceive to be the sense of this text, more to our purpose, than in its own language. The unqualified declaration that certain characters *shall not see life*, forever and eternally seals them with the seal of death. Matt, xii. 32. "And whosoever speaketh a word against the Son of man, it shall be forgiven him; but whosoever speaketh against the Holy Ghost, it shall not be forgiven him, neither in this world, neither in the *world* to come." Mark, iii. 29. "But he that shall blaspheme against the Holy Ghost hath never forgiveness, but is in danger of eternal damnation." Let it be remarked that the sin here spoken of, by some called the unpardonable sin, consisted in attributing to the agency of the devil, the miracles which Jesus Christ wrought by the power of the Holy Ghost. That this sin was committed by some of the Jews there can be no doubt. Of these it is said, they shall not be forgiven, neither in this world, nor in the world to come. Now, without forgiveness there can be no salvation, as we have already shown in Chap. IV. which is devoted exclusively to this subject. But universalists attempt to evade this by rendering the expression, "neither in this world, neither in the world to come," neither in this dispensation, neither in the dispensation to come; that is, this offence shall not be forgiven, under the Jewish, nor gospel dispensation; but this does not in the least relieve them, for if men are ever saved, they must be saved under or during the gospel dispensation; and as there is no forgiveness of this offence under this dispensation, those who commit it can never be saved. This conclusion is farther supported by two other expressions in the text. It is said, "he that blasphemeth against the Holy Ghost hath *never* forgiveness." An expression stronger than this cannot be framed. He that hath *never* forgiveness can *never* be saved. Now if the text does not deny *forgiveness* to the blasphemer, during all ages to come, then the writer in the above declaration has not denied *salvation*, during all ages, to such as have never forgiveness. If when Christ says the sinner hath *never* forgiveness, he does not deny that he will be forgiven at any future time, then, when the writer says the sinner can *never* be saved, he asserts nothing contrary to the sinner's salvation at some future time. Again it is said in the text, that those of whom it speaks, are "in danger of eternal damnation." This shows that forgiveness and damnation are opposed to each other; he who is forgiven is not damned, and he who is not forgiven, must be damned; hence, as the blasphemer hath *never* forgiveness, his damnation is *eternal*. We think we have now shown that the scriptures absolutely deny salvation to certain persons and characters.

IX. The scriptures represent the punishment of the wicked as their end, their last state, and their portion. Ps. lxxiii. 12. "Behold these are the ungodly who prosper in the world." Of these characters the Psalmist adds, verse 18, 19, "Thou casteth them down into destruction—they are utterly consumed with terrors." Note, this is their *end* which the Psalmist learned in the sanctuary of God, and if their end is to be cast down into destruction, and to be utterly consumed with terrors, they cannot be saved. Universalism says, the end of every man shall be salvation or eternal life; but the Bible says, the end of the wicked is to be destroyed and consumed with terror. If they are eternally saved, then salvation must be their end; hence, as their end is to be destroyed, they can never be saved. Psa. xvii. 14. "Men of the world which have their portion in this life." If then certain of the wicked have their portion in this life, in distinction from others who do not have their portion in this life, they can have no part in the inheritance that is incorruptible. If these persons are to have eternal life, then, that would be their portion, in which case they would not have their portion in this world; hence, as they have their portion in this life they cannot have eternal life. Of these characters Dr. Clark remarks in his notes on this text, "who never seek any thing *spiritual*—who have bartered heaven for earth and have got the *portion* they desired." Jer. xvii. 11. "He that getteth riches and not by right, shall leave them in the midst of his days, and at his end shall be a fool." If he is saved at last he will not be a fool at his *end*, but will be "wise unto salvation." It might be said of such an one that he was a fool; but now in his end or last state he has become wise; but the text says, "at his *end*, he shall be a fool," which cannot be said of any one whose end is salvation. On this text Dr. Clark remarks thus: "*And at his end shall be a fool*; shall be reputed as such. He was a fool all the way through: he lost his soul to get wealth, and this wealth he never enjoyed. To him are applicable those strong words of the poet:

> "O cursed lust of gold, when for thy sake
> The wretch throws up his interests in both worlds.
> First starved in this, then damned in that to come."

Matt. xxiv. 51. "And shall appoint him his portion with the hypocrites." Luke xii. 46. "And will appoint him his portion with the unbelievers." Here the punishment of the unfaithful is said to be their *portion*; and hence they cannot be heir to eternal life. 2 Cor. xi. 13. 15. "For such are false apostles, deceitful workers, whose *end* shall be according to their works." This text certainly predicts no good of these false teachers, but evil. Their works are bad, and their *end* is to be according to their works; their end therefore must be bad, hence, they cannot be saved, for salvation would be a good and glorious end. Their *end* is to be according to their works, but there can be no agreement between their works and salvation; hence, their *end* cannot be salvation. Phil, iii. 18. 19. "Enemies of the cross of Christ, whose *end is destruction*." No man, made finally holy and happy, can have his end in destruction. Heb. vi. 8. "But that which beareth thorns and briers is rejected, and is nigh unto cursing, whose end is to be burned." This was spoken of apostates, who should fall away after they had been made partakers of the Holy Ghost, &c. and if their end is to be burned, salvation cannot be their end.

X. The punishment of such as shall be judged at the last day and sentenced to a punishment in hell, is shown to be endless, from a consideration of the nature of the divine penalty, and the immutability of God, the Judge, by whose sentence it will be inflicted. If it can be shown that the penalty is, in itself, endless, and that the sentence of the judge is irrevocable, the endless punishment of the condemned will follow as an unavoidable consequence. These points we propose to establish.

1. The penalty of the divine law is, in itself, an endless curse. To establish this point, it is only necessary to repeat what has been said in Chapter III, when arguing the necessity of an atonement. It was there stated that the penalty of God's law is death. Death was the penal sanction of the first precept given to man, Gen. ii. 17. "In the day thou eatest thereof thou shalt surely die." Ezek. xviii. 20. "The soul that sinneth it shall die." Rom. vi. 23. "The wages of sin is death." Rom. viii. 6. "To be carnally minded is death." James i. 15. "Sin when it is finished bringeth forth death." Now death, whether natural or moral, must be in its own nature endless. What is death? It is the negation of life, the absence of that life to which its [sic] stands opposed. If death is made to consist in moral depravity, it is the negation of that holiness, that conformity to the divine will and likeness, which constitutes moral or spiritual life. If death is made to consist in the dissolution of the body, it is the negation of those vital energies which constitute natural or animal life. When

a person dies morally or naturally, it is the principle or power of the opposite life that is overcome; life becomes extinct and death reigns. Now, when a person is dead, on this principle, self resuscitation is utterly impossible; life has become extinct and nothing but death reigns and pervades the whole system; hence, death left to the tendency of its own nature, must hold on to its subjects with an eternal grasp, unless it be said that death can produce life, or that inertia can produce animation; for as there is nothing but death now pervading the once animated sphere of the fallen, the energies of life can move there no more forever, unless they can spring from death, or out of nothing rise! It is certain then, so far as moral or spiritual death is concerned, on which this argument is predicated, that persons once dead, must remain dead forever, unless God, who said "thou shalt die," speak to the dead, and say, thou shalt live, and thereby revoke the sentence of his righteous law. We see then, that there is no way of being delivered from the penalty of the law, but by a pardon; for when the penalty of the law takes effect in the death of the sinner, as death is in its own nature endless, holding the criminal under its dominion, any subsequent deliverance by the communication of life by God, from whom it must proceed, must be regarded in the light of a pardon, since in such case the offender does not endure all that the sentence imports; death being endless of itself.

2. The sentence which will be passed upon sinners, by the righteous judgment of God, at the last day, will be irrevocable. This must appear from a consideration of the immutability of God, the judge. Immutability is that perfection of God, which renders him eternally unchangeable. "He is immutable," says Mr. Buck, "in his *essence*, in his *attributes*, in his *purposes*, in his *promises*, and in his *threatenings*." "We are not however," says Mr. Watson,

"so to interpret the immutability of God, as though his *operations* admit no change, and even no contrariety, or that his mind was incapable of different regards and affections towards the same creatures under different circumstances. He creates and he destroys, he wounds and he heals, he works and he ceases from his works, he loves and he hates, but these as being under the direction of the same immutable wisdom, holiness, goodness and justice, are the proofs, not of changing, but of unchanging principles." We will illustrate the principle, here laid down, by supposing a case. It is said in the gospel, "he that believeth shall be saved, and he that believeth not shall be damned." This is an immutable principle in God, that saves the believer and damns the unbeliever. Now, suppose two persons, A and B; A is a believer, and B is an unbeliever; A has the promise of salvation, and B is threatened with damnation; it is also in accordance with the immutable principles of God, to save A, as a believer, and to damn B, as an unbeliever. Now, suppose A makes shipwreck of his faith and becomes an unbeliever, and B repents and believes the gospel, and it is in accordance with the immutable principles of God to damn A, on whom the threatening now rests, and to save B, to whom the promise now relates. In all this, it is clear that God has not changed but the change is in A and B, his creatures. But if when A, who first had the promise of salvation as a believer, becomes an unbeliever, God should still save him, it would imply change or mutability; for he has sworn to save the believer only, and to damn the unbeliever. We have given this illustration, lest our reasoning from the immutability of God, which follows, should be misunderstood or perverted. The above view amounts to this, that the immutability of God must render his administration unchangeable in view of moral principles; that is, what God does or sanctions at one time, he must do or sanction at all times, under circumstances involving the same moral principles. If God condemns a sinner to day, he must always condemn him, so long as he possesses the same moral character; but if the sinner reform and become a different moral being from what he was when God condemned him, we admit God may deal differently with him and still be immutable; but such a change we purpose to show impossible with sinners in hell. Suppose a sinner arraigned at the bar of God, at the last day, and sentenced and sent to hell, and if God be immutable he must forever remain under the sentence. To suppose that God may sentence a sinner to hell, at one time, and then revoke the sentence and take him out of hell, at another time, most clearly implies mutability in God. To this it may be replied that the sinner may be delivered from hell by first becoming morally reformed. This we will now show to be impossible.

The atonement or merits of Christ's death, and advantages of his intercession, will, after the day of Judgment, no longer be available, and hence, all the benefits of the same, including the efficacy of prayer, and the agency of the Holy Ghost, will be forever lost. It has been already shown, in the preceding chapter, in proof of a general judgment, that Jesus Christ is to be the Judge, and that God is to judge the world by Jesus Christ. Now, when Jesus Christ becomes our judge, he will no longer be our mediator and intercessor with the Father. Christ is now our mediator, and as such administers a mediatorial government, prays the Father, obtains and sends the Holy Ghost into the world. 1 Cor. xv. 24. "Then cometh the end when he shall have delivered up the kingdom of God." This text shows that the present state of things will not always continue, that Christ will not always, as Messiah and mediator, administer the government, and then, "when he shall deliver up the kingdom to God," cease to be mediator and advocate with the Father, and become the judge of "quick and dead," the benefits of his atonement will be no longer available. Now, as we have shown, in Chap. III, that the atonement of Christ is the only ground of salvation, it follows that those who reject this atonement, and are sent to hell for having rejected it, will then have no means of moral reformation, and must be as effectually lost as though Christ had never died for their redemption. To suppose that Christ can act as the sinner's judge, and can sentence him to hell, and at the same time be the sinner's mediator and advocate, to procure his deliverance from hell, is palpably absurd. When therefore, Christ shall judge the sinner; and sentence him to hell, his gospel will no longer offer salvation—the blood of sprinkling will no longer plead, and the Holy Ghost will no longer strive with him or operate for the renewal of his heart; it is, therefore, clear that no moral reformation can take place with the inhabitants of hell, unless it be self-wrought. Now, no self-change can be wrought independent of the benefits of the atonement, including the graces of the Holy Spirit. In a future state of punishment, that is, in hell, the sinner must be acknowledged to be destitute of holiness; and possessing no moral quality but sin or unholiness, he can of himself under these circumstances, never produce or originate holiness, which alone can prepare him for heaven. As well might unholiness produce holiness, sin produce righteousness, death produce life, or damnation produce salvation, as for a guilty, condemned sinner in hell, to work himself into a holy candidate for heaven! It is clear then that no moral change can take place in the sinner for the better after the day of general judgment; and hence; the sinner, if sent to hell, must remain forever the same, and remaining forever the same in moral character, God can never, consistently with his own immutability, revoke the sentence. For God to condemn a sinner and send him to hell, at one time, and then revoke the sentence and recall him from his infernal prison, while he is yet the same in moral character, is to act differently at different times, in view of the same moral principles; which implies change or mutability. We trust we have now shown,

1st. That the penalty of the divine law which is death, is in itself an endless curse, so as never to terminate of itself, but being left to its own tendency will hold on upon its subjects with an eternal grasp.

2d. That the immutability of God, the judge of all, forbids the thought that the sentence will ever be revoked by the act of him whose word inflicted it. From these two points the conclusion is irresistible, that the sinner if condemned when judged at the last day, must remain under condemnation for ever, world without end.

XI. The relation, which the sinner will sustain to the divine administration after the day of judgment, will be such as to render his punishment endless. After the general judgment the sinner will not sustain to God's moral government the relation of a subject in a state of trial or probation; but of a subject in a state of retribution. Leaving out of the account the case of infants, which can have no bearing upon this argument, we say that men can sustain but two relations to the divine administration: the first is that of a state of trial or probation, during which they are held accountable to answer for their conduct at the judgment of the last day; the second is a state of retribution, in which they enjoy or suffer the reward of their conduct in their state of trial, as it may have been good or bad. These two relations which men sustain to the divine government, are separated from each other by the judgment. Probation ends at death, and retribution commences at the judgment; the intermediate state being only a state of arrest preparatory to the judgment. The reader will perceive that this argument proceeds on the supposition, that there is a day of general judgment; this point having been proved in the preceding chapter. Not only so, but Restorationers, against whose theory this argument is directed, without much reserve admit the fact of a general judgment. On this ground then, we say the judgment, including the intermediate state, is the dividing period between these two states of trial and retribution, dividing man's existence into two grand portions, the first of which is a state of trial, and the second a state of retribution. Now, as there are but these two states in man's whole existence, and as the judgment divides between these, it follows that all prior to the judgment must be a state of trial, and that all after the judgment is a state of retribution. This clearly renders the retribution endless, both of the righteous and wicked; hence, those who are condemned at the judgment, having to spend the whole of their remaining existence in a state of retribution, must remain under such sentence of condemnation so long as they exist; and, therefore, must be the subjects of endless punishment.

Should it be insisted, in opposition to this argument, that probation or a state of trial will extend beyond the judgment, we object to such a hypothesis on the following ground:

1. Such a position, would suppose the judgment not final, and that another judgment must take place, subsequently to the one of which we read in the scriptures, and to which we refer when we talk of a general judgment to come. It must be clear that if the present state of trial is to be closed by a general judgment, calling its subjects to render an account for their conduct during the same, it must appear reasonable that every other state of trial which may follow should end in the same way, by a general judgment; and as it is matter of fact that some do mis-improve the present state, we see the principle which would assign to man a state of trial after the general resurrection and judg-

ment at the end of this world, would lay the foundation for an alternate succession of trial and judgment through the coming ages of eternity; nor can it appear, on this principle, that all will be saved; for as men do abuse the present state of trial, they may on the same principle, abuse every subsequent state of trial, and hence, never respond to the fearful claims of their probation.

2. If the future state, after the judgment, is to be a state of trial, no good reason can be given why it will not be such to the righteous as well as to the unrighteous; and if all are to be in a state of trial, it may be the occasion of the fall of some of the good, as well as of the repentance of some of the bad; hence, nothing will be gained to the cause of universalism by this unscriptural and visionary notion of probation in the future world. This appears still stronger in view of the facts already established—that both Adam and angels fell into sin from a holy state.

XII. The circumstances of the sinner, after the day of judgment, will be such as to preclude the possibility of his salvation, on *gospel terms*. There will be no opportunity in the future state to comply with the conditions of salvation, as it is offered in the gospel. We here particularly insist upon faith, and its concomitants, as being essential to salvation. Mark xvi. 16. "He that believeth shall be saved and he that believeth not shall be damned." John iii. 36. "He that believeth on the Son hath everlasting life and he that believeth not the Son shall not see life." Heb. xi. 6. "Without faith it is impossible to please God." Now, we maintain that it will be impossible for man to believe, in a gospel sense, in the future world, after the day of judgment. This must appear from the nature of faith itself. St. Paul has given us the following definition of faith, Heb. xi. 1. "Now, faith is the substance of things hoped for, the evidence of things not seen." From this text we learn,

1. That as "faith is the substance of things hoped for," it can exist only in the absence of the things which are the object of our hope.

2. As "faith is the evidence of things *not seen*" it can exist only in the absence of the things to which it relates, of which it is the evidence; hence, faith always stands opposed to *sight*. 2 Cor. v. 7. "We walk by *faith*, and not by *sight*." Now, no such faith can exist in the future world. Can the sinner, in the future world, believe that there is a God when he shall have seen him as he is, and while he shall be suffering under the penalty of his righteous law? Can he believe in Jesus Christ, as his saviour who died for him, after he has been judged by him and condemned for not having believed through the evidence which the gospel affords in this life? Surely there could be no virtue in such faith; or, rather, it would not be faith but knowledge, forced upon the understanding with all the solemnities of the judgment day. The day of judgment will furnish ocular demonstration of all the essential truths of the gospel, which we are now required to believe on other testimony, leaving no possible room for the exercise of faith; hence, as faith is the only condition of our justification, when a sinner dies in unbelief and passes into the invisible world, he is at once beyond the reach of gospel justification, and must reap forever the reward of his unbelief, where he will be made to know irresistibly, what he refuses to believe in this life on gospel testimony.

Faith will also be impossible after the day of judgment, in another point of view. We have shown in the preceding argument, that at the day of judgment Christ will resign the mediatorial kingdom; that he will *judge* sinners at the last day, and not *intercede* for them. He will then no longer be our intercessor, our advocate with God, our propitiation and our atoning sacrifice at the throne. How then can the sinner believe in Jesus Christ, in a gospel sense, after the day of judgment? Can the sinner believe in Jesus Christ as his intercessor and advocate with God at the day of judgment, when he shall be condemned by him as his judge? It is impossible. Indeed were the sinner to believe this, he would believe a falsehood which could not save him, and yet without faith in Christ there can be no salvation. It must appear plain in view of the above facts, that to believe in Christ after the day of judgment, as the gospel now requires us to believe in him, would be to believe what will not then be true; therefore, gospel faith, and consequently gospel salvation, will be impossible after the day of judgment.

Should universalists attempt to take advantage of this argument, by supposing it to cut off all the heathen and infants from salvation for want of faith, we reply, that the argument has nothing to do with them. That the heathen who never have heard the gospel, and infants whose rational powers are yet locked up in the immature organs of the earthly tenement, cannot believe, we admit; and the argument asserts nothing concerning these, but is founded wholly on the case of adult sinners, who hear the gospel in this life, and are capable of believing it. If universalists will undertake to prove that if adult sinners, who hear the gospel and are capable of believing, cannot be saved for want of faith, that therefore the heathen who do not hear the gospel, and infants who are not capable of faith, cannot be saved, they will assume ground both unscriptural and unreasonable.

XIII. To suppose that the punishment of the wicked, in a future state, will be of limited duration, must involve the divine administration in injustice. After the frequent and clamorous charges of injustice, which universalists have brought against the doctrine of endless punishment, it may startle the reader to sec this charge returned upon its authors and urged against the doctrine of limited punishment in a future state. It may also be thought a strange position to maintain, that endless punishment is just, and limited punishment unjust; but we have only to ask for an attentive hearing on this subject and hope to satisfy the candid reader that the position is tenable. That this argument may be clearly understood, we will distinctly state the several points from whence the conclusion is drawn.

1. There is to be a day of general judgment, as we have heretofore proved, when sinners will be judged and receive a sentence consigning them to a punishment proportioned to their demerit. That the punishment of sinners will be proportioned to their guilt, cannot be denied. Romans ii. 6. "Who will render to every man *according to his deeds*." 2 Cor. v. 10. "We must all appear before the judgment seat of Christ that every one may receive the things done in his body *according to that he hath done* whether it be good or bad." Common sense and common justice say, if the sinner is punished on principles of justice, his punishment must be proportioned to his guilt.

2. If the sinner is to be punished according to his works, having his punishment proportioned to the amount of sin he has committed, he must be sentenced to endure a term of punishment of definite length, if it be not endless. If punishment be endless it must be proportioned in *degree* to suit the degree of the sinner's guilt; but if it be limited in duration, it must be proportioned in *length* according to the degree of the sinner's guilt, and for a definite amount of sin, the sinner must receive a definite amount of punishment, *definite in length*."

3. If the sinner is still within the reach of salvation, and under the gospel dispensation, as he must be to be within the reach of gospel salvation, he may repent, believe the gospel and be saved, at any time or not at all, just as sinners are capable of doing in this life. Nothing can be more clear than that the gospel offers salvation in the present tense. Its language is, "to day if you will hear his voice," "now is the accepted time;" "ho, every one that

thirsteth, come ye to the waters;" "in the day that thou seekest me with all thy heart, I will be found of thee." &c. &c. Now, so long as the offers of salvation are held out to the sinner, he may accept at any time and be saved, and when the offers of the gospel shall no longer be held out to the sinner, it will be forever too late for him to secure salvation. From this it must appear, that if the sinner in hell has the offers of salvation he may accept at any time or not at all; for sinners are capable of receiving or rejecting the gospel. If then the sinner be consigned to hell for a term of punishment of definite length, and still have the offers of salvation, he may accept, before the expiration of his term of punishment, or may defer until a period far beyond the expiration of his term of punishment; either of which must involve the divine administration. Suppose then, that the sinner has lived in sin and unbelief fifty years, for which he deserves to be punished fifty years in the future world; that is, he deserves to be punished fifty years for the wrong done in this life. Suppose again that this sinner repent of all his past sins, and turn to God with all his heart at the expiration of the first year of his term of punishment, which is perfectly a possible case. Now, we have presented to view in this case, an individual, having repented of all his sins, turned to God with all his heart, praying with his eyes lifted to his holy throne; and at the same time this individual is under a sentence of condemnation which dooms him to forty-nine years' suffering in hell, he having been sentenced for fifty years, but one of which has elapsed.

What can God himself do with such a case? To punish the sinner longer would be a violation of every principle of the gospel, which alone promises salvation to any of our fallen race. It would be a violation of the promises which God has made to sinners in the gospel. John iii. 28. Christ says, "He that believeth on him is not condemned." But this doctrine of limited punishment, after the day of judgment, says the sinner may believe and still remain under condemnation and suffer for ages. This is a violation of truth and justice both, on the ground that God has promised in the gospel to save when the sinner will accept, saying, "now is the accepted time, now is the day of salvation." This shows, beyond all dispute that the offers of the gospel cannot be continued to sinners after the day of judgment. Such a sentence as we have shown will be passed upon sinners at the day of judgment, cannot take place, and the gospel offers be continued at the same time; for the sentence and the gospel must be directly opposed to each other. The gospel says, "now is the accepted time," but the sentence says, now is not the accepted time—the sinner must suffer for fifty years, less or more, before he can be saved. God cannot sentence the sinner to endure a punishment in hell of any length, without contradicting the gospel, which ever offers salvation in the present tense, saying "to day, now," &c. We will now suppose the case to be a different one. Suppose the sinner to be judged worthy of fifty years' punishment in hell, as above stated, and that this term expires and the sinner remains impenitent still. This is a possible case; for if sinners have the offers of the gospel in the future world, they may reject them. This view presents us with the case of a sinner, who has been sentenced to endure a term of punishment of definite length, and having endured it all, he is impenitent, and just as unholy and unfit for heaven as he was the moment God passed sentence upon him. Now, we ask what God can do with such a character? He cannot take him to heaven, for he is an impenitent sinner, and morally unfit for the society of the blest; and he cannot keep him longer in hell, for he has already suffered all he deserved to suffer, and all that the divine sentence determined he should suffer; hence, to keep him longer in hell must be unjust. Should it be said, in reply to this, that though the sinner in this case has suffered all the punishment due to the sin committed in this life, for which only he was judged, yet he now deserves to be punished longer, for the sin which he has committed since the judgment, during the period of his punishment in hell, and therefore he may remain longer in hell on principles of justice, we reply,

1. This would require another judgment, and another sentence, of which the scriptures are entirely silent.

2. If it be admitted that the sinner is responsible, and liable to punishment for his conduct in hell, it will involve him in an eternal necessity of remaining in sin and punishment.

We have supposed the sinner to deserve fifty years' punishment, for having spent fifty years in sin, in this life. Now, nothing can be more plain than that this fifty years spent in punishment can form no part of the sinner's obedience; for the law no where requires suffering, as a duty, but inflicts it as a penalty for having failed of our duty. If then it be admitted that the sinner is responsible for these fifty years spent in punishment, it cannot be denied that at the expiration of this term of punishment, the sinner will be just as guilty as at its commencement; and on this principle one age of punishment will only prepare the sinner to enter upon another *ad infinitum*.

Should it be said, in reply to the above argument, that God will bring the sinner to repentance by irresistible grace at the expiration of his term of punishment, we reply, that if it be consistent with the principles of the divine government irresistibly to save sinners, it would appear more to the advantage of the divine wisdom and benevolence, to save sinners in the commencement of their career, and thereby prevent an age of suffering in hell. It must appear evident that God can as easily save a sinner from going to hell as he can save him from hell after he has fallen into the gulf of perdition, especially if it is to be done by irresistible grace.

XIV. If sinners in the future world are still subjects of grace and salvation, they must be subjects of prayer also, and we should pray for the dead as constantly and fervently as for the living. The Romish church does offer prayers for the dead, and, if the doctrine of universal restoration be true, they must be correct in this, however erroneous they may be in relation to other matters. Among all the Restorationers we ever heard pray, we never heard one offer a petition for his brethren, who have gone to try the realities of the future world, and are, like the rich man lifting up their eyes in hell, (*hades*) being in torment. If they really believe that sinners in the future world are still subjects of grace and salvation, why do they not pray for the death of the worm that never dies, and that the fire may be quenched, which shall never be quenched?

VII
A Reply to the Arguments employed by Universalists

HAVING CLOSED THE ARGUMENT in favour of our own theory, we will devote a brief chapter to the consideration of the arguments of our opponents. Universalists generally argue in the use of negative propositions, which are intended to prove that certain points are not true; yet they sometimes advance direct arguments, in proof of the doctrine of Universal Salvation, and to the principal of these we will now offer a reply. We may not consider them in the same order in which a universalist would state them; but as universalists have no standard work, in which their sentiments are stated, and the arguments by which they pretend to prove them, systematically arranged, we shall have to pursue the order which to us appears most consistent.

I. Universalists argue the salvation of all men from the perfections of God. As there are several arguments professedly drawn from the divine perfections, we will first offer some general remarks on the uncertainty of any conclusions drawn from the divine attributes, on this subject, and then notice each argument separately. Rev. Mr. Morse, in a controversial letter published in *The Christian Advocate and Journal*, Vol. VIII. No. 2. holds the following language: "The attributes of God form the basis of religious truth." To this we object, and make our appeal to the word of God for a decision on all points of faith and practice. This we do on the ground that the attributes of God, aside from revelation and matter of fact, do not furnish sufficient data from whence to deduce conclusions concerning man's future destiny. In support of this position we offer the following considerations:

1. God cannot make a full revelation of himself; to us, in view of our want of capacity to comprehend infinity. The attributes of God can be fully known only to himself; hence, any conclusions drawn from the divine perfections, are deductions drawn from premises which we do not understand, and our conclusions must be as uncertain as our knowledge of the premises is imperfect We do not say that we cannot know what some of the divine perfections are; God has revealed to us that he is almighty, wise, just, holy and good; but we cannot so understand these perfections, as to be able to determine from them, aside from scripture and matter of fact, what is, and what is not, consistent with them. We can determine what is, and what is not, consistent with the attributes of God, only by what we see actually exist, or from what God has said in the scriptures. If universalists will prove from the bible that all men will be saved, we shall be bound to admit that it is consistent with the divine perfections to save, in a future world, those who only abuse his mercies in this, and die in unbelief and contempt of his authority; and if we can prove from the scriptures, that some men will be endlessly miserable, universalists must be bound to admit that endless punishment is consistent with the divine attributes, though they may not be able to see any

reason in the divine attributes why it should be so. That we cannot discover what is, and what is not, consistent with the divine perfections is clear, from the simple fact that providence has already developed many things for which we can see no reason in the divine attributes. We presume universalists can see no reason in the divine goodness, why a holy, devoted and useful minister should be put to the rack, and caused to suffer a most painful death *by the hand of an ungodly sinner*; and we can see no reason in the divine justice, why God should *take the murdered and the murderer to the same heaven.*

2. The perfections of God do not enable us to determine what the desert of sin is; a point which must be settled before it can appear that endless punishment is not consistent with divine justice and goodness. Can universalists, from any knowledge they have of the divine perfections, clearly determine the extent of the evil of sin, and what and how much punishment the sinner is liable to endure? If they can, they will confer a favor on the world to speak out, and say just what, and how much the sinner must endure to answer the claims of the divine law; and if they cannot determine from the divine perfections, what, and how much the sinner deserves, they cannot know but that a punishment worse, and much longer than they have imagined, may be consistent with the perfections of God. We believe these points must be settled by the law and the, testimony of God's word, and not by some rule of consistency, in our own imaginations, by which we would direct the attributes of God in the government of the world.

3. The perfections of God, in our opinion, do not of themselves, so far as we are enabled to understand them, prove the immortality of the soul or the resurrection of the body. What is there discoverable in the perfections of God, that proves that the spirits of men, that go upward, are any more immortal than the spir-

its of beasts, that go downward; or that our bodies will be raised any more than theirs? And if a future state is not clearly discoverable from the perfections of God, they cannot, independently of direct revelation, prove the final salvation of all men.

4. If the future destiny of man can be determined from the perfections of God, no good reason can be given why every other point in theology cannot be proved in the same way. Now, will universalists pretend that they can discover what is truth, and what is error, from their knowledge of the divine perfections? If they can, then all those portions of the scriptures which do not relate to the attributes of God, are not necessary in order to a correct theory of religion; and if universalists cannot determine from the attributes of God what is, and what is not religious truth, it cannot appear that they can prove from this source what will be the punishment of sin or what will be the sinner's final destiny. It must be perfectly plain, that if we have a view of the perfections of God sufficiently clear, to enable us to determine what is, and what is not consistent with them, we can need no farther revelation than that which relates directly to God and his attributes; for whatever is consistent with the divine attributes, must be true, and does or may exist; and whatever is not consistent with the divine perfections must be false, and does not and cannot exist.

5. So far as any thing can be proved from the perfections of God, on this subject, the argument is in our favour. Though we cannot discern what is consistent with the perfections of God, from any view we have of his perfections; yet, we can determine that some things are consistent with them from the actual existence of the things themselves. We know that whatever does exist must be consistent with the divine perfections; hence, when we behold the existence of any thing and infer from thence that such thing is consistent with the perfections of God,

we reason from matter of fact, and not from the perfections of God. We cannot prove from the divine perfections that the existence of sin and misery are consistent with such perfections, yet this point can be proved from matter of fact; for sin and misery do exist, and therefore, we know from their actual existence that they are consistent with the perfections of God. This throws the weight of the argument into our side of the scales, for matter of fact says that it is consistent with the divine perfections that sin and misery should exist, while matter of fact cannot be brought to bear on the other side of the question. Matter of fact cannot prove that it is consistent with the perfections of God to save all men, whatever may be their conduct, for all men are not saved. Not only so, but as it is now consistent with the divine attributes that sin and misery should exist, and as those attributes are unchangeable, the inference is a fair one that it may always be consistent with the divine perfections that sin and misery should exist. We think we have now removed the entire foundation of every argument drawn from the perfections of God, in favour of universalism; hence, the arguments must fall; but as this is the strong ground of universalists we will examine the arguments separately.

Universalists argue the salvation of all men from the divine goodness, love and mercy. We connect goodness with the love and mercy of God in one reply, because universalists blend them together in the same argument. In the letter above referred to, Mr. Morse says, "The love of God is unbounded. All christians believe in the universal goodness of God." In proof of this he quotes Mark x. 18. "There is none good but one, that is God." From this it is clear that the terms in question are used reciprocally for each other. Not only so, but it must appear plain that a reply to an argument drawn from either the goodness, love or mercy of God, must be, in point of fact, a reply to an argument drawn from each or all of these perfections. Mr. Morse, in the above named letter, introduces his argument thus: "All will be finally holy and happy, because the universal parent of creation possesses love underived, uncaused, unbounded, unchangeable, and endless." Here are five reasons rendered why all men will be saved. It is said,

1. All men will be saved "because the love of God is underived." We admit that the love of God is underived, but deny that it follows from thence that all men will be saved. If universalists could prove that the love of God has just been derived from some foreign source they might argue that all will now be saved as the fruit of this new accession to the divine perfections; but as God's love has always existed the same, it must be difficult to see why it should be any more efficacious in the destruction of sin and misery than it was in preventing them.

2. It is said, "the love of God is uncaused." The object of this proposition was, to furnish occasion to show that the death of Christ did not produce the divine love. This we admit; but maintain that the death of Christ, as our atoning sacrifice, is the only medium through which we can enjoy the love of God; and that therefore we may be saved because Christ died, rather than for the reason that the love of God is uncaused.

3. It is said, "God's love is unbounded." By this it is meant that God's love extends to all his creatures; but it cannot prove the final holiness and happiness of all men; since it did not keep them holy and happy when they were so. The argument would have applied to Adam and Eve in the garden of Eden, in proof that they could never become unholy and unhappy, with the same propriety that it does to us, in proof that we cannot remain unholy and unhappy. It might have been said to them, God's love is boundless; he loves all the creatures he forms, you cannot therefore become unholy and wretched; and as it

would have been false in view of what is past, so it is not to be relied upon in view of what is to come.

4. It is said, "the love of God is unchangeable." This cannot prove the salvation of all men; for if the love of God is unchangeable, it is the same now that it was when sin and misery first entered the world; and if it change not, no good reason can be given why it will not suffer them to remain on the same terms that it admitted them at first. If universalists could prove that the love of God will change at some future period so as to operate very differently in the moral system from what it now does, they might argue the salvation of all men as the result of such change.

5. It is said, that "the love of God is endless." That the love of God is endless in itself, we have no doubt, but this cannot prove that all men will be saved. For God to be love is one thing; but for men to enjoy God is something quite different. God's love exists independently of all his creatures; but man's enjoyment of God depends upon his moral state. Again, for God to love sinners is one thing, and for sinners to love God is something else. God loves all men, as his creatures, but all men do not love God, as their Creator.

Now, as no man can be holy and happy who does not love God, it is for universalists to prove that all men will love God endlessly, and not that God's love is endless. God loves sinners now; but sinners are not now saved, and if present love does not produce present salvation, it cannot appear that endless love will certainly produce endless salvation.

But to strengthen this argument, drawn from the divine goodness, universalists call in the wisdom of God to its aid. Mr. Morse reasons thus: "If any created being will be endlessly miserable, God knew it before that being was created. *Goodness* would have prevented such creation." To this we reply,

1. It is fallacious to consider the creation of such as may be endlessly miserable, separately from the creation of those who shall be saved, or from the whole. God could not prevent the existence of such as may be lost, without preventing the existence of such as shall be saved; for their existence, in the order of things, is alternately derived from each other. The question then, with divine goodness and wisdom must be, not whether those who will be finally lost shall be created or have an existence, but whether our race shall exist as a whole, taking lost and saved together. This leads us to remark,

2. That God might have seen that any other race of beings which he might have created, would sin and become as wicked and miserable as have the human family. It must appear clear that God could not have created a race of intelligent and accountable beings without a liability to sin, for beings cannot be accountable subjects of a moral government unless they are moral agents, and moral agents may sin. If then any other race of beings which God might have created would have been equally liable to fall into sin and misery, the question is narrowed down to this: Is it consistent with divine goodness that such a race as the human family should exist, on the supposition that sinners are liable to endless punishment, divine wisdom foreseeing this issue? This leads us to remark,

3. That a greater amount of good than evil will be the final result of the creation of the human family, though some of our race be forever lost; and if a greater amount of good than evil result from the existence of the human family, then their creation was an act of goodness. In making an estimate of the comparative good and evil that results from the creation of the human family, we are not to draw our conclusions from what is the actual result, but from what the system would produce, were not its operations turned aside from their proper issue by the

abuse of moral liberty on the part of the creature. Taking this view, we see that divine goodness stands unimpeached, though sinners perish forever. The system which God put in operation, would have eventuated in the happiness of all his creatures, had it not been turned aside from its natural course by mal-conduct on the part of the creature; hence, divine goodness and wisdom are to receive credit for having originated a system which, in itself, was calculated to produce happiness without the least degree of misery, while what evil has arisen from this system argues, not a defect in divine goodness, but a fault in the conduct of man as a moral agent. But it may be said in reply to this, that though God created a system which was in itself calculated to produce good, and only good, yet he knew that evil would grow out of it. This may be true, but still it will follow that he knew at the same time that much more good than evil would be the result; hence, to suppose that goodness was bound to withhold existence from our race, because wisdom saw that some evil would be the result, is no less than to say that wisdom is bound to sacrifice a greater good to prevent a less evil, which is absurd. As a greater amount of good than evil is the actual result of the existence of the human family, on the supposition that some are endlessly lost, it follows that their creation is an act of goodness and not an act of cruelty, as universalists affirm; for cruelty would not produce more good than evil. It only remains to be shown, on the supposition that the doctrine of endless punishment is true, that more good than evil will still be the result of creation. This will appear when we consider that the number that is saved will far exceed the number of the lost.

1st. All infants will be saved, it is admitted on all hands, and they form a considerable portion of the human family.

2d. All pious adults, of every period, land and nation, will be saved. This number will increase in proportion to the whole, just as piety becomes more and more general in the world. Suppose then, as is the general opinion of the church, that christianity is yet to fill the world, and that time will then measure out some thousands of years of millenial glory, when the human family shall be much more numerous than at any former period, and we may imagine the ranks of the redeemed so filled up as to render the lost but a small portion of our entire race.

Should it still be urged that goodness would not suffer the existence of those whom wisdom saw would be lost, we reply,

1. Goodness could not have prevented their existence, without preventing the existence of those who are saved, as remarked above. This would have prevented more good than evil, which would have rendered it, in view of the whole, an evil act instead of a good one.

2. Those who are lost have the same opportunity to secure salvation as those who shall be finally saved; and that they do not secure salvation is their own fault. Both the saved and the lost are ushered into being under circumstances precisely the same, and hence, the act of producing both must be the same in moral quality; and as it cannot be denied that the creation of such as are saved is an act of goodness, so on the other hand, it cannot be affirmed, in truth, that the creation of those who may be finally lost is not an act of goodness.

But universalists argue from the fore-knowledge of God, and contend that the circumstance that God knows what will be their end, lays them under necessity, or an irresistible fate. To this we reply,

1. The knowledge of God can have no influence over the conduct of moral agents. If we apply the term *foreknowledge* to God, it is doubtless to describe the knowledge which he possesses of things yet future. Now, we ask on what ground, the fore-knowledge of God is maintained? We answer, it must be on the ground of the cer-

tainty of his decree, or the perfection of his knowledge. Now, the first of these cannot be admitted; for it is worse than trifling to argue the certainty of an event from the fore-knowledge of God, when that fore-knowledge is made to rest upon a decree: Why not argue from the decree itself? The moment the doctrine of decrees is introduced, fore-knowledge is excluded from the argument, and can have nothing to do in the case; for if it can be proved that God has unchangeably decreed all things that come to pass, we will admit the necessity by which every thing comes to pass, without making the certain decree still more certain by an argument drawn from the fore-knowledge of God, which fore-knowledge is made to depend upon the decree itself. If, then, any argument is drawn from fore-knowledge, such fore-knowledge must be maintained on the ground of the perfection of God's knowledge—that God's knowledge being perfect, he must know all things, as things past, things present or things to come, or as things which might be, but still will not be. If then the argument is made to rest upon the perfection of God's knowledge, we maintain that as the knowledge of God is perfect, he must know things just as they are, certain or contingent, necessary, or merely possible. Now the fact in the case is, the sinner, who shall be finally lost, is a moral agent and might do differently from what he does and be saved; and if so, God knows this as a thing possible. Now, if the sinner were to do differently and be saved, still there would be no disappointment in the divine mind; for as the perfect knowledge of God arises from a view of the facts, and not the facts from his knowledge, were the acts and end of the sinner different, the knowledge of God on these points, would be different. Thus we plainly see that the knowledge of God can have no influence in producing events, while we see equally plain how events, growing out of the moral agency of man, might be different from what they are, and still be in accordance with the fore-knowledge of God. We have now shown that no argument can be drawn from the wisdom and goodness of God combined, to prove the final salvation of all men, or to disprove the doctrine of endless punishment.

But Universalists also call to the assistance of this argument the power of God. Mr. Morse says, in the above mentioned letter, God "possesses power to annihilate hell and sweep its inhabitants into the dark abyss of non-existence:"—What God has power to do, when power alone is consulted, and what he can consistently do in view of all the perfections of his nature, are points quite different from each other. It cannot be denied that God has the same power to annihilate a limited hell that he has to annihilate an endless hell; and this he does not see fit to do. Some, who contend for the final salvation of all men, admit that there is a hell in the future world in which sinners will be punished for ages, and all universalists pretend to believe that sin is punished in this world or the next; and they cannot deny that sin, sorrow and death have reigned in this world for nearly six thousand years. Now, God can have no more power to destroy sin and misery than he had to prevent them; if indeed his power slumber over the reign of sin and misery, over sighs and groans, and death, for six thousand years, no argument can be drawn from the power of God to prove that he will ever see it consistent to destroy sin and misery, or annihilate its wretched subjects.

To the above, universalists sometimes add the holiness of God, in farther proof that he will destroy sin and misery. The argument is founded upon a supposed absurdity that a *holy* God should perpetuate *unholiness* forever. There can be no force in this. If sin and misery cannot exist forever without being perpetuated by God, then they cannot exist for six thousand years without being perpetuated by him for that length of time; and if a holy

God can perpetuate the existence of unholiness for six thousand years, his holiness can form no objection to its endless existence.

To bring up the rear of the arguments drawn from the perfections of God, universalists introduce the will of God. The argument is sometimes stated as follows:

What the goodness of God wills or proposes, and his wisdom plans, his power will execute. It is said that God wills the salvation of all men, and whatever he wills he has power to execute. If he does not will the salvation of all men, he is wanting in goodness, and if he does will the salvation of all men, and does not effect it, he must be deficient in power. To this we reply,

1. That God does not will the salvation of all men irrespectively of their moral agency. We admit that God wills the salvation of all men on gospel terms; but all men, as moral agents, do not comply with the terms of the gospel.

2. The will of God is not done in all things, by moral agents. The text, on which universalists rely to prove that God wills the salvation of all men, is 1 Tim. ii. 4. "Who will have all men to be saved and come unto the knowledge of the truth." This text as clearly proves that it is the will of God that all men should "come unto the knowledge of the truth" as it does that he wills that all men should he saved. Now, it is clear that all men do not come to the knowledge of the truth, and those who defeat the will of God in this respect, will also find it defeated in its purposes of their salvation. God wills the salvation of all men now, and that they should come to the knowledge of the truth as the means of effecting it, but all men are not saved now. It is said to the Laodiceans, Revelations iii. 15. "I know thy works that thou art neither cold nor hot: I *would* that thou wert cold or hot." Here God plainly declares that they were not what he *would* that they were; hence, his will was frustrated in the moral character of

this luke-warm church. It is useless to waste time and paper to prove that the will of God is not done in all things by man; for every sin is a violation of the divine will. God has given us his commands and what he has commanded, he wills that men should do; but men do them not. The law that speaks in deep toned thunders from the cloudy summit of Sinai, and the gospel that breathes a pardon upon the repenting sinner, in the milder voice of a crucified Redeemer, alike declare that the will of God has been violated. But universalists often quote Isa. xlvi. 10. "My counsel shall stand and I will do all my pleasure." This text does not relate to the final salvation of all men, but to the events which transpired under the reign of Cyrus. The counsel of God described in this text, was his purpose to overthrow Babylon and deliver the Jews from their captivity by the hand of Cyrus. But what has this to do with the salvation of all men? Just as much and no more than his counsel to destroy the old world by water, or to overthrow the Jews by the Romans.

We have now done with the arguments drawn from the divine perfections, and whether or not we have furnished a sufficient reply we leave the candid reader to judge.

II. Universalists argue the salvation of all men from the corrective nature and design of punishment. The argument may be thus stated: "All divine punishment is designed to reform the sufferer, but endless punishment cannot reform the sufferer, therefore no divine punishment can be endless." The fallacy of this argument lies in the major proposition, which asserts, that all punishment is designed to reform the sufferer. We deny this proposition and offer the following reasons for so doing.

1. There is no evidence to support it. That the scriptures teach that God does sometimes correct with a view to the reformation of the subject we heartily admit; but such corrective dispensations are mostly confined to those who are the people of God, in distinction from others,

and are always limited to this life, during which sinners are in a gracious state of probation. Because God corrects his children to render them more fruitful, or because he punishes sinners during their day of gracious probation, to bring them to repentance, to infer from thence that all punishment, under all circumstances, is designed to reform the sufferer, is to draw a conclusion much broader than the premises from whence it is deduced. The following is one of the principal texts produced in proof of the point in question, when any effort is made to prove it from the word of God. Lam. iii. 33. "For he doth not afflict willingly, nor grieve the children of men." It must be perfectly plain that the Prophet, in this text, has exclusive reference to the afflictions of the Babylonish captivity; hence the subjects of the punishment were God's covenant people, and the time of its infliction was this life, therefore the prophet says, verse 39, "Wherefore doth a living man complain, a man for the punishment of his sins." Now because God punished the Israelites for their idolatry with a view to their reformation, to infer from thence that sinners in hell are punished with no other design than their own benefit, is preposterous. But allow all that can possibly be claimed, namely, that the text relates to all sinners, proving that God punishes no sinner willingly, and still it will not furnish the least shadow of proof that all punishment is designed to reform the sufferer. If God punishes men not willingly, because he sees it is for their good, he may on the same principle punish them endlessly, because he sees that it is for the good of the whole moral system. Those who believe in the doctrine of endless punishment are very far from supposing that God inflicts any punishment, limited or endless, unnecessarily. There is then no evidence that all punishment is designed to reform the sufferer.

2. We object to the sentiment that all punishment is corrective, on the ground that it entirely overlooks the

sinner's desert. What the sinner *deserves* as a just punishment for his sins, and what he *needs* as a remedy for his spiritual disease, are two distinct points vastly different from each other. Taking this view, to suppose that all punishment is designed to make the sinner better, is to say that he deserves no punishment as a reward for his sin, but only needs it as a remedy for his disease. If all punishment is designed to benefit the sufferer, he can receive no more nor less of it than will really do him good; hence, the amount of punishment which the sinner is liable to endure, does not in the least depend upon what he *deserves*, but wholly upon what he *needs*. This is unscriptural, because the scriptures uniformly represent the sinner as guilty and deserving of punishment, and his punishment as a curse and real evil. Let us compare this sentiment with a few scriptural expressions. Gal. iii. 13. "Christ hath redeemed us from the curse of the law." By the curse of the law must be meant punishment. Now, if all punishment be designed to reform the sinner, then, Christ has redeemed us from what would have done us good, and from what God designed as the means of bringing us to repentance and salvation. Matt. iii. 7. "Who hath warned you to flee from the wrath to come." Wrath here must mean punishment, and if this is designed to make men better, the text should read, "who hath warned you to flee from what is designed by God to do you good, and make you better." Rom. iv. 15. "The law worketh wrath." Is not the law then the most efficient agent in man's salvation, if wrath be intended to effect it? Rom. v. 9. "Much more then, being now justified by his blood, we shall be saved from wrath through him." As wrath is punishment, and as punishment is designed to make us better, on the above principle, this text must teach that Christ saves us from what is desired by God as the means of salvation from sin. 1 Thess. i. 10. "Jesus which delivered us from the wrath to come;" that is, from a merciful remedy for our spiritual disease. 2 Thess. i. 9. "Who shall be punished with everlasting destruction." What then is everlasting destruction with which the sinner is threatened? Awful to relate! it is the only efficient and gracious means which God can employ to make sinners good and happy! Can any one in the light of these scriptures say that the Bible threatens no punishment only as a gracious discipline, and effectual remedy for the intellectual and moral disease of the sinner? Such a sentiment is not only unscriptural, but it is unreasonable and an insult to common sense. The sinner is represented as being punished according to his *works*, not according to his *wants*. Every man is represented as receiving *"according to that he hath done in the body,"* and not according to *that which is necessary to save him.* Christ says, "Behold I come quickly, and my reward is with me to give unto every man *according as his works shall be,"* not *according to what is necessary to bring him unto repentance.* Again the sinner is said to be *cursed*, to be *punished*, to endure *wrath, wrath without mixture, indignation, fiery indignation,* to *perish,* to be *destroyed,* &c. Now, if all these mean no more than what is for the sinner's good—no more than what is essential to his best interest—no more than what unmingled mercy deals out as the most tender physician administers a bitter medicine to a patient, there were never greater misnomers. Then are wrath and love the same; then between vengeance and mercy there is no difference; then is punishment the means of salvation from sin, the cause of punishment, and an effect proves a remedy for its own cause; then is a curse a blessing, and death leads to life!

3. To suppose that all punishment is designed to bring the sinner to salvation, entirely overlooks the atonement of Christ, the efficacy of the gospel, and the influence of the Holy Ghost. As we have shown, in a preceding chapter, that there will be a day of general judgment when

sentence will be passed upon sinners, it follows that if punishment is still inflicted with a design to reform the sufferer, it must be as a last resort, after all other means have failed. It must be perfectly plain that all the means connected with the gospel must be resisted by the sinner before the judgment, for it is for rejecting these that he is punished; hence, if punishment be inflicted after judgment, to reform the offender, it must be a last resort. This supposes punishment to be more efficacious than all other means. The gospel is preached without effect, the story of the Father's love and of the Redeemer's suffering, are insufficient to reclaim the hardened sinner; and the Holy Ghost woos him, but wins him not. Now, if after all this the sinner is to be reformed by punishment, then must wrath do more towards winning the sinner than mercy; then must hell fire do more towards reforming transgressors than the blood of Christ, the preaching of the gospel, and the Holy Ghost combined; and then must the sinner be more indebted to hell torments for his reformation than to all other means which God employs to bring sinners to repentance.

4. To contend that all punishment is designed to reform the sufferer is to abandon one of the main principles of universalism, viz. that love is the only proper incentive to obedience. Oft have their presses teemed with this sentiment; oft have their pulpits resounded with the unmingled delight of that sentiment which triumphs over all fear of punishment, and with sarcastic declamations on the slavish fear and perpetual horror of darkness, which must pervade the minds of those who believe in an endless hell. As a mere specimen of these very lofty strains, we will introduce the following from Mr. Morse's reply to the Rev. J. Parker, page 20. Concerning those who believe the doctrine of endless punishment Mr. M. enquires as follows: "We are induced to ask, do christians worship the true God, 'who is good to all,' or do they worship a

moloch burning with immortal vengeance, and pouring the sulphureous [sic] streams of never ending wrath on millions of his own creatures." This quotation clearly shows how universalists treat the views of those who appeal to the fears of sinners to excite them to repentance from a dread of the punishment which awaits them; and yet by holding to the corrective design and nature of punishment, as they do, they make this very dread of punishment the strongest incentive to repentance that can be brought to bear upon fallen spirits. Punishment becomes the sinners last safe hope, which will surround him and force him in when he shall have broken through every other barrier in his course to ruin. Thus we sec that no class of people declaims so vehemently against the fear of punishment, as an incentive to obedience, as universalists do, and yet no class depends so much upon its efficiency in effecting the sinner's salvation. In this they are inconsistent with themselves. They must cease to urge the corrective design and nature of punishment, or else give up one of their first principles, viz. that love is the only incentive to obedience, and preach hell torments and the horrors of the damned as the means of bringing sinners to repentance.

5. If it were admitted that all punishment is designed to reform the sufferer, still it would not prove the salvation of all men. The gospel is designed to bring sinners to repentance, and yet it does not effect this object universally; for if it did, there would be no necessity of corrective punishment, and if so, punishment, though designed to reform the sufferer, may, notwithstanding, fail to secure this end. The scriptures unequivocally teach that sinners sometimes harden themselves and grow worse under the dispensations of divine punishment as has been shown. Chapter VI. Argument V. Taking this view, we see that if it were admitted that all punishment is designed to reform the

sufferer, still his reformation would remain a matter of uncertainty.

III. Universalists sometimes argue the salvation of all men from the universality of the atonement made by Christ. They contend, that as Christ died for all men, all will be saved. So far as this argument is urged by that class of universalists who deny all future punishment, it possesses no force, and is undeserving a reply; for they deny the atonement outright, and contend that the death of Christ does not save sinners from one pang of deserved suffering, that every man suffers for all the sin he commits. Now, we ask if the death of Christ does not save sinners from the least degree of deserved punishment, how can his death for all men disprove the endless punishment of obdurate sinners? But this argument, when urged by restorationers appears somewhat plausible, and is entitled to serious consideration. We admit the premises, that Christ died for all men, but deny the conclusion, that all will therefore be saved. The fallacy of the argument consists in supposing that the death of Christ *unconditionally* and *absolutely* secures the object for which he died. If it be shown that the death of Christ does not absolutely secure the object for which he died, the argument vanishes at once, and universal salvation will not *necessarily* follow from a universal atonement. Now, it is a sufficient reply to any argument, or a sufficient refutation of any principle, to show that it contradicts plain matter of fact. We will then show that to suppose that the death of Christ necessarily secures the object for which he died, in those cases where moral agency is concerned, does contradict matter of fact and the argument will be finished.

1. Christ died to save all men here in this life, yet all are not saved here. We can allow no evasion on this point. Christ died to save all men in this life, or he did not. If he did not die to save all men in this life, several

absurdities follow. First, the fact that sinners are not saved in this life, argues no defect in their conduct, but a defect in the atonement of Christ. Secondly, if Christ did not die to save all men in this life, it follows that some sinners cannot be saved here, or else that they can be saved independently of the death of Christ, which cannot be allowed; for if sinners can be saved independently of the death of Christ, his death is an unnecessary interference; and to argue that all will be saved because he died for all, when they might be saved without are his death, is absurd. On the other hand to say that there [are] some for whom Christ did not die, to save in this life, and who consequently cannot be saved here, while others are saved, would be no less than to say that the ways of God are not equal. Again if Christ did not die to save *all* men in this life, and yet did die to save *some*, as some are saved, which cannot be denied, it follows that Christ died for some in a sense in which he did not die for others, and was therefore partial in his death, which cannot be allowed by universalists. It is clear then, that Christ died to save all men in this life. Now, nothing can be more plain than that all men are not saved in this life, wherefore the death of Christ does not absolutely secure the salvation of those for whom he died.

2. Christ died to save sinners from going to hell, and yet Restorationers admit that some will go to hell and be punished for a season, at least until they repent and reform. It cannot be denied that Christ's death was intended to save sinners from going to hell, and yet sinners do go to hell, universalists themselves being judges; it is therefore futile to argue that all will be saved because Christ died for all. Christ's death was as much intended to save men from going to hell as it was to bring them out of hell, and we think more so, for we admit the former, and deny the latter. Now, as it manifestly fails in the first of

these objects, it is absurd to contend that it will certainly succeed in the latter.

3. We would remark in conclusion that the death of Christ, or the atonement, was never intended unconditionally to save any adult sinner, as has been shown in Chapter III. in reply to objection II.

IV. Universalists argue the salvation of all men from those scriptures which speak of reconciliation, restoration and restitution, by Christ. We will consider the principal of their proof texts on this subject.

Acts. iii. 20, 21. "And he shall send Jesus Christ, who before was preached unto you: Whom the heavens must receive until the times of the restitution of all things, which God hath spoken by the mouth of all his holy prophets since the world began." The argument drawn from this text rests on the expression, *"restitution of all things."* If this means the restoration of every individual human being to the favour and image of God, it may argue something in favour of universalism; but if it do not mean this it can prove nothing to the purpose of universalists. Now, that the text does not mean this, appears from the following consideration.

1. The *time* of the restitution of all things, clearly proves that universal salvation cannot be meant by it. At what time will the restitution of all things take place? An answer to this question is to be drawn from an expression in the text, *"whom the heavens must receive until the time of the restitution of all things."* This expression refers to Christ's ascension to heaven, there to remain until he shall come again at the end of time to judge the world. The second coming of Christ to judge the world we have already proved in Chap. V. Arg. XV. and to this event the text clearly refers. The meaning appears to be this: Christ has ascended to heaven and shall remain there until the restitution of all things, when he shall again be revealed from heaven. This shows that the restitution of all things,

here spoken of, is to take place before the second coming of Christ, which proves that it cannot mean the salvation of all men; for all men will not be saved when Christ shall come to judge the world. Some will be judged by him and be punished for their sins, as has been abundantly proved in the argument above referred to.

2. The connection shows that universal salvation cannot be meant. Verses, 21, 22 and 23. taken in connection read thus: "Whom the heavens must receive until the times of the restitution of all things, which God hath spoken by the mouth of all his holy prophets since the world began. For Moses truly said unto the Fathers, a prophet shall the Lord your God raise up unto you of your brethren like unto me, him shall ye hear in all things whatsoever he shall say unto you. And it shall come to pass that every soul which will not hear that prophet *shall be destroyed from among the people.*" This restitution, which has been predicted by all the holy prophets since the world began, is so far from meaning the salvation of all men, that it includes the destruction from among the people of all who will not hear Jesus Christ, who will not receive and believe his gospel. But it may be asked what is to be understood by the restitution of all things if it does not mean the salvation of all men? We answer that it most probably means that state of things which the Gospel will ultimately effect; implying the restoration of all things that will ever be restored. When the gospel shall have been fully preached in the world, when it shall have been offered to all to whom it will ever be offered, and when all shall have accepted of it and shall be saved, who will ever accept of it and be saved; then will the restitution of all things have taken place in the sense of this text. It may relate exclusively to the restoration of harmony aid piety in this world.

Suppose a time is to come when all on the earth shall become pious, and righteousness and holiness prevail;

when the long looked for day of millennial glory shall rise resplendent, and dispel the gloom of moral night from the earth, when the North shall give up and the South keep not back, when Ethiopia shall stretch out her hands to God,

"And western empires own their Lord,
And Savage tribes attend his word;"

then will the restitution of all things be effected in the sense of this text; but this will not restore or save those who have lived and died in sin, and gone to hell during the darker ages of wickedness.

1 Cor. xv. 24, 25, 26, 28. "Then cometh the end, when he shall have delivered up the kingdom to God even the Father; when he shall have put down all rule and all authority and power. For he must reign until he hath put all enemies under his feet. The last enemy that shall be destroyed is death. And when all things shall be subdued unto him, then shall the Son also be subject unto him that put all things under him that God may be all in all." This text, though often urged by universalists in proof of universal restoration, has, we think, no direct bearing on the subject. It speaks of Christ's putting down all rule and all authority, and of his subduing all enemies under his feet; but this does not imply their restoration. An enemy may be subdued without being restored to favour. "The Apostle," says Mr. Isaac, "here undoubtedly alludes to the custom of conquerers treading upon the necks of their enemies. The captains of Joshua put their feet upon the necks of the five kings they had subdued; but this was preparatory to their destruction, not to their restoration." That the text does not prove the salvation of all men, is evident from the time when its predictions are to take place. All authority and power are to be put down, and all enemies are to be put under his feet prior to his deliv-

ering up the kingdom to God, which will take place at the end of the present state of things, or end of time, and at the day of judgment, as has been shown in Chapter V. Argument XV. Christ will reign until he shall have subdued all enemies under his feet, and then will deliver up the kingdom to God. Now, as this delivering up the kingdom to God is to take place at the day of judgment, and as all men will not be saved at the day of judgment, if they ever are, it follows that the text does not predict the salvation of all men, since its predictions are to be fully accomplished at a period when it is manifest all will not be saved. There is no way to evade the force of this without maintaining that all will be saved prior to the general judgment, which idea is without foundation; for there are no scriptures that speak directly of a general judgment, which do not associate with it the punishment of some of the human family.

Some lay great stress on the expression, "that God may be *all in all*, as though sin and misery can no longer have an existence in the universe, when God shall be all in all. That the expression furnishes no such proof is clear from the fact that God will be "all in all" when Christ shall deliver up the kingdom to him at the day of judgment, which will be the very time when sinners will be condemned and punished. Now, as God will be *"all in all,"* and sinners suffer punishment at the same time, the circumstance of God's being "all in all" cannot prove universal salvation. God's being *"all in all,"* is the result of Christ's delivering up the kingdom to him, and not of the salvation of all sinners. The expression, that God will be all in all, has reference to authority or dominion, and means no more than that God the Father will then govern the universe in his own person, and not as he now does, through the medium of his Son. It is said, "then shall the Son also himself be subject unto him, that God may be all in all," implying that if the Son should not deliver up the kingdom and become subject, God could not be all in all, in the sense intended in the text. This proves, beyond all doubt, that reference is had to authority, and that by God's being all in all, nothing more is meant than that he will then govern the universe in his own person, as he did before all power in heaven and in earth was given into the hands of Christ, as he declares it to be. Matt, xxvii. 18.

Eph. i. 10. "That in the dispensation of the fullness of times he might gather together in one, all things in Christ, both which are in heaven and which are in earth." This text simply speaks of the purpose of God in giving his Son to redeem the world, which was that he might gather together in one all things in Christ. Now, were we to admit that all things, in this text, include every individual, and that their being gathered together in Christ implies their salvation; still it would not prove the salvation of all men. The text does not say that all things, in this universal sense, will be gathered together in Christ, but simply that it is the divine purpose to gather all things together. But this purpose is not to gather them irrespectively of man's moral agency; hence, though God proposes to gather all in Christ, yet man as a moral agent may refuse to be gathered. Christ says. Matt. xxiii. 37. "O Jerusalem, Jerusalem, how often would I have gathered thy children together as a hen gathereth her chickens, under her wing, but ye would not." Here then is a plain case of some who had the offer of being gathered together in Christ and would not, and the consequence was, they were not gathered. If the gathering together of all things in Christ, implies the salvation of all men, it follows that God does not propose to gather all things in Christ, only upon the terms on which he proposes to save men; and salvation we have already proved to be conditional, see Chap. VI. Argument, III. It has been abundantly shown, in reply to the argument drawn from the will of God, that man as a moral agent, may defeat the purpose of the divine will in relation to his own salvation; therefore the fact that God proposes gathering all things together in Christ cannot prove the salvation of all men.

Though the above is a sufficient reply, we will add that the most probable meaning of the text under consideration, is that the gathering together of all things in heaven and in earth signifies the union of the Jews and Gentiles in one gospel church; and how this can take place, without implying the salvation of every individual, may be as easy to conceive as it is to understand how Jerusalem, and *all* Judea, and *all* the region round about Jordan could be baptized by John, without supposing that every individual within the specified districts received the ordinance. See Matt. iii. 5, 6.—Col. i. 20. is also urged by universalists in proof of universal restoration, but the above remarks are as applicable to this text as they are to the one on which they have been offered.

Rom. xiv. 11. "For it is written, as I live saith the Lord God, every knee shall bow to me and every tongue shall confess to God." This text has been considered a strong hold by universalists, but a little attention to it must convince all that it contains nothing in proof of universal salvation. The argument drawn from this text takes for granted what should be proved, viz. that bowing and confessing to God imply true repentance on the part of the sinner, and gracious reception on the part of God. Now, the connection absolutely forbids such an exposition. Take it as it stands connected with the verses that precede and follow it, and it reads thus: "Why dost thou judge thy brother? for we shall all stand before the judgment seat of Christ. For it is written, As I live saith the Lord God, every knee shall bow to me, and every tongue confess to God. So then every one of us shall give account of himself to God." From the whole, it is clear that the oath of God, that every knee shall bow, and every tongue confess, relates to universal judgment, and not to universal salvation. What this confession will be, as the text would be understood by a Jew, we may learn from the following very remarkable extract from Josephus' Discourse to the Greeks, on Hades. For all men, the just as well as the unjust, shall be brought before *God the Word,* for to him hath the *Father committed all judgment;* and he, in order to *fulfill the will of his Father,* shall come as judge, whom we call *Christ.* This person exercising the righteous judgment of the Father towards all men, hath prepared a just sentence for every one according to his works; at whose judgment seat, when all men, and angels, and demons shall stand, they will send forth one voice, and say, JUST IS THE JUDGMENT: the rejoinder to which will bring a just sentence upon both parties, by giving justly to those who have done well, an *everlasting fruition;* but allotting to the lovers of wicked works *eternal punishment.*" From this we see that Josephus supposed that men and devils could confess to God at the judgment seat without being restored to the divine favour. We also see that it was his opinion that sinners will confess the authority of the court, and the justice of the sentence, though it will hurl them down to hell; and this no doubt is the meaning of the apostle in the above text.

Phil. ii. 10, 11. "That at the name of Jesus every knee should bow, of things in heaven, and things in earth, and things under the earth; and that every tongue should confess that Jesus Christ is Lord, to the glory of God the Father." On this text we remark,

1. That the bowing and confessing, of which it speaks, most clearly imply an acknowledgment of the authority of Jesus Christ as the moral governor and judge of all rational beings. The preceding verse says, "God hath highly exalted him and given him a name that is above every name; that at the name of Jesus every knee should bow," &c. By this we understand that Christ has received,

as he declares, himself, all power in heaven and in earth, and that he is, as Messiah, constituted the moral governor of the universe, and that all are therefore bound to obey him, as saith the poet:

> "Jesus, the name high over all.
> In hell, or earth, or sky;
> Angels and men before it fall.
> And devils fear and fly."

But this does not prove the salvation of all men; for this confession commenced among the devils more than eighteen hundred years since, when they cried out saying, Luke iv. 34. "Let us alone, what have we to do with thee, thou Jesus of Nazareth? Art thou come to destroy us? I know thee who thou art, the Holy one of God;" but we are not informed that his satanic majesty or any one of his Angels are yet restored.

2. If it were admitted that the text speaks of true worship, still it will not follow that it will ever be performed by all men. The expression, "that at the name of Jesus every knee should bow, and that every tongue should confess that Jesus is Lord," expresses no more than the obligation which rests upon all intelligent beings, in consequence of his exaltation. That men *should* worship Jesus Christ, that God exalted him that men *should* worship him we are willing to admit; but to infer from thence that all men will discharge this duty, is as absurd as it would be to argue that all men do, and must of necessity do, every thing which God has made their duty. God has exalted Jesus Christ, that all men should now bow and confess in this sense; but all men do not discharge this duty.

We have now examined the principal texts which are urged in proof of universal restoration, and we venture that every candid and prudent mind will require stronger proof of so important a sentiment, than any thing contained in these scriptures, before they will venture their everlasting all upon its truth.

V. Universalists argue the salvation of all men from the promises of God, especially from the promise made to Abraham. So much stress is laid upon this promise, that we often hear them call universalism *"the Abrahamic faith."* In order to show the ground taken by universalists on this subject, we will give an extract from the pen of the Rev. Pitt Morse. In giving an account of a public, oral debate, which he once held with the writer of these pages, he makes the following statement. "Then came up the all engrossing subject of *conditionality*. I took the position that God can control the human will without doing violence to human freedom. — This was sustained by argument, and confirmed by the unconditional covenant recorded in the thirty-first chapter of Jeremiah and the eighth of Hebrews. I proved that the promises are universal and unconditional, that they contain spiritual blessings, that there is no law against them, and that they are confirmed by the oath of God." See Magazine, &c. published at Utica, N.Y. for Nov. 3, 1832. On the all engrossing subject of conditionality, as Mr. M. calls it, the reader is referred to what has been said in the preceding Chapter, Argument III. In this place we shall only attend to the promises which Mr. M. says, "are universal and unconditional." In speaking of the covenant, recorded Jer. xxxi. we suppose he refers to the 33d verse, which reads thus: "But this shall be the covenant that I will make with the house of Israel; after those days saith the Lord, I will put my law in their inward parts, and will write it in their hearts; and will be their God, and they shall be my people." It would appear from Mr. M's own account that he relied upon this as a principal text in support of his theory; we will therefore show that it furnishes no support to universalism.

1. The text does not speak of all men, but of the house of Israel in distinction from all other men. Mr. M. says, "I proved that the promises are universal," and refers us to this text as one of the proofs he introduced on the occasion. From this, the reader can judge how well he sustained his cause. "This is the covenant I will make with the house of Israel; I will put my law in their inward parts," &c. This, with Mr. M., is a universal promise, i. e. the house of Israel includes not only every individual of the descendants of Israel, but all the gentile world. Such conclusions are only worthy of the cause of error. Should it be said that the text relates to the days of the gospel, and that it includes all believers as the spiritual Israel of God, we grant it; but still it is not universal, for it can include only such as believe the gospel, experimental christians, in distinction from such as do not receive the gospel. Now is the time in which God said he would do these things, and all true christians enjoy the blessings promised in the text; but does it follow from thence that swearers, and liars, and filthy drunkards, have the law of God written in their hearts?

2. It is evident that the promise contained in the text is not unconditional, as Mr. M. supposes. It is true there is no condition expressed in the text, but still scripture, matter of fact, and the experience of all christians, prove that the blessing here promised, is conditionally enjoyed. A few observations must be sufficient to show this fact. The nature of the blessing must convince all of its conditionality. "I will put my law in their inward parts, and write it in their hearts." This implies that renewal of the moral man, which is termed in the New Testament being "born again," being "saved by the washing of regeneration and renewing of the Holy Ghost," being "after God, renewed in righteousness and true holiness," &c. It implies the difference between a true christian and one who is not. Now

that all this is conditional, is evident from the following text, John i. 12. "But as many as received him, to them gave he power to become the sons of God, even to them that believed on his name." It is true that the work of renewing the heart is the work of God, which none but God can do, as the 13th verse shows; but still that God may do this work for us, may put his law within us, and write it in our hearts, the text above quoted shows that we must receive Christ, and believe on his name; the blessing therefore is conditional. Again, the promise in the text is shown to be conditional from a consideration of the agent by which God performs this work for us. This agent is the Holy Spirit. It cannot be denied that it is by the Holy Spirit that God writes his law in the hearts of men. Now, we have shown in the preceding chapter that the influence of the Spirit, as well as all the other means which God employs to save sinners, may be resisted by the sinner himself; it must therefore be conditionally that God promises to write his law in our hearts. Once more, the promise in the text under consideration, is shown to be conditional from its partial fulfilment. In order to see this, it is necessary to fix on the time in which God has promised to do this work for us. "*After those days*, saith the Lord, I will put my law in their inward parts," &c. After what days, or at what time, we enquire? This most clearly refers to the coming of Christ, and describes the indwelling of the Holy Spirit in the hearts of christians, which was given after his ascent to heaven. From this it appears that now is the time in which God promised to do these things for the house of Israel; that this time commenced with the opening of the gospel dispensation. The question then is, Does God write his law in the hearts of all men? This cannot be pretended; as we have remarked above, drunkards, liars, thieves, murderers, and all the abominable, cannot have God's holy law written in their hearts. This presents a dilemma for the consideration of universalists, holding out three alternatives from which they must choose, any one of which will ruin their cause. First, the covenant does not embrace all men; or secondly, the covenant promise is conditional; or thirdly, God does not fulfill the promise in all those cases in which his law is not written in the heart. This must fully settle the question of the conditionality of the divine promises. Heb. viii. 10. to which Mr. M. also alludes as containing an unconditional promise, is a literal quotation of the words of the Prophet, on which we have just been remarking; and hence, must be the same in meaning, and therefore is sufficiently explained in what has been said on the original.

The above is a sufficient reply to the argument drawn from the promises of God, which appear to include all men; for it is a matter of fact that the promises generally, which universalists urge in proof of their theory, speak of blessings which are the privilege of christians in this life, and which all men do not enjoy. Here again, plain matter of fact rears its unyielding front, against which universalist's arguments batter in vain; for as the promises of God speak of blessings to be enjoyed in this life, and as matter of fact says all men do not enjoy these blessings, it follows beyond dispute that the promises do not unconditionally and absolutely secure the blessings of which they speak. These remarks will apply to the Abrahamic, as well as to the general promises of the gospel. We will notice a few of those promises on which universalists base their argument, and then dismiss this subject. The promise which God made to Abraham may be found, Gen. xii. 3.—xviii. 18.—xxii. 18.—xxxvi. 4.—xxviii. 14. This promise is given in these words: "In thy seed shall all the nations of the earth be blessed." In one of the places above referred to, the word, "families" is substituted for "nations;" but this cannot alter its meaning, for the word *families* is undoubtedly used in this place to signify nations or tribes. We cannot, without transcending our intended limits, go into a full investigation of the Abrahamic covenant, but we will attempt to show, in few words, that it does not unconditionally secure the personal salvation of one individual adult sinner; which must be sufficient so far as this controversy is concerned.

1. It is perfectly easy to conceive that all nations of the earth, and all the families of the earth, can be blessed with the gospel of Christ, without supposing that every individual of all nations must consequently be saved. We as a nation, are now blessed with the gospel, or are blessed in the seed of Abraham, but every individual of our nation is not blessed with personal salvation from sin.

2. The apostle most clearly makes a conditional application of this promise, showing that none can enjoy the blessing of Abraham, who are not imitators of his faith. Rom. iv. 11, 22, 23, 24. "He received the sign of circumcision, as a seal of the righteousness of the faith which he had, yet being uncircumcised, that he might be the father of all them that believe. And therefore it was imputed to him for righteousness. Now it was not written for his sake alone, that it was imputed to him, but for us also, to whom it shall be imputed, if we believe on him who raised up Jesus our Lord from the dead." Gal. iii. 9, 26, 29. "So then they which be of faith are blessed with faithful Abraham. For ye are all the children of God by faith in Christ Jesus; and if ye be Christ's, then are ye Abraham's seed, and heirs according to the promise." These quotations from the apostle clearly show that the promise of God to Abraham was conditional, so far as it related to the salvation of individual sinners, and that none but believers can be Abraham's children and heirs with him to the promised blessings. But Mr. M. says, the promises "are confirmed by the oath of God." This is

granted; but it does nothing towards proving the salvation of all men, since no one contends for the doctrine of endless punishment on the ground that the covenant will be violated on the part of God. The oath of God renders the covenant sure for its true intent and purposes, but we have abundantly shown that it contains conditions to be complied with on the part of man; and by a non-compliance with these, the sinner may forfeit his interest in it and come short of the promised blessing, though God remain ever true to his word. We suppose Mr. M. refers to Heb. vi. 17, 18. "Wherein God willing more abundantly to show unto the heirs of promise, the immutability of his counsel, confirmed it by an oath: that by two immutable things, in which it was impossible for God to lie, we might have a strong consolation, who have fled for refuge to lay hold on the hope set before us." It cannot be over-looked that this text limits the object of the oath to those who flee to lay hold on the hope set before them; hence, the oath of God secures the blessing to no others. We ask then, have all men fled to lay hold on this hope? This cannot be pretended. True believers in Christ Jesus only have done this: sinners, drunkards and scoffers, have not fled to lay hold on the hope that is set before them. Until it be proved that all men embrace the gospel, and by faith lay hold on the hope it holds out to our fallen race, this text can prove nothing in favour of universalism; but this point cannot be proved. Of many, the words of Christ are now as true as when he uttered them. "Ye will not come unto me that ye might have life."

We think we have now shown that no argument can be drawn from the promises of the gospel in proof of unconditional universal salvation. We do not pretend that we have examined every promise that universalists quote in proof of their doctrine, but we have examined the principal of them, and the remarks which have been made will apply to the promises of the gospel generally; it is therefore unnecessary to pursue this subject farther.

VI. Universalists often urge in proof of their theory those scriptures which predict the universal reign of grace and piety. In reply to the argument drawn from this class of texts it will be necessary to offer but few remarks.

1. Let it be noted that this class of texts relates to the present world. It is the earth, that is, this world that is to be filled with the knowledge of God.

2. Admitting that such a day is to come, when "all shall know the Lord, from the least to the greatest," and when "the knowledge of God shall cover the earth," and it will not prove universal salvation; for a general reign of grace and piety on earth, cannot, save or in the least affect those who may have lived and died in sin, and gone to perdition, before this day shall dawn to bless this now dark and sinful world.

VII. Universalists argue the salvation of all men from the nature of faith, and the duty of all men to believe in Jesus Christ. The argument is sometimes thus stated: All men are required to believe that they have eternal life in Jesus Christ—they must therefore have eternal life in him, whether they believe it or not; otherwise they must be required to believe a lie; for believing cannot make a thing true which was not true before. If men have eternal life in Jesus Christ, then their unbelief cannot deprive them of it, or make it less true that they have such life in him.

The fallacy of this argument consists in supposing that men are required to believe that they have eternal life unconditionally given them in Jesus Christ. That there is eternal life in Jesus Christ we admit; but that it is unconditionally given to sinners, or that they are unconditionally made the partakers of it we deny. The simple facts are these; there is life in Jesus Christ, life for all who will accept of it on gospel terms; but in order that the sinner may be made the partaker of this life, he must believe and be connected with Christ by faith as a branch is connected with the vine. John xv. 5, 6. "I am the vine, ye are the branches: If a man abide not in me, he is cast forth as a branch and is withered, and men gather them and cast them into the fire, and they are burned." From this it must appear, that though there is life in Christ, yet it cannot save the sinner, who does not believe in him, any more than the life and nourishment which is in the vine can preserve the branch, when severed from it. There is life in Jesus Christ, but what good can this do that class of sinners of whom Christ says, John v. 40. "Ye will not come unto me that ye might have life."

VIII. It is very common for universalists to appeal to the sympathies of our common nature, in proof of the salvation of all men. To give the argument the greater force, we are told that God is the common parent of all men, and then an appeal is made to the throbbing bosoms of fathers and mothers, and the question is asked if they would punish their children forever; and if not, how they can believe that God, who is better than any earthly parent, will punish his children forever. To this we reply,

1. That the sympathies of human nature can be no just rule, by which to determine what is right and proper to be done by the divine administration. Earthly parents are not always governed by strict justice, nor true mercy. This must appear from the fact that most parents, if not all, are disposed to punish their own children less than they are others, for the same offence. We have a most striking instance of this in the conduct of one of the governors of a neighboring state, who pardoned his own son, notoriously guilty, and condemned to death. Now, it is evident that the governor would not have pardoned any other person under the same circumstances, which clearly shows that a parent's feelings and conduct towards a child are not always the offspring of strict justice or true mercy, and therefore can prove nothing at all what God will do,

who does not act from sympathy, but from his own eternal and immutable justice.

2. Earthly parents and all good governments, do punish offenders, and aim at punishing according to the magnitude of the offence; and if so, it cannot be unreasonable to suppose that God will punish sinners all they deserve. Taking this view, we see that the argument to which we are replying, entirely overlooks the sinner's desert; it takes for granted that the sinner does not deserve endless punishment, which is a mere begging of the question. If the sinner deserves endless punishment, he will certainly be punished endlessly, and the circumstance that God is our creator, preserver, and good benefactor, serves to deepen the turpitude of sin, and render the sinner more deserving of punishment than he would otherwise be. From this it appears that if God be our Father, the sinner is stamped with the guilt of rebellion against a kind and heavenly parent; if God be good to sinners, so much worse, and morally corrupt sinners must be to hate and disobey him. Has God made a great display of divine compassion in the gift of his Son, to suffer and die for sinners? So much greater must be the sinner's guilt for rejecting this Saviour, and spurning offered mercy through a crucified Redeemer. How clear is it then, that just in proportion as universalists dwell upon the circumstance that God is the Father of all, and that he is good unto all, exercising tender mercy over all his works, they enhance the sinner's guilt and heighten the fearful picture of his final doom.

3. If the argument could prove any thing, it would prove that sin and misery could never exist. What parent would suffer his child to be miserable for a year, a month, a week, or even a day? But this does not prove that God will not suffer his creatures to be miserable for a year; for matter of fact declares that they are miserable for years on years, and if so, the fact that a parent would not pun-

ish a child forever, cannot prove that God will not punish sinners forever.

We have now done with the examination of universalist's arguments, and though we do not pretend to have noticed every idea that has been advanced in favor of Universalism, yet we have noticed the principal; insomuch that we think but few arguments will be found, in any vindication of that doctrine, or met with in any oral discourse, which may not be classed under some one of the above heads. And having examined the evidence in favor of universal salvation, we make an appeal to the candid reader, and ask him, if after reading this brief reply, he can still see proof sufficient to justify him in venturing the eternal interest of his undying soul upon the supposition that all are to be saved, irrespectively of their conduct in this life.

VIII
Objections to Universalism Stated

IN THIS CHAPTER WE PROPOSE to consider some of the most prominent objections to universalism, which render it defective as a system of religious faith and practice. It must be the object of true religion to better the condition of man, both in this life and that which is to come. It cannot be denied, by those who contend that universalism is the religion of the Bible, that it involves our future and eternal interests. It must appear then, that any system of religion, on which is suspended such a vast and eternal interest, should present strong claims on our credulity before it is embraced. Nothing short of the following qualities can justify us in the reception of any system of religion. It should be consistent in its parts, direct and clear in its proof, reforming in its tendency, especially comforting to its true votaries, and secure in its hope. These qualities, we maintain, universalism does not possess; hence, we urge their opposites as so many objections to the theory.

1. Universalism is discordant in its parts and self-contradictory. This is peculiarly true in two respects.

I. It contradicts itself, respecting the time when all men are to be saved. The grand point is assumed, that all men will be saved, but if an attempt be made to tell *when* all men will be saved, the system is presented in a variety of forms.

Some say that all will be saved at death, or as soon as they are dead. It is known that a large portion of universalists at the present day, deny all punishment after death, and maintain that all enter upon a state of happiness so soon as they leave the world. This appears to be the sentiment of Rev. H. Ballou, as all know, who are acquainted with his writings. The same opinion seems to be held by Mr. Balfour, who has written a volume, in which he attempts to annihilate the very existence of a future hell. The same may be said of Rev. Pitt Morse, who has cut Mr. Balfour's laboured work much short, by a bold assertion that "Christ never taught a hell beyond the grave."

While the above is strongly insisted upon by many universalists, others take different ground and maintain that sinners will be punished after death, during the intermediate state, but that all will be saved at the resurrection, making that the new birth or regeneration.

A third class admit that there will be a day of general judgment after the resurrection, when sinners will be judged and punished, but contend that they will still, at some subsequent period, be redeemed from hell, and be made forever holy and happy. Universalists of every class agree in asserting that all will be finally saved; but the moment they undertake to tell when, the system is broken into fragments. They generally agree also in maintaining that sin cannot go unpunished; but when and how it is punished are questions concerning which there are almost as many opinions as there are advocates for the system. Universalists are themselves aware of these discrepancies in their theory; and hence, make every possible effort to prevent public investigation and discussion on these points. To show that these charges are well founded, the reader is presented with universalist testimony which cannot be doubted on this subject. The following is quoted from the editorial department of a universalist periodical published at Utica, N.Y. The articles from which we quote are headed "Peace Maker;" the object of which is to dissuade universalists from discussing points of difference which exist among themselves, as the language will show for itself. The writer says, "I wish to be distinctly understood, that I am not opposed to the discussion of any of these subjects in the abstract, at any time, and in any manner which may not endanger our peace and unity. But I do not consider the present juncture the time for such a discussion, if publick, and least of all in our periodicals. Though warmly attached to my own peculiar opinions, I am more attached to universalism at large. Many universalists, it is well known, who believe in *post mortem* punishment, [punishment after death,] do not believe the Bible teaches it expressly and directly, but only by inference—others believe it merely on reason and analogy, independent of the scriptures—some make it merely a deprivation of present holiness and happiness—some confine it to a very short period of time—others to an indefinite period—others to the intermediate state between death and the general resurrection. If we were inclined to divide, where would we draw the line—at what doctrinal point shall *we begin*, and at what doctrinal point *end* the separation? In a denomination like our own, where there is such an extent of christian freedom, and such a consequent diversity of opinion, the only bonds of union must be some great and leading principle of theology, which can be universally applied and practiced. To prove this let a brief examination be made: supposing *ante* and *post mortem* punishment, [punishment *before* and *after* death,] to be the line of separation.

"1. To which party shall A belong, (a respectable class of valued brethren,) who has not yet made up his mind on the subject—is yet undecided which side, has the truth?

"2. B deems *ante mortem* punishment [punishment before death] *merely probable*—C thinks *post mortem* punishment [punishment after death] merely probable.— Neither believes his opinion in any wise revealed, but infers it from reason and analogy alone. Where will you place these?

"3. D not only deems *post mortem* punishment *probable* but finds *inferential* testimony for it in the Bible. E believes exactly the reverse, on *inferential* testimony to the contrary, or for want of any testimony on the subject.

"4. F believes in *post mortem* punishment, believing it expressly taught in the Bible; while G believes it expressly denied by the same authority.

"5. H believes in the sleep of the soul and *post mortem* punishment—I believes in an immediate consciousness of future existence and denies punishment after death.

"6. J believes with I, as it respects the soul, [that it has a conscious existence after the death of the body,] but with H as it respects punishment, [believing that sinners are punished after death,] while K is diametrically opposed to J [believing that the soul sleeps in death with the body, and that sinners are not punished after death.]

"7. L believes that the sleep of the soul is prolonged in proportion to the viciousness of its character, and is thus punished *negatively*, by a deprivation of holiness and bliss. M believes that the sleep of death will be instantaneously broken at the general resurrection, and perfect holiness and happiness succeed it.

"8. N believes that immediately after death, or after

the resurrection, if he believe in the sleep of the soul, the soul has the same *moral* character which it had at death, from which state it advances gradually to perfection. O, on the contrary, believes that immediately after deaths or the resurrection, if he believe in the sleep of the soul, the soul is freed from all immorality, and filled with the fullness of knowledge, holiness and bliss.

"9. P believes in a gradual and progressive improvement, in the intermediate state, of all the moral and intellectual powers at death, until holiness becomes the characteristic, when all are thenceforward equal in bliss according to capacity. Q believes that immediately after death, or the resurrection, all are alike divested of the immoral character, but left different in mental powers, and thus progress through eternity." See *Magazine and Advocate for April 26, and May 3,* 1824. In the above quotations the words included in brackets have been added with a view to render the sense more conspicuous; by omitting these the reader will have the extract in the precise words of the original. We think this comment on universalism is a good one, perfectly worthy of its source, and fully answering the purpose for which we have quoted it. We regard it as an epitome of universalism, on which we beg leave to submit a few remarks of our own.

1. This must be regarded as an honest testimony, respecting the discordant views, which prevail among universalists. The writer is a teacher of universalism both from the pulpit and the press, and therefore ought to understand the system; and being a member of the fraternity, and as he tells us he is "more attached to universalism at large" than to his "own peculiar opinions" he can have no motive to misrepresent it.

2. The article under consideration represents universalists as being so discordant and contradictory in their views, as to be held together as a denomination, only by closing their eyes against the light of investigation

concerning the means by which they are to arrive at the grand conclusion at which their theory aims, and blindly rushing forward to an anticipated result without ever considering the way, the process, and time of arriving at their fondly anticipated issue. They must fix their eyes on the one individual and most distant point, the salvation of all men; and this object must be viewed with, a fixed gaze, which overlooks all that intervenes. The moment attention is diverted from this assumed point, by the enquiry concerning the way of coming at it, they are represented as broken to pieces, and as wandering off in different directions though professedly going to the same place.

Here are sixteen ways marked out by which to arrive at the grand conclusion, the salvation of all men. These theoretical paths cross at right angles, and in almost every other direction, in a manner to contradict and destroy each other, insomuch that but one out of the whole sixteen can be true. Now on the truth of one of these theories universalism depends; for it must be true in some one of these forms if true at all, unless the number of theories be increased by multiplying divisions, which will render it still more doubtful; and as all these theories are embraced by universalists with equal tenacity, each being equally confident that he has the truth, it follows that fifteen universalists out of sixteen must be mistaken, and can never obtain salvation in the way they anticipate. If then fifteen forms of universalism out of sixteen must be false, it is reasonable to conclude that it is false in all its forms. This conclusion is the more reasonable, wben we consider that the main question at issue, and the only question which universalists are willing to agitate, is whether or not any of these forms are true.

3. It is too plain to be overlooked that the above account of the sentiments of universalists, savours strongly of infidelity. In two respects the features of infidelity are

developed in the extract we have made. First, it appears that many universalists do not themselves believe that some very important points in their religious creeds have any foundation in the word of God. The writer says, of those who believe in punishment after death, and those who deny it, "neither believes his opinion in any wise revealed, but infers it from reason and analogy alone." The meaning of this is, some universalists believe that sinners will be punished in the future world, and at the same time do not believe it is taught in the Bible; and others believe that sinners will not be punished after death — that they receive all their punishment in this life, on the ground of natural reason, not believing it taught in the word of God. It is clear then, if we may believe a universalist witness, that many suppose that some very important points in their creeds, have no support from the scriptures; and if the question, are sinners liable to punishment after death or not, can be decided both affirmatively and negatively with equal tenacity, without even an appeal to the law and testimony, we think universalists can have but little use for the scriptures; nor does it appear to us that persons who can decide such momentous theological points without the aid of the scriptures can have but little confidence in them as a full and perfect system of revealed religion.

Secondly, another feature of infidelity, which the extract contains is the denial of the immortality of the soul. Of H, (a class of universalists,) the writer says, he "believes in the sleep of the soul." This sentiment he applies to five other classes of universalists, making it probable that at least one third part of universalists "believe in the sleep of the soul;" that is, that the soul dies with the body and with it sleeps in the grave. This not only shows that universalism is indefinite and self-contradictory, but also that it is infidelity outright. No man honestly believing the scriptures, can believe in the sleep of the soul. Does the soul of Enoch, who was translated, sleep in death? Does the soul of the prophet, whom the fiery chariot of the Lord bore to the heavenly world, sleep in death? Do the souls of Moses and Elias, who appeared and conversed with Christ on the mount, hundreds of years after the dissolution of their bodies, sleep in death? Do "the souls of those who were slain for the word of God" whom the revelator saw under the altar and who cried, "saying, how long O Lord, holy and true, dost thou not judge and avenge our blood;" sleep in death? See Heb. xi. 6. 2 Kings ii. 11. Matt xvii. 3. Rev. vi. 9, 10.

4. Universalism is self-contradictory in the means through which the grand object is to be obtained. One argues that all men will be saved because sin does not deserve endless punishment. A second contends that all will be saved because God is good to all—that he is the tender parent of all men; and because he is gracious to forgive the iniquity of his people, &c. &c. A third is sure that the doctrine of universal salvation is true because Christ has died for all men to redeem them from the curse of the law. These positions of which universalism is made to rest, are directly opposed to each other, and cannot all be true. If all are to be saved because sin does not deserve endless punishment, then they cannot be saved on the ground of divine mercy and forgiveness, nor on the ground of Christ's death; for, in such case, they may be saved without either. Again if men are to be saved because God is merciful even to the forgiveness of sin, as universalists often argue, then the circumstance that sin does not deserve endless punishment, cannot be the ground of salvation, since a pardon would secure salvation even if sin did deserve endless punishment. Nor can the death of Christ be urged as the ground of salvation, if God's forgiving mercy secures it; for if mercy can extend pardon to offenders without the death of Christ, then sinners can be saved without it, and therefore the death of

Christ cannot be the ground of salvation. Once more, if the death of Christ be urged as the ground of salvation, or as a reason why all men will be saved, then neither the small demerit of sin, nor the pardoning mercy of God can be urged as such ground, or reason. If endless punishment be unjust, and if Christ, notwithstanding, died to save men, then he must have died to save them from an evil which they did not deserve, or to prevent God from being unjust. Thus it is plain that universalism is discordant in its parts and self-contradictory, and therefore is defective as a system of religious faith.

II. Universalism is indirect and confused in its proof.

This must follow to some extent, from the confused and contradictory views of universalists stated above. Where there are so many and contradictory views taken of the same theory, there will be a proportionate confusion in the modes of proving it; for though all aim at the same point, yet as they have different modes of coming at it, each will argue as he conceives most consistent with his own peculiar views, and as there are so many contradictory views taken of the system as a whole, so the arguments employed to support it will clash with each other just as they are suited to the different forms in which it is held and defended. We will notice a few instances of the indirectness and confusion of universalists arguments.

1. Universalists labour more to disprove the sentiments of others than they do to build up their own theory by direct arguments. The reason of this is plain; they can constantly assail others in this way without hazarding any thing in the warfare. It is much easier to oppose a system even of pure truth, than it is to rear a fortress of error, which will stand an assault; hence, universalists, by keeping their own system indefinite so as to present nothing tangible to be demolished, can, after the manner of infidels, carry on an offensive warfare without hazard. No one who has read many universalist books, or

heard much universalist preaching can fail of being convinced that their arguments consist mostly of negative propositions, designed to prove that such and such things are not true. Mr. Ballou, under the pretence of writing a treatise *on* the atonement, has written one *against* it, in which the principal effort consists in denouncing the opinions of others. His exposition of the parables is in a similar style. Mr. Balfour has written an entire volume of three hundred and forty-eight pages, to disprove the existence of a place of punishment called hell. The same author has produced a second volume to disprove the existence of devils or evil spirits. This last effort is no more than justice might seem to demand of the author; for if in his first he has annihilated hell, as he pretends, it appears no more than right that he should, by another blow, strike the devils from being, and not leave them to linger in a homeless existence. In like manner universalist criticism is usually spent in attempts to prove that some pre-conceived notion of the sacred text is absurd—that such and such texts do not mean so and so. Now, we ask why is this so, if universalism be the plain and obvious sentiment of the Bible? If the scriptures in their most plain and natural construction, are not opposed to universalism, why is all this labour and criticism spent to prove that they do not mean what common readers generally understand by them? This kind of proof though it may have some bearing on the subject, is indirect and of itself insufficient. Should they succeed in proving every argument advanced by their opponents false, still it would not follow that their theory is certainly true.

2. Universalists employ arguments which contradict and destroy each other. We will give a few instances as specimens. It is common for universalists to urge Christ's death for all men, in proof of universal salvation. They contend that as Christ died for all men, all must be saved; for, say they, he could not die in vain. Let us then see how

8-OBJECTIONS TO UNIVERSALISM STATED | 359

this will agree with other arguments which they employ. They urge the salvation of all men from the corrective design of punishment. This is a favorite argument, entering into the very composition of universalism, and is directly opposed to the argument drawn from the death of Christ. If men are to be saved because punishment is designed to make them better, then the death of Christ cannot prove their salvation; for if punishment can effect it, the death of Christ is superfluous and can prove nothing on the subject; and if punishment cannot effect the salvation of sinners, then the argument drawn from its corrective nature and design must fall. The two arguments are opposed to each other, and therefore they cannot both stand. Again, universalists argue from the goodness of God, which is directly opposed to the argument drawn from the death of Christ. If the goodness of God secures the salvation of all men, irrespectively of the atonement or any conditions, then the death of Christ cannot have secured their salvation, and therefore cannot prove it. If sinners might have been saved without the death of Christ as an atonement for sin, then it cannot have secured their salvation, and hence cannot prove it; and if sinners could not have been saved without the death of Christ as an atonement for sin, the goodness of God does not secure salvation, and therefore cannot prove it. We see then that to argue the salvation of all men, both from the death of Christ and the goodness of God, is to contradict one's self.

Universalists also introduce the justice of God to prove universal salvation, or to disprove the doctrine of endless punishment, which also contradicts the argument drawn from the death of Christ. If the endless punishment of sinners would be unjust, as is insisted, then no sinner could have been endlessly punished if Christ had never died for our redemption, since it cannot be admitted that God could do an act of injustice. Now, as no sinner could have been punished forever without a violation of divine justice, Christ cannot have died to save men from endless punishment; for this would suppose that he died to prevent a violation of divine justice. We say then as Christ did not die to save men from endless punishment, on the supposition that such punishment would be unjust, it follows that his death cannot disprove endless punishment on one hand, nor prove endless, universal salvation, on the other. The arguments then drawn from the death of Christ and the justice of God clearly contradict each other.

Once more, universalists contradict themselves in their exposition of terms. They often urge the term *destruction*, in proof that the devil and sin will have an eternal end, because this term is applied to the devil and his works; but when it is said that sinners shall be destroyed, they turn in defence and attempt to maintain that *destruction* means nothing more than some temporal evil, which is perfectly consistent with an eternal and happy existence. The above points have been produced as mere specimens of the contradictions which exist between the arguments employed by universalists. We ask then, will the reader venture the cause of his eternal salvation on evidence so contradictory?

III. Universalism is not calculated to reform community, but is demoralizing in its tendency. We are perfectly aware that this objection will be highly resented by many universalists, and be condemned as false and slanderous; but our appeal is to the candid, who will please to remember that it is not *universalists* that we here assail, but *universalism*. Let facts speak for themselves.

1. Universalists as a religious community have not done, and are not doing so much for the spread of the gospel and the advance of the Messiah's kingdom, as christians of other denominations. As a denomination they have not made the least effort to spread the saving influence of the truth beyond the circle of our own already christianized congregations. Christianity is evi-

dently designed to fill the world, and to bless all nations; and if universalism be true, its heralds should fly on mercy's wings to proclaim it to the ends of the earth; and yet a universalist minister was never known to step over the line of christendom to scatter the light of the gospel in the pathway of the benighted heathen. All other denominations are making praiseworthy efforts to bring the heathen under the influence of the gospel, while universalists instead of coming up to the work, so far as they have done any thing on the subject, have actually opposed. Those among christians, who believe that they must live a sober, righteous and prayerful life here, in order to be saved in heaven, are entitled to their unmingled pity, while the degraded savages excite no sympathy, and Hindoo widows can perish upon the funeral pile; and they have not a tear to shed, nor an effort to make, to have it otherwise.

The following article, which is copied from the Magazine and Advocate, a universalist paper published at Utica, N.Y. goes to prove the effect which universalism produces in drying up the streams of benevolence, and paralizing [sic] the efforts which are made for the support of the gospel under the influence of other sentiments. As the article is short we copy it entire.

"For the Magazine an Advocate.
WHY IS THIS?
I know men who, while they were Partialists, paid from forty to sixty dollars per annum, for the support of these doctrines. They are now universalists, and are as able as ever—but they complain of being unable to afford ten to twenty dollars per annum to support the doctrine they profess! Did they love Partialism more—Universalism less, or their *money most of all*? WHY IS THIS?"

We answer, because if universalism be true, all will be

just as well off in the end, without the preaching of the gospel as with it.

2. No visible reformations take place under universalist preaching. When and where have universalist preachers entered the neighborhood of sabbath-breakers, drunkards, and of vice in general, and had them transformed under their ministry into a sober, praying and moral people? Such an instance has never fallen under our observation, though we have often seen these fruits follow the labours of those who preach the doctrine of endless punishment.

3. Men do not generally become more pious, better citizens and neighbours, when they abandon the doctrine of endless punishment and embrace universalism; but men do, on the other hand, generally become more moral and pious when they abandon universalism and embrace the doctrine of endless punishment. This cannot be denied.

4. Some who have committed crime, have afterwards confessed that a belief in universalism led them to perpetrate the deed, but no one ever made a contrary confession. It is perfectly easy to conceive that men may, through temptation, be led to commit sin because they think they shall not be punished endlessly for it; but it is not possible to conceive that a belief in the doctrine of endless punishment could, under any circumstances, be an incentive to crime. But it may be said that universalism teaches, that if men sin they must be punished for it, and that there is no way of escaping it. To this we reply, that while universalism teaches that there is no way of escaping the punishment of sin after it is committed, it has never told the sinner what his punishment must be, but that it is endured in some way here as he passes along through life. Taking this view, the sinner can have no cause much to fear a universalist hell, for he is taught that he has been in it ever since he began to sin; and hav-

ing found it quite supportable, and most of the time quite comfortable, he can have but little to fear for the future. We think the above array of facts most clearly proves that universalism is demoralizing.

IV. Universalism is not especially comforting to the truly pious, but administers consolation to none but the ungodly. The godly have every assurance of salvation whether it be true or false; hence, their own hope of salvation does not depend upon the truth of universalism, but upon a knowledge of their present acceptance with God, being justified by faith and already in the way to heaven. Should it prove true that those who live and die in sin will be forever lost, it would not endanger the salvation of those who fear God and keep his commandments. Taking this view, we see that so far as relates to personal hope and comfort, universalism can administer nothing to the truly pious which they may not enjoy without it, or which they might not enjoy knowing it to be false. But while universalism administers nothing to the personal comfort of the pious, it really administers to the comfort and hope of the wicked of every description, so far as they believe it. It says to them that sin cannot endanger their final salvation. Universalism says to the drunkard that though he must suffer here in the loss of property, character, and the aching of a feverish brain, yet drunkenness cannot endanger his final salvation; that just in proportion as he shortens his life by intemperance he will hasten his flight to heaven; and if at any time he shall drink so much as to destroy life, or if he meet with some fatal accident in a defenseless hour of intoxication, for such last drunken-fit he will have no after pain, but will awake in heaven and find himself shouting among the angels and redeemed spirits. Universalism says to the murderer, that though he must be somewhat disturbed with the horror of a guilty conscience, and be hanged by the neck if he be detected, yet all the murders he can commit cannot shut him out of heaven at last; that should he be called to expiate his crimes upon the gallows, yet it will be but a momentary pang, from whence he will make a precipitate retreat to heaven where he will meet the victim for whose murder he was hanged, and will have the opportunity of congratulating him on their premature arrival in glory.

Universalism says to the man who may be tired of contending with the ills of the present life, that suicide is a shorter way to heaven; that though it looks like a harsh work to take one's own life, yet he must die at last, and probably suffer more in dying than he will by an act which will end his life and suffering together in an instant. From this view it must be seen that universalism administers no special comfort to the devoted, praying christian; gives no special encouragement to virtue; but absolutely comforts the wicked in their sin, and strengthens the hands of the workers of iniquity.

V. Universalism is unsafe. It makes salvation depend upon a disputed point; disputed too by the voice of the church, and by the principal writers and commentators of every age. How unsafe then must it be, to hang our immortal hopes upon the truth of a point so generally and ably contested? There are many no doubt, whose only hope of heaven depends upon the truth of universalism, and should it fail, which it may do, their prospects are blasted in eternal night. Unless universalists pretend to popish infallibility, they must admit that they may be mistaken, and if mistaken, all who depend upon it for salvation will be ruined forever. But this is not the case with those who hold the opposite doctrine.

Should those who believe in the doctrine of endless punishment, and are living, watching and praying in view of it, after all find themselves mistaken, it will be attended by no lasting evil — they will still be saved. If there be no hell, our believing that there is one, cannot be the cause of our going to hell, and if there be no eternal damnation, we cannot be eternally damned; and if the doctrine of endless punishment be false, our believing it to be true will not render us liable to be punished endlessly. An old and just proverb says, "there can be no harm in keeping upon the safe side." "Their rock is not as our rock, our enemies themselves being judges."

THE END.

MEMBERS OF SCHMUL'S WESLEYAN BOOK CLUB
BUY THESE OUTSTANDING BOOKS AT 40% OFF
THE RETAIL PRICE

Join Schmul's Wesleyan Book Club by calling toll-free:

800-$S_7P_7B_2O_6O_6K_5S_7$

Put a discount Christian bookstore in your
own mailbox

Visit us on the Internet at
www.wesleyanbooks.com

Schmul Publishing Company | PO Box 776 | Nicholasville, KY 40340

www.ingramcontent.com/pod-product-compliance
Lightning Source LLC
Chambersburg PA
CBHW071734150426
43191CB00010B/1570